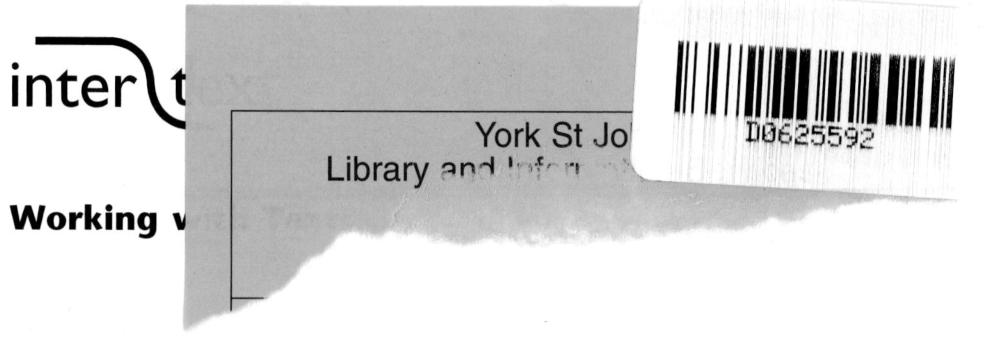

Working with Texts: A core introduction to language analysis is a well established textbook that introduces students to the main principles of language analysis, through contemporary text examples. Covering a wide range of language areas, the book uses an interactive, activity-based approach to support students' understanding of language structure and variety. The third edition includes:

- new material on analysing sound
- an updated range of texts, including literary extracts, advertisements, newspaper articles, comic book strips, excerpts from popular comedy sketches, political speeches, telephone discourse and internet chat
- new extension work to support student-directed study
- detailed suggestions after each unit for further reading within the Intertext series as a whole
- an updated list of URLs.

Ronald Carter is Professor of Modern English Language in the School of English Studies, University of Nottingham. **Angela Goddard** is Head of Subject for Languages and Linguistics at York St John University, and Chair of Examiners for English Language A-Level. **Danuta Reah** is a Chief Examiner for English Language A-Level, and a published novelist writing under her own name and as Carla Banks. **Keith Sanger** was Principal Moderator for English Language A-Level Investigation. **Nikki Swift** is Head of Programme for English Language and Linguistics at York St John University. **Adrian Beard** is a Visiting Lecturer in English Language and Linguistics at York St John University and a Chief Examiner for A-Level English.

The Intertext series

- **Why does the phrase 'spinning a yarn' refer both to using language and making cloth?**
- **What might a piece of literary writing have in common with an advert or a note from the milkman?**
- **What aspects of language are important to understand when analysing texts?**

The Routledge INTERTEXT series will develop readers' understanding of how texts work. It does this by showing some of the designs and patterns in the language from which they are made, by placing texts within the contexts in which they occur, and by exploring relationships between them.

The series consists of a foundation text, *Working with Texts: A core introduction to language analysis*, which looks at language aspects essential for the analysis of texts, and a range of satellite texts. These apply aspects of language to a particular topic area in more detail. They complement the core text and can also be used alone, providing the user has the foundation skills furnished by the core text.

Benefits of using this series:

- **Unique** – written by a team of respected teachers and practitioners whose ideas and activities have also been trialled independently.
- **Multi-disciplinary** – provides a foundation for the analysis of texts, supporting students who want to achieve a detailed focus on language.
- **Accessible** – no previous knowledge of language analysis is assumed, just an interest in language use.
- **Comprehensive** – wide coverage of different genres: literary texts, notes, signs, advertisements, leaflets, speeches, conversation.
- **Student-friendly** – contains suggestions for further reading; activities relating to texts studied; commentaries after activities; key terms highlighted and an index of terms.

The series editors:

Adrian Beard lectures in English Language and Linguistics at York St John University and is a Chief Examiner for AS and A-Level English Literature. He has written extensively on the subjects of literature and language, his publications including *Texts and Contexts* (Routledge) and *The Language of Sport, The Language of Politics, Language Change* in this series.

Dr Angela Goddard is Principal Lecturer and Head of Subject for Languages and Linguistics at York St John University. Her publications include *The Language of Advertising* and *Language and Gender*, both in this series. Her current research interests are in aspects of identity and language use in computer-mediated communication. She is Chair of Examiners for English Language A-Level at a major national exam board.

Core textbook:
Working with Texts: A core introduction to language analysis (3rd edn; 2008)
Ronald Carter, Angela Goddard, Danuta Reah, Keith Sanger, Nikki Swift

Satellite titles:

The Language of Advertising: Written texts
(2nd edn, 2002)
Angela Goddard

Language Change
Adrian Beard

The Language of Children
Julia Gillen

The Language of Comics
Mario Saraceni

The Language of Conversation
Francesca Pridham

The Language of Drama
Keith Sanger

The Language of Fiction
Keith Sanger

Language and Gender
Angela Goddard and Lindsey Meân Patterson

The Language of Humour
Alison Ross

The Language of ICT: Information and communication technology
Tim Shortis

The Language of Magazines
Linda McLoughlin

The Language of Newspapers
(2nd edn, 2002)
Danuta Reah

The Language of Poetry
John McRae

The Language of Politics
Adrian Beard

Language and Region
Joan C. Beal

The Language of Science
Carol Reeves

The Language of Speech and Writing
Sandra Cornbleet and Ronald Carter

The Language of Sport
Adrian Beard

The Language of Television
Jill Marshall and Angela Werndly

The Language of War
Steve Thorne

The Language of Websites
Mark Boardman

The Language of Work
Almut Koester

Working with Texts

A core introduction to language analysis

Third Edition

- Ronald Carter
- Angela Goddard
- Danuta Reah
- Keith Sanger
- Nikki Swift

Edited by
Adrian Beard

LONDON AND NEW YORK

First published 1997
Reprinted 1998, 1999, 2000 (twice), 2001
Second edition published 2001
This third edition published 2008
by Routledge
2 Park Square, Milton Park, Abingdon, Oxon OX14 4RN

Simultaneously published in the USA and Canada
by Routledge
270 Madison Ave, New York, NY 10016

Routledge is an imprint of the Taylor & Francis Group, an informa business

Typeset in Stone Serif and Stone Sans by
Florence Production Ltd, Stoodleigh, Devon

Printed and bound in Great Britain by
The Cromwell Press, Trowbridge, Wiltshire

British Library Cataloguing-in-Publication Data
A catalogue record for this book is available from the British Library

Library of Congress Cataloging-in-Publication Data
Working with texts: a core introduction to language analysis/
Ronald Carter . . . [et al.]; edited by Adrian Beard. – 3rd ed.
p. cm.
Includes bibliographical references and index.
1. Linguistic analysis (Linguistics) I. Carter, Ronald, 1947–
II. Beard, Adrian, 1951–
P126.W67 2007
420.1′41 – dc22

ISBN10: 0–415–41421–0 (hbk)
ISBN10: 0–415–41424–5 (pbk)

ISBN13: 978–0–415–41421–0 (hbk)
ISBN13: 978–0–415–41424–1 (pbk)

contents

notes on the authors

Ronald Carter is Professor of Modern English Language at Nottingham University. He has written a range of books and articles in the fields of language and education, applied linguistics and the teaching of English. Recent books include: *Language and Creativity* (Routledge, 2004) and *Cambridge Grammar of English* (with Michael McCarthy; CUP, 2006). Professor Carter is a Fellow of the Royal Society of Arts, a Fellow of the British Academy for Social Sciences and was Chair of the British Association for Applied Linguistics (2003–6).

Angela Goddard teaches at York St John University and is Chair of English Language for AQA. Publications include *Researching Language* (Heinemann); *The Language of Advertising* (Routledge); *Language and Gender* (Routledge); *Writing for Assessment* (Routledge).

Danuta Reah has published academic books and articles and works as Senior Examiner for Edexcel. She has also published six novels, two under her pen name, Carla Banks.

Keith Sanger has taught English at secondary school and sixth-form college level. Until recently he taught English Language and Drama at New College, Pontefract. He has an MA in Modern English Language from Leeds University, and is a team leader for A-level English Language examiners. His publications include *The Language of Fiction* (Routledge, 1998) and *The Language of Drama* (Routledge, 2000).

Nikki Swift is Head of Programme for English Language and Linguistics at York St John University. She is a University Teacher Fellow and her research interests include phonological variation in regional varieties of English, and online learning.

notes on the editor

Adrian Beard was for many years Head of English at Gosforth High School, Newcastle upon Tyne. He now lectures at York St John University. He is a senior figure in A-Level and GCSE examining in English. His publications include *The Language of Sport, The Language of Politics* and *Language Change,* all in the Routledge Intertext series.

acknowledgements

Pret-a-Manger Sandwich packaging. Reproduced with permission.

The Co-operative Bank advertisement. Reproduced with permission.

Warning signs from Highway code. Reproduced under the terms of the Click-Use Licence, Office of Public Sector Information.

Martin T. Davies 'Gamers don't want any more grief'. *The Guardian* 15 June 2006. Copyright © Guardian News & Media Ltd 2006. Reproduced with permission.

Dorian Lynskey 'We need heroes'. *The Guardian* 29 November 2006. Copyright © Guardian News & Media Ltd 2006. Reproduced with permission.

Text and illustrations of Fray: 26th Century Slayer™ © 2007 Joss Whedon. Published by Dark Horse Comics, Inc.

Excerpt from 'Buffy the Vampire Slayer' © 2002. Courtesy of Twentieth Century Fox Television. Written by Jane Espenson and Drew Goddard. All rights reserved.

Tucson Word Center, reading concordances. Reproduced by permission of John Sinclair and Elena Tognini Bonelli.

From *Sandman: The Doll's House* © 1990 D.C. Comics. All rights reserved.

Karl Plewka 'City Slick'. *The Observer* 26 May 1996. Copyright © Guardian News & Media Ltd 1996. Reproduced with permission.

Waitrose Letter. Reproduced with permission.

Orange advertisement. Reproduced with permission.

Christian Aid advertisement. Reproduced with permission.

'This is a Photograph of Me', from *Selected Poems*, 1965–1975 by Margaret Atwood. Copyright © 1976 by Margaret Atwood. Reprinted by permission of Houghton Mifflin Company. All rights reserved.

'This is a Photograph of Me', from *The Circle Game* by Margaret Atwood. Copyright © 1966, 1998 by Margaret Atwood. Reprinted by permission of House of Anansi Press, Toronto.

'This is a Photograph of Me', from *Eating Fire: Selected Poetry*, 1965, 1995 by Margaret Atwood, 1998. Reproduced by permission of Little, Brown Book Group Limited.

Wildlife and Habitats: Friends of the Earth Free Booklet Series, copyright © 2004 Friends of the Earth. Reproduced with permission.

Illustration and text extract from *Keywords with Ladybird – Boys and Girls* © Ladybird Books, Ltd, 1964, 2004.

Yakult advertisement. Reproduced with permission.

BA advertisement. Reproduced by permission of Kate Ridyard (kate@3fishinatree.com) at 3 fish in a tree.

United Utilities notice. Reproduced with permission.

The Prostate Cancer Charity advertisement. Reproduced with permission.

Port Salut advertisement. Reproduced with permission of Bel UK Ltd.

Two-minute transcript from Scott Mills show Radio 1, 19/1/06. Reproduced with permission of Radio 1 and IXtra.

Transcript from Andrew Marr, *Sunday AM Show*. Reproduced with permission.

Boddingtons advertisement. Reproduced with permission of InBev UK.

Excerpt from *Ladder of Years* by Anne Tyler. Reprinted by the permission of Russell & Volkening as agents for the author. Copyright © 1995 by Anne Tyler.

From *Ladder of Years* by Anne Tyler, copyright © 1995 by Anne Tyler. Used by permission of Alfred A. Knopf, a division of Random House, Inc.

From *Ladder of Years* by Anne Tyler, published by Chatto & Windus. Reprinted by permission of The Random House Group Ltd.

'Not waving but drowning' by Stevie Smith, from *Collected Poems of Stevie Smith*, copyright © 1972 by Stevie Smith. Reprinted by permission of New Directions Publishing Corp. and the Executors of James MacGibbon.

Subaru Justy advertisement. Reproduced with permission of Subaru (UK) Ltd.

High Peak Borough Council leaflet on conservation areas. Reproduced with permission.

'Off Course' by Edwin Morgan, from *Collected Poems,* Carcanet Press Ltd, 1996. Reproduced with permission.

The following are gratefully thanked for their contribution of material to Unit 2: Kate Whisker and Ralph, Astrid and Hedy Clark. Thanks also to Dodie Clark for her contribution to Unit 1.

While the publisher has made every effort to contact copyright holders of the material used in this volume, they would be happy to hear from anyone they were unable to contact.

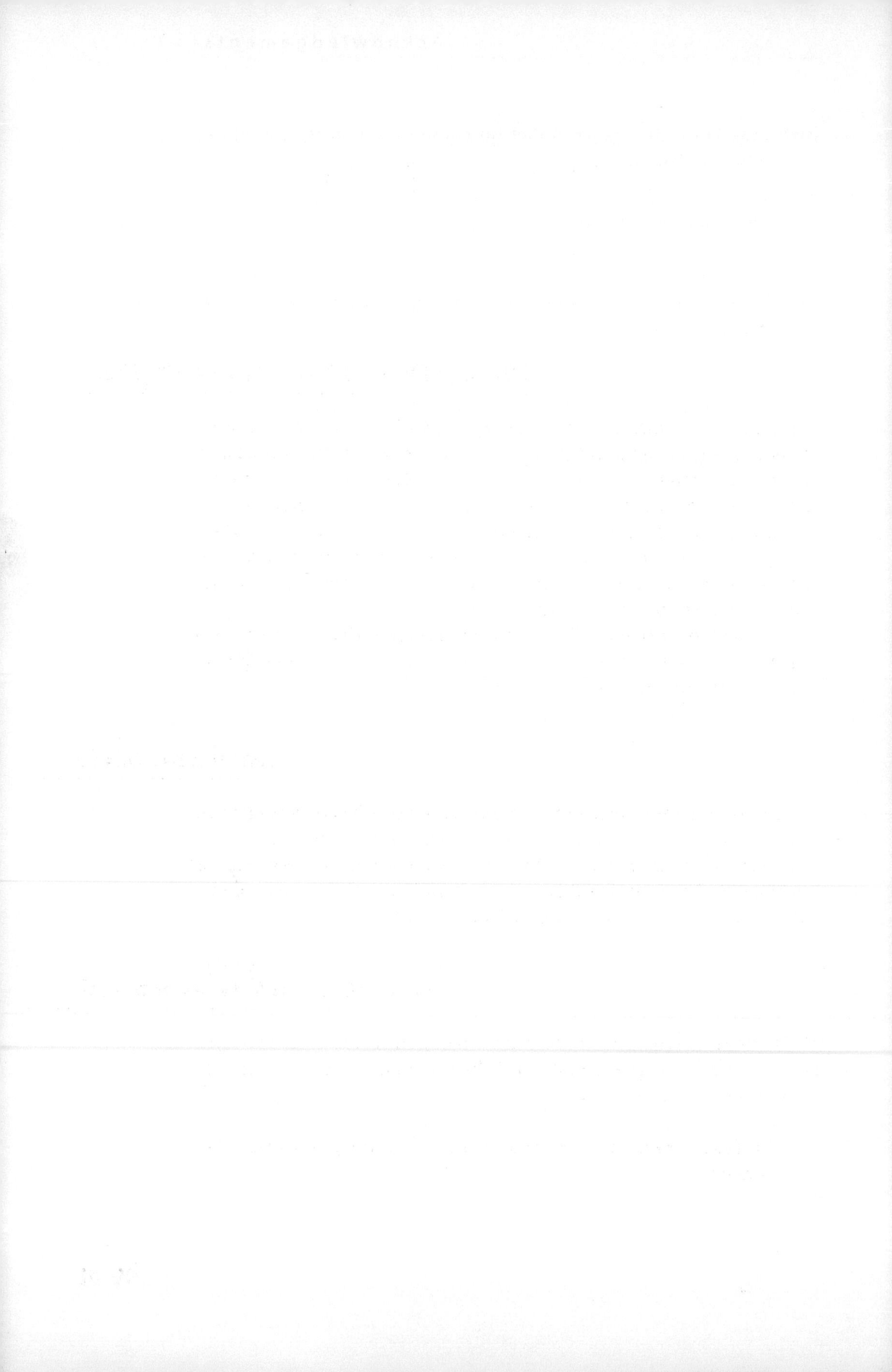

introduction

Third edition of *Working with Texts*

Welcome to the third edition of *Working with Texts*. This third edition has been revised in a number of ways and for a number of reasons. Based on feedback from users, this new edition is made easier to use through a clearer structure and more consistent application of key organisational features. At the same time it reflects developments that have taken place in linguistic study, with reference to language corpora and especially to computer-mediated communication. New texts are added as examples where they help to highlight these developments.

In addition references have been updated and clear links between this book and the satellite texts in the Intertext series are highlighted. There is also a brand new unit on 'Sounds'.

Aim of this book

The aim of this book is to provide a foundation for the analysis of texts, in order to support students in any discipline who want to achieve a detailed focus on language. No previous knowledge of language analysis is assumed; what is assumed is an interest in language use and a desire to account for the choices made by language users.

How this book is structured

The book is divided into seven units which, taken together, cover the main aspects of language that it will be important to consider in any rigorous textual description:

- **Unit one: Signs** explores some aspects of meaning in written sign systems;

- **Unit two: Sounds** explores some of the ways in which sounds are represented and why thinking about sound is important in the study of texts;
- **Unit three: Words and things** examines the nature of the lexical system;
- **Unit four: Sentences and structures** considers the effects of various types of grammatical patterning;
- **Unit five: Text and context: written discourse** focuses on the cohesive devices that tie texts together across sentence boundaries;
- **Unit six: Text and context: spoken discourse** looks at some important aspects of spoken varieties, both in naturally occurring and in mediated texts.
- **Unit seven: Applications** points forward to the ways in which language and analysis can be taken further into investigative research.

Although the units represent distinct areas of language, in practice, when language is actually being used, these areas are not independent of each other. For example, written symbols are combined to form words, and lexical patterning is an important aspect of written discourse. But in order to study language rather than simply use it, some systematic ways of paying attention to its various components are necessary.

When working through this book, it is obviously important to understand each of the language areas being considered in the units; but it is equally important not to lose sight of language as a whole system while thinking about its parts. Practical reminders about the holistic nature of language occur in this book in a number of ways:

- in cross-references between the units, where some features of language are considered more than once, but from different perspectives;
- in analytical activities, where questions and commentaries on texts will focus on certain salient features, but will also suggest the larger picture to which these features contribute;
- in the developmental structure of the book, where later units will enable earlier skills to be reapplied and further enhanced;
- in a range of extension activities at the end of each unit; and
- in the focus of the final unit, where students are pointed towards the planning of their own research projects.

The book also puts aspects of language study into wider context by cross-referencing this core book in the INTERTEXT series with the full range of satellite texts which are also available. These references can also be found at the end of each section.

The intention, then, is that the book should build a composite picture that enables students to appreciate the nature of texts as a whole while being able to discuss meaningfully the contributions made by different aspects of language.

Ways of working

Wherever possible, the features of language referred to are shown in operation, within texts. This means the book is not intended to be a passive reading exercise but, rather, a set of active learning materials: instead of simply being told about features, readers are asked to consider how they work within texts and in particular contexts. The wide range of different genres covered is intentional, to show that skills in analysing language can be successfully applied whatever the text, and to break down the idea that only high-status texts such as literary forms are worthy of scrutiny: literary texts are considered here, but there is equivalent, if not more, discussion of such texts as notes, signs, advertisements, informative leaflets, speeches and spontaneous conversation. For students of literature, comparative studies across a range of textual types can enable interesting questions to be asked about the nature of literary language.

Commentaries are provided after many of the activities. Where they form part of the learning process, they appear immediately after the activity. Where they are used to check the learning has taken place, they are put at the end of the unit, to allow the activity to be completed before the commentary is seen.

These commentaries, which highlight and discuss some of the main points of language use, are not intended to be model answers or definitive accounts: rather, they are a way to compare readers' perceptions with those of the authors. It is hoped that readers will use these commentaries in the way that best supports their own learning.

While this book may form the basis for work in groups, it can also be used by individuals working alone. However, when readers work alone, the feedback from other group members will not be available, so the commentaries can, at least in part, make up for that.

At the end of each unit, suggestions are given for extension work. It is a common feature of many A-Level and undergraduate courses that students undertake their own language investigations. The ideas within the 'Extension' sections have this type of work in mind. As a core text, this book can only offer brief suggestions and pointers; the satellite titles that form part of the INTERTEXT series as a whole are designed to pursue many of these topics in considerably more detail.

Terminology and further reading

Because no previous knowledge of language analysis is assumed, the first usage of what is considered to be a technical term is emboldened in the text. Some of these terms are explained in context, but a brief explanation of most of these terms can be found in the 'Index of terms' at the back of this book. Suggestions for further reading are also provided.

Unit one

Signs

Aims of this unit

The aims of this unit are to explore some of the visual aspects of writing and to show various ways in which written texts contain more than just printed words.

What is a sign?

Language is sometimes referred to as a **semiotic** system.

This means that it is thought to be a system where the individual elements – 'signs' – take their overall meaning from how they are combined with other elements. The analogy that is often used to illustrate this principle is the system of road traffic lights: the red, amber and green lights work as a system, and the whole system has meaning which is not carried by any one of the lights alone, but by the lights in a certain combination and sequence. In the same way, written letters of a language are signs that have to be in a certain order to make sense to the reader, and the sounds of a language are signs that only have meaning to a hearer when they occur in predictable groups. To take this idea to its logical conclusion, it is clearly possible for the elements mentioned to occur in unpredictable ways – such as for a red and green light to occur simultaneously in a set of traffic lights, or for an invented word to have a non-English-looking spelling, such as 'mldh'; but, in these cases, we still make sense of what is happening – by explaining away these occurrences as 'breakdowns' or 'mistakes'. We are still therefore referring back to a system of rules, in defining such phenomena as deviating from what we expect.

Cultural analysts would go beyond language to look at all aspects of society as systems of signs: for example, films are a system where different signs are combined in patterned ways; dress codes embody rules where different elements can occur in many varied combinations; the area of food contains many rules about what can be combined with what, and when different foods can be eaten. In all such aspects of culture, conventions are highly culture-bound – in other words, different cultures have different semiotic systems.

Activity

This activity will focus on signs in the most traditional sense – road signs – and will explore the idea of how we read them. Look at the signs in Text 1:1. These are all from an edition of the British Highway Code published in the 1930s.

The originator of the idea of semiotics – the Swiss linguist Ferdinand de Saussure – suggested that there were at least two types of sign in cases such as these: **iconic** and **symbolic.** An iconic sign tries to be a direct picture of what it refers to (although this may consist of a generalised line drawing rather than a picture in the photographic, literal sense). A symbolic sign is not a picture of what is being referred to (**referent**), but a picture of something that we associate with the referent.

- Which of these signs are iconic, and which symbolic?
- Where a sign is symbolic, how does it work – what are the associations (**connotations**) that are in your mind?

There is a commentary on this activity at the end of the unit.

Text 1:1

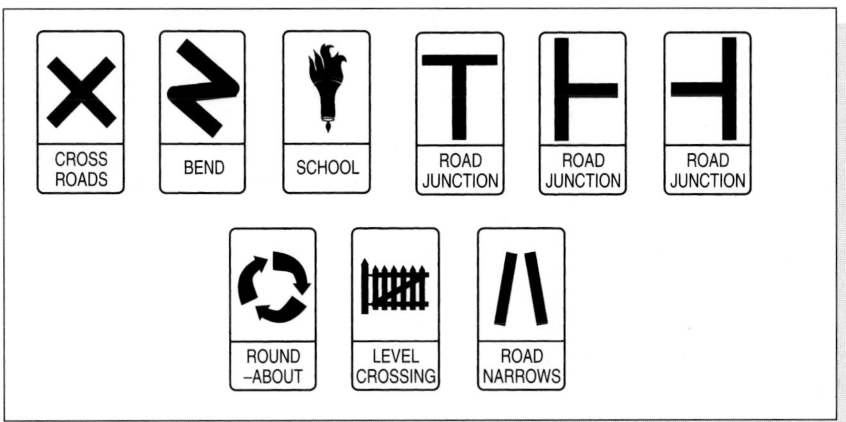

Activity

Now look at Text 1:2, where you will see some contemporary versions of the same signs, from a Highway Code published in 2004.

- What changes, if any, are in evidence?
- How do you explain any changes that have occurred?

Note that there is no commentary on this activity.

Text 1:2

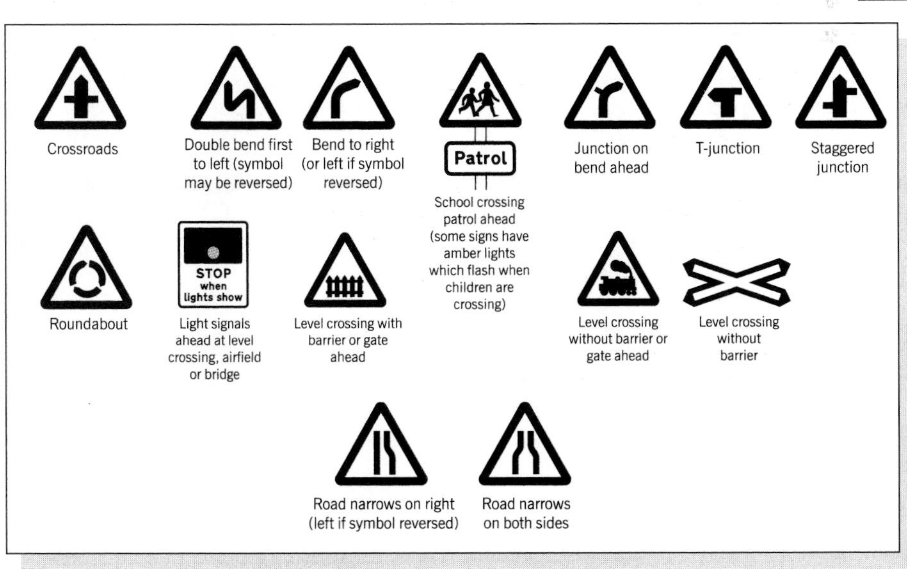

Although there were changes in evidence in the two sets of road signs you have been studying, the signs have been, and continue to be, understood by the community of road users they were designed to serve. To that extent, the signs represent a level of shared knowledge within a culture.

Being able to rely on shared knowledge within a culture allows members to take shortcuts, so that not everything has to be spelt out every time we communicate. But having ideas remaining unstated also has other side-effects: it means that attitudes and values can be called up quickly, below the level of conscious thought. This is a powerful facility for advertisers to tap into.

Activity

At the end of this unit (Commentary, pp. 27–8), we can see how the makers of Boddington's beer use the semiotics of the torch symbol, as well as that of 'cream', to promote their product. Now look at the pieces of advertising below (Text 1:3), which use **intertextual** references to road signs to help them formulate their message. Can you explain in each case what the role of the road sign is?

There is a commentary on this activity at the end of the unit.

Text 1:3

Chefs at work
'Just made' with preservative-free, fresh, natural ingredients.

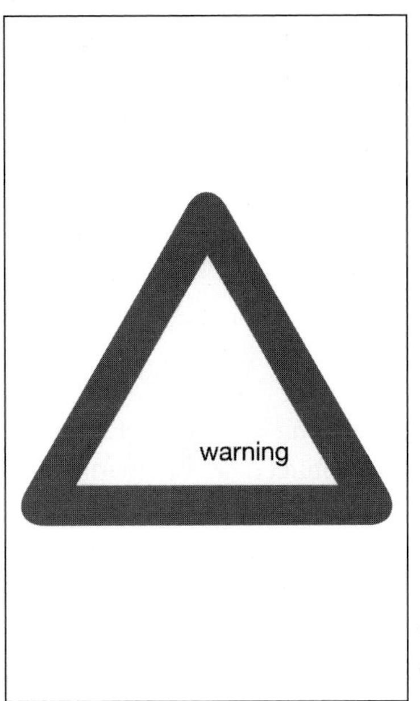
warning

2
ROYAL MAIL
POSTAGE PAID GB
HQ233
Your RAC cover has expired
Renew your RAC membership from just £33*
Reply within the next seven days and you can save £10 off usual renewal prices which start at £57. Save an extra £14 when you switch to payment by annual Direct Debit. We will also send you a Free Road Atlas when you renew.
Call now quoting LAPS31/LAP010/ATLAS
0870 333 2492
Please have your payment details to hand.
Lines open 8am-9pm Monday-Friday, 8.30am-5pm Saturday.
Calls may be recorded and/or monitored.
If you have renewed your membership recently, please ignore this reminder.
This offer is only available to reinstated members renewing on an annual basis. Prices quoted are based on payment by continuous methods and are correct at time of going to press. Subject to terms of membership – available on request.
*£33 is for Roadside assistance only.
Provided by RAC Motoring Services and/or RAC Insurance Limited. RAC Motoring Services (Reg'd No: 01424399 Reg'd office: RAC House, 1 Forest Road, Feltham TW13 7RR) in respect of insurance mediation activities only and RAC Insurance Limited (Reg'd No: 2355834 Reg'd office: as above) are authorised and regulated by the Financial Services Authority within the jurisdiction of the Financial Ombudsman Service and the Financial Services Compensation Scheme. There is a complaints procedure, details can be found in the Terms of Membership which are available on request. Full terms and conditions apply.
-14 Triangle 02/06
RAC Design 2073/11.03
Miss A Goddard
21 Scarcroft Hill
York
YO24 1DF
10144192029
RAC
always there

So far, this section has focused on the way a system of signs can rely on shared, culturally embedded meanings which can then be used in other contexts for their connotative power. While the signs listed in the Highway Code are clear examples of signs, there are other sign systems that may not draw attention to themselves in such an obvious way. The next activity is designed to explore signs at a slightly more subtle level.

Activity

There are many signs that circulate in our everyday texts in the form of the logos produced by companies and institutions to represent their products and services. Looking at these in a systematic way can give us quite a lot of information about the shared assumptions at work in the culture from which the signs have been taken.

The signs in Text 1:4 are logos taken from texts advertising goods and services. Although each one is a picture of a bird, in each case the advertiser was using the bird image for its associations or connotations.

For each logo, write down the connotations that come to mind when you see it. Don't try to guess which product or service was being advertised, but rather concentrate on the image itself.

There is a commentary on this activity at the end of the unit.

Text 1:4

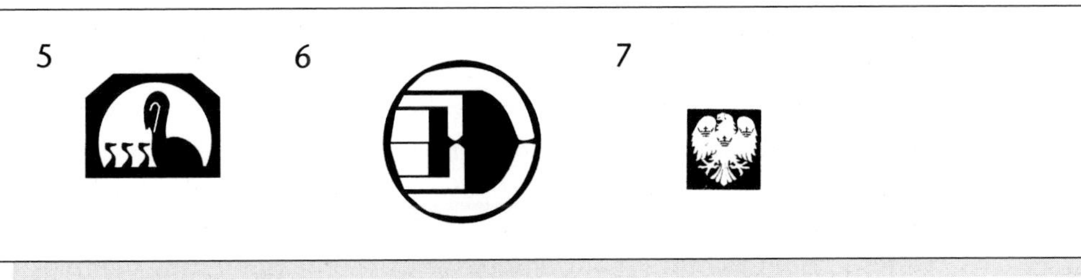

There is nothing natural about the associations we have for these images: for example, the owl is, in fact, blind at night; and it would be absurd to suggest that a swallow felt 'freer' than a sparrow, that a sparrow thought of itself as cheeky, or that a seagull knew what a seaside resort was. These ideas are imposed on members of the animal kingdom by humans – a process so well recognised that we have a name for it – **anthropomorphism** (from Greek 'anthropos', human, and 'morph', shape). Further examples of this would be the 'cuddly' bear, the 'cunning' fox, the 'evil' snake. They are not universal ideas, but are culture-specific, and different cultures may well have very different connotations for the same animal.

As well as cultural associations, individuals of course bring their own experiences and feelings to images: a cuddly bear may not seem so cuddly if you've been attacked by one.

Signs such as the ones you have just been studying are powerful rhetorical devices, for a number of reasons: they call up strong associations in the mind of the reader; they are economic, using no verbal language at all, and taking up minimal space; meanings can be fluid, so there is space to manipulate, adapt and change; signs can suggest several ideas at once, so they can be multi-purpose.

The ideas behind such signs – here, animals having certain characteristics – are used frequently in literary texts as forms of symbolism: for example, a poem could use a verbal description of a bird to suggest ideas about personal freedom. Such a poem could go further, by also setting out its lines in the shape of a bird's wings. The use of verbal text as a visual art form in poetry is often referred to as 'concrete poetry', and you can probably remember occasions in school when you were asked to create a text of that kind.

As simple as ABC

So far, we have been dealing with some quite complex levels of **representation** and interpretation. In comparison, the written alphabet that we know and use on an everyday basis might seem like child's play. But looking at the whole business of written language – even the everyday variety – from a child's point of view reveals some interesting complexity too.

THE FUNCTIONS OF LITERACY

By the time we have reached adulthood, most of us have forgotten what it felt like to move from spoken to written language, and to encounter, not just a whole new set of conventions in terms of the features of writing, but a new set of rules about functions as well: just what are the purposes of written language? Why bother to have it at all? Why pay so much attention to it?

Activity

Read through the comments in Text 1:5 and Text 1:6. They are from classes of 7–8 year olds, asked about the purposes of writing and reading. What ideas come through here, and how do their ideas compare with your own – what do *you* see as the functions of written language?

Bear in mind that these children were interviewed before computer-based writing became a commonly used method of communication.

There is a commentary on this activity at the end of the unit.

Text 1:5

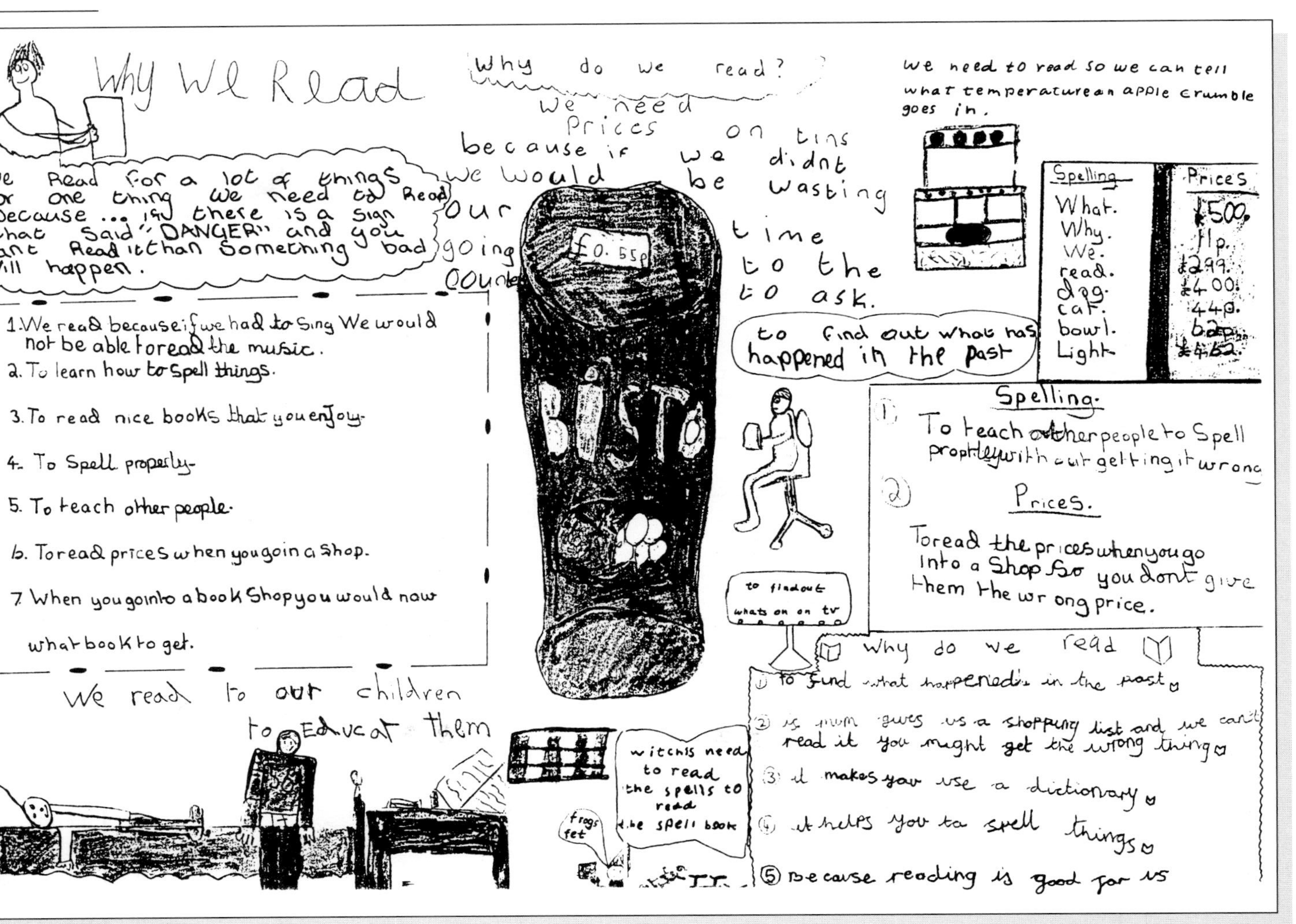

Why We Read
We Read for a lot of things for one thing We need to Read Because ... if there is a sign that said "DANGER" and you cant Read it than something bad will happen.
1. We read because if we had to sing We would not be able to read the music.
2. To learn how to spell things.
3. To read nice books that you enjoy.
4. To Spell properly.
5. To teach other people.
6. To read prices when you go in a shop.
7. When you go into a book Shop you would now what book to get.
We read to our children to Educat them
Why do we read?
We need Prices on tins because if we didnt we would be wasting our time going to the counter to ask.
£0.55p
BISTO
to find out what has happened in the past
to find out whats on on tv
witchis need to read the spells to read the spell book
frogs fet
We need to read so we can tell what temperature an apple crumble goes in.
Spelling
What. Why. We. read. dog. cat. bowl. Light.
Prices
£500. 1p. £2.99. £4.00. 44p. 62p. £4.62.
Spelling.
1 To teach other people to Spell properly with out getting it wrong
2 Prices.
To read the prices when you go into a Shop So you dont give them the wrong price.
Why do we read
1 to find what happened in the past
2 is mum gives us a shopping list and we can't read it you might get the wrong thing
3 it makes you use a dictionary
4 it helps you to spell things
5 Because reading is good for us

Text 1:6

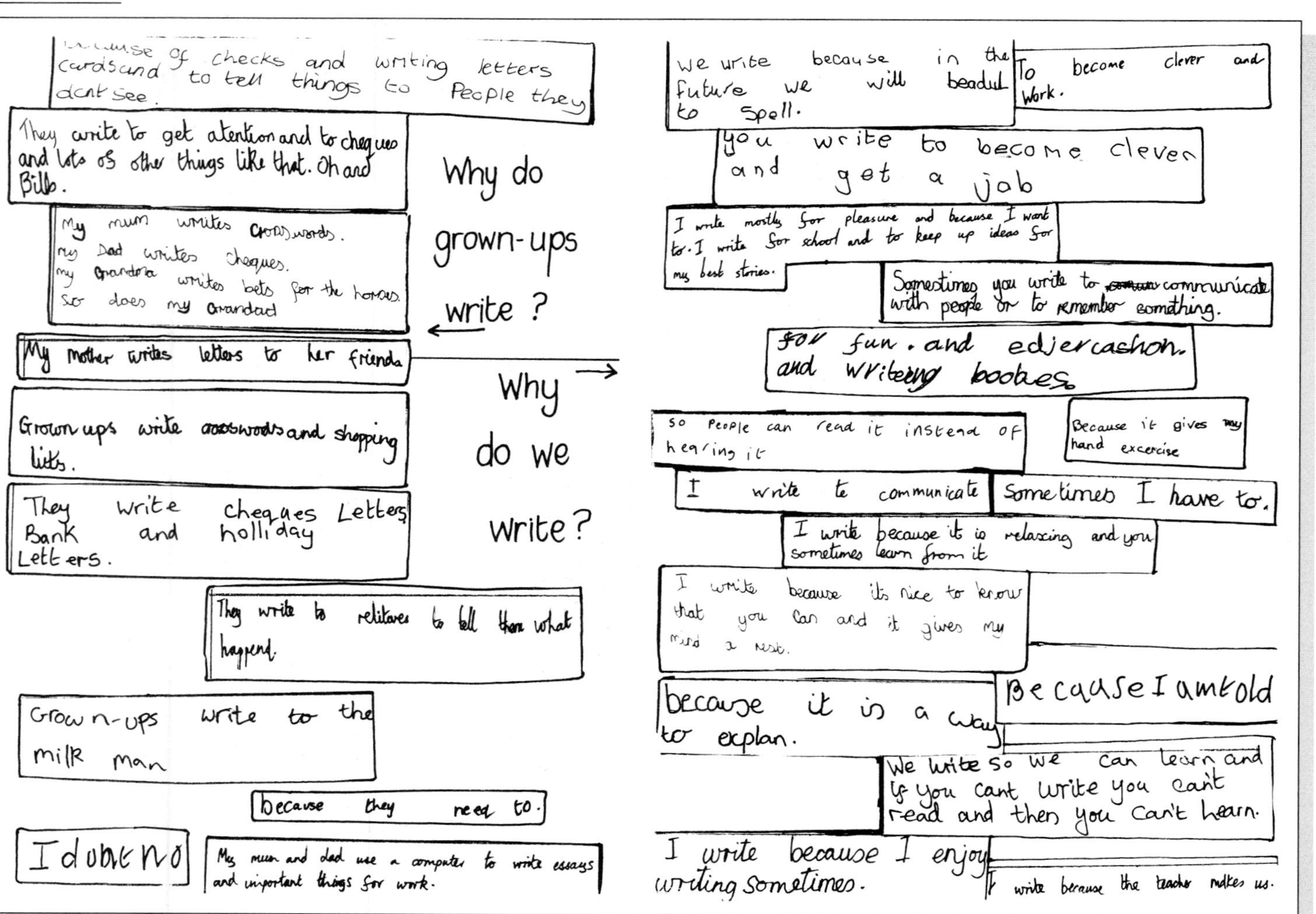
Why do grown-ups write?
because of checks and writing letters cardsand to tell things to People they dont see.
They write to get atention and to cheques and lots of other things like that. Oh and Bills.
My mum writes crosswords. my Dad writes cheques. my Grandma writes bets for the horses. So does my Grandad
My mother writes letters to her friends
Grown ups write crosswords and shopping lists.
They Bank Letters. write and cheques holliday Letters
They write to relitaves to tell them what happend.
Grown-ups write to the milk man
because they need to.
I donk no
My mum and dad use a computer to write essays and important things for work.
Why do we write?
we write because in the future we will beadul to spell.
To become clever and work.
you write to become clever and get a job
I write mostly for pleasure and because I want to. I write for school and to keep up ideas for my best stories.
Sometimes you write to communicate with people or to remember something.
for fun. and edjercashon. and writeing bookes.
so People can read it instead of hearing it
Because it gives my hand excercise
I write to communicate
Sometimes I have to.
I write because it is relaxing and you sometimes learn from it
I write because its nice to know that you can and it gives my mind a rest.
Because I am told
because it is a way to explan.
We write so we can learn and if you cant write you can't read and then you can't learn.
I write because I enjoy writing sometimes.
I write because the teacher makes us.

LITERATE STRATEGIES: ABBREVIATIONS

As you will already have realised, observing children in the process of learning to understand and produce written language can give us many insights into how written texts work for us as adults.

Activity

Text 1:7 is a piece of writing by Jonathon, age 4, reporting on his day out to Blackpool. In it, the writer uses initial letters to stand for whole words; the child's teacher wrote the full lines of text, after Jonathon read his writing back to her. Can you see how Jonathon's writing strategy is a logical approach to the cognitive demands that literacy makes on beginning writers?

There is a commentary on this activity at the end of the unit.

Text 1:7

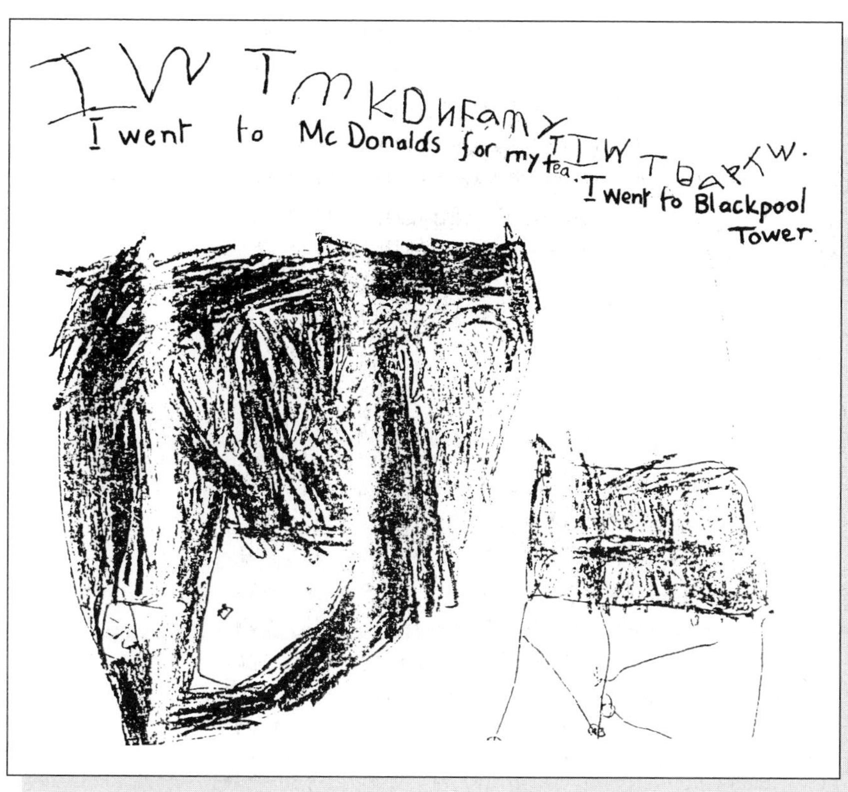

I went to McDonalds for my tea.
I went to Blackpool Tower.

Where, in adult texts, do we use single letters or abbreviated forms of words on a regular basis? How do such alterations work? Are our reasons for doing this the same as Jonathon's?

Activity

To get you thinking about the above questions, read through Text 1:8, then abbreviate the words as far as you can without removing the ability of the reader to reconstitute them.

There is a commentary on this activity at the end of the unit.

Text 1:8

BEAUTIFULLY RESTORED nineteenth-century farmhouse with two reception rooms, a large kitchen, three bedrooms, a bathroom and separate toilet. There is gas central heating throughout the house. Outside the property, there is a substantial double garage, and extensive gardens and outhouses. All the carpets and curtains are included in the selling price, which is £85,000 or nearest offer.

The reasons for our uses of **initialisms** and **acronyms** in adult texts could be determined by any one or several of the following factors: financial cost of advertising space (e.g. estate agents, personal ads); demands on the memory made by having to remember the whole word or series of words (e.g. acronyms); the need for speed in writing (e.g. shorthand), reading (e.g. road signs) or speaking (e.g. initialisms which enable us to refer quickly to institutions or artifacts – BBC, TV, CD-ROM, PC).

LITERATE STRATEGIES: SOUND EFFECTS

Another area where children can teach us a lot about the resources of written texts is that of sound effects. The writing system has a range of ways to call up some of the aspects of sound that we learn to pay attention to as part of the meaning of spoken language.

Activity

Read through the two children's stories in Texts 1:9 and 1:10. How are these children using aspects of written language to try to suggest sound?

There is a commentary on this activity at end of the unit.

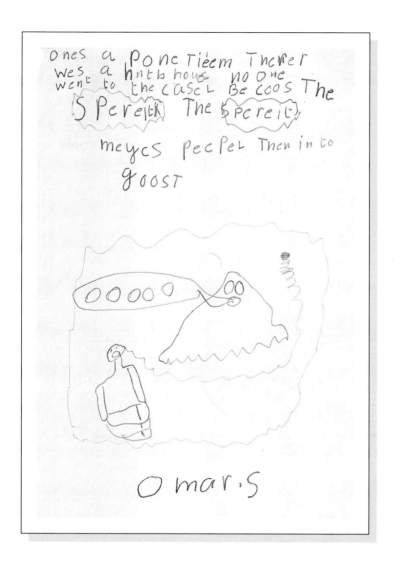

Text 1:9

Text 1:10

~~The~~ my brithday

When it was my brithday I went to
a island for a picnic.. I take
Simone and megan. We went in a boat
Waen we got there we played for
a bitr Then we had. The picnic.
~~then~~ we come to going home the
boat had gone I Started to
cry. I whant to go home
Simone had a ~~Idey~~ Idea We can
make a ward out of pebbles.
What is the ward going to
Say ~~hdpt~~ help??? yes Side
megan. lasts get going I ho
I ho its of to work we
go There ~~we have~~ ~~were~~
Wave finish. At home mum
and dad had Send a
Sertch party. At the island
the were sitting wating.
A helicopter they Saw the
words h.e.l.p then we all
Side hepp. the helicopter
came with laders we ~~clamad~~
clamnd up.

Lauren.

If writers can use aspects of writing to suggest sound, this is unlikely to remain unnoticed by the advertisers of hi-fi equipment.

Activity

Text 1:11 is an advert for personal stereos. Identify the written language devices being used by the advertisers to refer to or represent aspects of sound.

Note that there is no commentary on this activity.

Text 1:11

Lots of people settle for any old personal stereo –they jusst put up with the hissSing and accept that sometimes only one earpiece works at a time. They TURN UP THE VOLUME until the sound is so distorted that its just a NIGHTMARE Then, just when they're listening to their favourite music, their batteries *conk out on them.....* or their headphones drop to bits in their lap.

Not with Metz & Rahmen.

EEZZZy listening that's a dream .

(((M&R)))

Writers of fiction often try to give the reader a sense of spoken language, in a variety of ways: they may want to construct a 'voice' for the narrator, so that the reader can distinguish this address from the language used by the characters; there are the various voices of the characters themselves when they are talking to each other; and there are 'inner voices' in the form of the thoughts of the characters, relayed to readers by the narrator.

Activity

Text 1:12 shows an extract from *Ladder of Years,* by Anne Tyler, published in 1995. It is the opening of the novel.

- How does the writer use graphological features – in particular, punctuation and variations in typeface – to suggest aspects of spoken discourse?
- How much cannot be conveyed by such features, but has to be explained by the narrator directly, in the form of description?

There is a commentary on this activity at the end of the unit.

Text 1:12

LADDER OF YEARS

This all started on a Saturday morning in May, one of those warm spring days that smell like clean linen. Delia had gone to the supermarket to shop for the week's meals. She was standing in the produce section, languidly choosing a bunch of celery. Grocery stores always made her reflective. Why was it, she was wondering, that celery was not called 'corduroy plant'? That would be much more colorful. And garlic bulbs should be 'moneybags,' because their shape reminded her of the sacks of gold coins in folktales.

A customer on her right was sorting through the green onions. It was early enough so the store was nearly empty, and yet this person seemed to be edging in on her a bit. Once or twice the fabric of his shirt sleeve brushed her dress sleeve. Also, he was really no more than stirring those onions around. He would lift one rubber-banded clump and then drop it and alight on another. His fingers were very long and agile, almost spidery. His cuffs were yellow oxford cloth.

He said, 'Would you know if these are called scallions?'

'Well, sometimes,' Delia said. She seized the nearest bunch of celery and stepped toward the plastic bags.

'Or would they be shallots?'

'No, they're scallions,' she told him.

Needlessly, he steadied the roll of bags overhead while she peeled one off. (He towered a good foot above her.) She dropped the celery into the bag and reached toward the cup of twist ties, but he had already plucked one out for her. 'What are shallots, anyway?' he asked.

She would have feared that he was trying to pick her up, except that when she turned she saw he was surely ten years her junior, and very good-looking besides. He had straight, dark-yellow hair and milky blue eyes that made him seem dreamy and peaceful. He was smiling down at her, standing a little closer than strangers ordinarily stand.

'Um . . .,' she said, flustered.

'Shallots,' he reminded her.

'Shallots are fatter,' she said. She set the celery in her grocery cart. 'I believe they're above the parsley,' she called over her shoulder, but she found him next to her, keeping step with her as she wheeled her cart toward the citrus fruits. He wore blue jeans, very faded, and soft moccasins that couldn't be heard above 'King of the Road' on the public sound system.

'I also need lemons,' he told her.

She slid another glance at him.

'Look,' he said suddenly. He lowered his voice. 'Could I ask you a big favor?'

'Um . . .'

'My ex-wife is up ahead in potatoes. Or not ex I guess but . . . estranged, let's say, and she's got her boyfriend with her. Could you just pretend we're together? Just till I can duck out of here?'

'Well, of course,' Delia said.

And without even taking a deep breath first, she plunged happily back into the old high-school atmosphere of romantic intrigue and deception. She narrowed her eyes and lifted her chin and said, 'We'll *show* her!' and sailed past the fruits and made a U-turn into root vegetables. 'Which one is she?' she murmured through ventriloquist lips.

'Tan shirt,' he whispered. Then he startled her with a sudden burst of laughter. 'Ha, ha!' he told her too loudly. 'Aren't you clever to say so!'

But 'tan shirt' was nowhere near an adequate description. The woman who turned at the sound of his voice wore an ecru raw-silk tunic over black silk trousers as slim as two pencils. Her hair was absolutely black, cut shorter on one side, and her face was a perfect oval. 'Why, Adrian,' she said. Whoever was with her – some man or other – turned too, still gripping a potato. A dark, thick man with rough skin like stucco and eyebrows that met in the middle. Not up to the woman's standard at all; but how many people were?

Delia's companion said, 'Rosemary. I didn't see you. So don't forget,' he told Delia, not breaking his stride. He set a hand on her cart to steer it into aisle 3. 'You promised me you'd make your marvelous blancmange tonight.'

'Oh, yes, my . . . blancmange,' Delia echoed faintly. Whatever blancmange might be, it sounded the way she felt just then: pale and plain-faced and skinny, with her freckles and her frizzy brown curls and her ruffled pink round-collared dress.

They had bypassed the dairy case and the juice aisle, where Delia had planned to pick up several items, but she didn't point that out because this Adrian person was still talking. 'Your blancmange and then your, uh, what, your meat and vegetables and da-da-da . . .'

The way he let his voice die reminded her of those popular songs that end with the singers just absentmindedly drifting away from the microphone. 'Is she looking at us?' he whispered. 'Check it out. Don't make it obvious.'

Delia glanced over, pretending to be struck by a display of converted rice. Both the wife and the boyfriend had their backs to her, but there was something artificial in their posture. No one could find russet potatoes so mesmerizing. 'Well, she's mentally looking,' Delia murmured. She turned to see her grocery cart rapidly filling with pasta. Egg noodles, rotini, linguine – Adrian flung in boxes at random. 'Excuse me . . .,' she said.

Writing as design

WRITING ON THE SCREEN

New technologies, such as computers, have offered us new contexts for writing. Writing online is very different from writing on a piece of paper, for many different reasons. When we do a piece of online writing, such as constructing our own homepage, or writing a blog, that writing has permeability: in other words, readers can click on sections and links, opening new windows to view new pages. In that sense, the kind of reading we do online may be non-linear – not reading from top to bottom of a page, but rather reading sections of text and then clicking through to new material. In fact, describing online writing as if it were conventional text is very misleading: although this paragraph has referred to 'pages', such a thing does not really exist in electronic **discourse**.

As well as giving us new audiences and purposes for writing, the Internet allows writing to be part of a richly **multimodal** system in ways that were not possible on paper. Keyboard symbols, themselves the basis of new art forms in the shape of **emoticons**, can take their place alongside sound files, video clips and animations where text can sing, dance and play. Online text can be interactive in ways that its paper-based cousin could only dream about. Online writers can be seen as textual designers, assembling different elements to create a kind of colourful assortment or **bricolage**.

Because online writing is potentially readable by a mass audience, it's possible to see the phenomenon of personal homepages as a form of instant publishing, and instant self-promotion – a way of advertising oneself to the world. Daniel Chandler (2006) talks of such texts as places where the writer's identity is permanently 'under construction', as writers change and adapt the elements that go to make up their site. Following the **metaphor** of site construction, he sees online writers as 'bricoleurs', people who assemble varied elements into a shape or pattern. It follows, then, that analysing such bricolages requires consideration of a wide range of textual aspects, termed by Chandler 'the bricoleur's webkit', as follows.

THE BRICOLEUR'S WEB KIT

Types of activity

- *Inclusion*. What different ideas and topics are included?
- *Allusion*. What ideas and topics are being referred to?
- *Omission*. What's left unsaid or is noticeable by its absence?
- *Adaptation*. How are materials and ideas added to or altered?
- *Arrangement*. How is everything organized on the page?

Types of content

- personal statistics and biographical details;
- interests, likes and dislikes;
- ideas, values, beliefs and causes;
- friends, acquaintances and personal icons (e.g. celebrities).

Types of structure

- written text;
- graphics – whether still or moving – and other artwork;
- sound and/or video (e.g. associated webcams);
- short screenfuls to long scrolls of text;
- single page or many interconnected pages;
- separate windows or frames;
- an access counter (i.e. number of people who've visited);
- a guestbook;
- links for other pages (e.g. a 'cool links' section);
- an email button or chat button.

(Adapted from Chandler's original list by Thurlow *et al.* 2004, p. 194)

The scope of this section, or even this book, does not allow for any detailed consideration of computer-based communication. But, as with our earlier exploration of conventional writing, it may be useful to consider the nature of online writing from a beginner's point of view.

Activity

Text 1:13, on pp. 22–3, is a paper representation of a young person's home page.

Dodie was 11 years old when she made the site, and this was her first attempt at creating her own homepage.

Transferring this site to paper, of course, has immediately limited its multi-modal nature: in its original form, there was a colourful background of mauve circles; the emoticons winked and smiled; and music played as the site opened.

Also, limitations of space in this book prevent any display of the linked pages Dodie had created, including her story page (where she had written a story about bullying), her favourite links (with her own reviews of the sites), her guestbook, chatrooms, and so on.

Looking at what has been reproduced here, analyse Dodie's home page by applying Chandler's 'bricoleur's webkit'.

There is a commentary on this activity at the end of the unit.

Text 1:13

Silverstar

the show must go on!

- Home
- Links
- Story time!
- have a safe chat
- Guestbook

Welcome to silverstar

0000000111

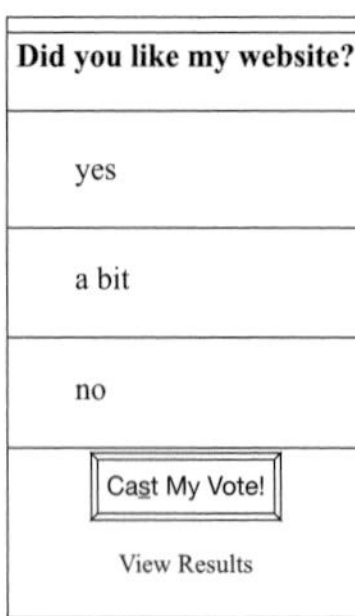

Hello, and welcome to silver stars, the coolest website ever! ☺

Look around this wicked site. ☺ It's soooo fun!

☺ Don't know what to do? Why not try play some cool games (courtesy of www.battleon.com and www.miniclip.com), click on one of the other sites, have a chat (if anyone is on) or simply tell me what I need to improve on in this site (write in the guestbook).

And don't worry, the games are free!

also, please don't forget to sign the guestbook. It will be fun to see who's been on my site!

(the links below are to some games from www.battleon. com.)

undeadassault.swf

firespawn.swf

---

this is a website made by Dodie Clark

Thanks for visiting. Click here to create you own FREE website at Freewebs.com!

Extension activities

1 Collect some signs in a systematic way and try to determine how that system works. Here are some examples to get you started:

- How do the signs in the contemporary UK Highway code compare with those used in other countries?
- To what extent are any signs universal? To help you think about this, look at Text 1:14 below, where you will see two signs from different cultures – Sweden and Canada, respectively. Can you understand their messages? If you do understand them, put yourself in the position of someone outside those cultures and think about what cultural knowledge you would need to have in order to make sense of them.

Text 1:14

Swedish sign

This sign, on a footpath where cyclists are also allowed, says 'You who cycle, be mindful of us'. The pictures then suggest who the 'us' refers to, viz. the elderly, children, dogs and lovers – all groups who are seen as unlikely to be paying full attention to vehicles on the path. The playful nature of the sign – particularly the comical hearts surrounding the lovers – might be seen as frivolous by British readers, who are used to official signs being rather more serious.

Canadian sign

This sign was placed on the bank of a large river in a Canadian city, and tells members of the public not to go any nearer to the edge. The sign harnesses the prohibitive meaning of the road sign system, but also warns that breaking this rule could cost trespassers a minimum of $75 in court. The legal system is symbolised by the gavel (judge's hammer) at the bottom of the noticeboard. The equivalent British signs sometimes say 'trespassers will be prosecuted', but it is unusual to see the force of the law symbolised by any image, such as that of the gavel here.

- Collect some more examples of particular types of sign (for example, the use of certain animals or objects) and explore some different cultural readings of them. For example, how are animal logos used in other cultures? What are the associations for particular animals in the culture in question? Are there examples of animals being viewed very differently by different cultures?

2 If you do any work with young children, or have children in your family, ask them for their views on the importance of reading and writing. See to what extent things have changed since the data presented here was collected (1992). For example: Does anyone still 'leave a note for the milkman'? Do people still write many cheques, or are bills paid more often via direct debit or online accounts? Do children automatically think of book-reading and handwriting when reading and writing are mentioned, or do they see the reading and writing of computer texts (such as websites) as forms of literacy?

3 Collect as many examples as you can find of texts that use abbreviations, initialisms and acronyms. When you have collected your material, sort your examples into groups according to the techniques they use. Try to draw some conclusions about the reasons for the usages you have collected. If you are unsure about the comprehensibility of some of your examples, test them out on some informants of your own.

4 One area that hasn't been covered, but which you could explore in your data collection, is that of jokes, puzzles and riddles that involve playing around with written symbols. For example, some use single letters (but not necessarily initial letters) to stand for whole words, as in the following hoarding outside a church:

WHAT'S MISSING FROM THIS CH-CH?

You might find some more examples like this in children's comics and magazines, or in some types of English school textbook.

5 Another area to consider is abbreviated language use in computer chatrooms, e-mails or text messages (SMS). For example, according to Thurlow (2001), the following are quite commonly used in texting:

gd	good
yr	your
lv	love
msg	message
2moz	tomorrow

Do you use abbreviations like these?

Do some research among your friends, and make a list of the most commonly used shortened forms.

Try to explain the literacy strategies used to abbreviate the words: why are some of the letters chosen, and not others? Are there words that can be abbreviated in a number of different ways?

6 Collect some texts that are using features of written language in order to suggest aspects of speech. You could focus on a particular area: for example, children's early writing; advertising; literature.

Commentaries/Answers to activities

COMMENTARY: ACTIVITY p. 2, TEXT 1:1

All the signs are iconic apart from the sign for 'school'.

The 'school' sign, rather than picturing a school, symbolises a school by using a torch. This type of torch is often used on public statues, and carries classical references to such ideas as 'shedding the light of knowledge on dark areas', 'lighting up a path towards progress and civilisation' – ideas which are represented by the torch still used to mark the Olympic games. This same idea is in the word 'enlightenment', which is often used to describe a particular period in history when people looked towards classical civilisation (Ancient Greece and Rome) as ideal states.

Such associations are being played with in the Boddington's beer mat below (Text 1:15), where the symbol (a cut-out shape) resembles both a torch and an ice-cream cone, and where the phrase 'the cream of' synthesises ideas of cream-as-luxury-foodstuff with that of high quality in general (as in 'la crème de la crème') and, ultimately, with the 'creamy' pint of Manchester-based beer.

Text 1:15

Although all the other signs are iconic, the sign for 'crossroads' is slightly different from the rest in that it doesn't necessarily suggest the actual shape of roads coming up: instead, it takes the idea of the cross as a written symbol, and bases itself on that shape. Note that, outside the context of road signs, this shape can have other, highly symbolic, meanings – such as a 'kiss' on a personal letter, 'wrong' when written on an answer, or 'multiply' in mathematics.

COMMENTARY: ACTIVITY p. 4, TEXT 1:3

Co-operative Bank advert

The leaflet is promoting the ethical values of the bank's investment policies. Inside the leaflet, each panel shows either an example of where investment was made in what the bank considers a worthy cause (for example, 'green' energy projects), or an example of an application turned down (for example, from a bank owned by an oppressive regime). Each panel has a 'yes' or a 'no' stamped across the information. The message is that the Co-op bank actively decides where to put its business, and that ethical considerations play as much of a part as profit margins.

The front of the leaflet uses the road sign to suggest the strongest possible version of 'no': road signs with red circles are prohibitive, giving orders that ban specific activities (for example, no waiting, no overtaking, no entry, etc). The fact that the 'o' of 'no' has been turned into a red sign of prohibition (the sign was red in the original text) therefore strengthens its negativity. It may also make it seem more authoritative, in that road signs are usually seen as encoding government legislation, for the benefit of the community.

There is an interesting double meaning to the word 'business' in 'it's our business to say no'. On the one hand, the statement can mean that it's the bank's job sometimes to turn down applicants for funds; but it can also mean that their refusal itself is part of what makes them money. In other words, the fact that they sometimes say 'no' makes them popular with customers who have a conscience.

Pret-a-Manger advert

Pret-a-Manger is a sandwich chain specialising in freshly made sandwiches. The text presented here is from the side of one of its sandwich boxes. The idea of 'men at work' connoted by the road sign, which would normally appear at road works, is here applied to chefs at work on edible ingredients rather than tar and asphalt. To anchor this idea, the parts of the road sign are made up of food – tomatoes make up the warning triangle, the worker's head is a slice of cucumber, his arms are prawns, and his spade handle is a spring onion. The intertextual reference to the road sign is therefore done in a humorous way, but there is a serious message too: the sandwiches sold are subject to the same serious labour and attention as that demanded by our highways and byways. In other words, the workers put their backs into their jobs.

RAC advert

This is slightly different from the other two ads studied here because it travelled through the postal system as a card or letter would. Evidence of this is shown on the reverse of the triangle, where the addressee's details appear. Although both the Pret-a-Manger advert and this one use the warning triangle, this one differs in specifying no particular 'hazard' on the front. The recipient of the card would therefore – if the card landed on the doormat 'warning' side up – have their attention drawn to the starkness of the message, with its red border and single, rather threatening, word. On the back of the triangle are the details that then translate this 'warning' sign into the rather more familiar 'reminder' notice for expiry of cover. It seems appropriate that a company that offers cover for vehicle breakdowns should use an intertextual reference to a road sign; the difference here, of course, is that regular road signs specify the nature of the danger they are warning us about.

COMMENTARY: ACTIVITY p. 6, TEXT 1:4

The products/services and possible connotations are as follows:

1 Owl: from a small ads/services page in a local paper. The column headed by the owl logo was advertising children's reading clubs. We have connotations of the 'wise kindly old owl'; perhaps the fact that the owl has large, forward-facing eyes makes us associate the bird with reading and therefore acquiring knowledge. Or it could be that we associate reading with night-time activity, a time when the nocturnal bird is alert.

2 Sparrow: the logo of a local paper, placed in the top right-hand corner of the front page, just below the title of the paper, which was the *Enquirer.* Sparrows are thought to be bold, inquisitive birds – qualities that the newspaper would presumably like to be associated with.

3 Seagull: from a holiday company. We associate seagulls with the seaside, and therefore leisure-time activities. The picture shows the seagull flying across the sun: to see the bird at this angle, we would have to be lying

on our backs – presumably basking in the warmth and sunshine of a summer's day.

4 Swallow: from a futon company. Associations we have for this type of bird are likely to include grace, elegance, freedom – soaring high in the air, swooping and diving. These birds also often feature in oriental art, and the futon itself is Japanese.

5 Pelican and chicks: from an insurance company. The adult pelican is known to peck out its own feathers in order to line the nest for its chicks. Whether all readers would bring this idea to the image is doubtful, but even so the image of an adult bird with its chicks calls up associations for us of protection and security.

6 Swallow: from an airline company. The idea of 'flying high' would be something any airline would like to suggest. The design of the picture is very stylised and mechanistic, so in contrast to the futon company's 'natural' image, this picture suggests power and man-made speed, calling up the shape of an aircraft with its engines creating a slipstream of air.

7 Eagle: a bank. The eagle suggests power and strength. It has been used to symbolise the power of nation-states, as in the famous American bald eagle. It therefore calls up ideas of large, powerful institutions with extensive resources at their disposal.

COMMENTARY: ACTIVITY p. 8, TEXTS 1.5, 1.6

Some of the ideas that are expressed by the children could be grouped as follows:

1 The importance of literacy in terms of day-to-day functioning: reading recipes, seeing signs for danger, not being cheated in shops, finding out what's on TV, leaving notes for the milkman, writing shopping lists and cheques, and putting bets on. These are all ways of controlling and negotiating our world, and illustrate the importance of reading and writing as forms of instrumental, everyday communication.

2 Written language is seen as the repository of knowledge and therefore a means of educating ourselves. Writing produces tangible permanent artifacts – books – and as such is the archive of a culture's ideas and attitudes. To gain access to this store, we need to be able to read.

3 Written language is associated with being 'clever' and getting a job. In contemporary society, we take for granted the idea that literacy should

be a universal entitlement. But compulsory schooling only started in 1870; traditionally, while spoken language was universal, writing was a very particular skill, learned only by those who were formally educated. In medieval times, writing was a professional skill – 'scribing' – for which money would be charged. Even though we now view literacy as a basic skill for everyone, we still have a legacy which connects literacy with power in all sorts of ways, from the most obvious – the importance we give to written exams and application forms, the way we pay large sums of money to lawyers to write our legal documents and 'translate' them for us – to the slightly more subtle – the importance of signing your name (as opposed to giving a verbal agreement), the way libel is seen as a valid legal concept, while slander is not taken as seriously.

4 Both the pleasure and the labour of using literacy skills come across here. Unlike speech, which is spontaneous and feels relatively effortless, both writing and reading are skills which require concentration and subtle co-ordination of hand and eye movements, aside from all the different types of linguistic processing that they entail.

COMMENTARY: ACTIVITY p. 11, TEXT 1:7

Using initial letters to stand for whole words is a common stage for early writers: it signals that a crucial connection has been made between speech and writing, but that not enough of each whole word can be mapped out in order to represent it graphically. Initial letters can be a useful aide mémoire, to recall the whole word if necessary at some later stage (as here – it was two days later that Jonathon read his text back to the teacher); in learning the manual skill of writing, the hand quickly tires. This method is therefore a good way of writing a long text – something any teacher would encourage. Note also the importance of drawing in early texts such as these, where pictures are often an integral part of the writing. It is only the adult world that puts strong boundaries around these two types of activity, putting them into the separate categories of 'art' and 'writing'; for children who have yet to learn about the way adults divide up the world of representation, one type of symbolic mark must be much like another. It is well known that early drawing, what adults sometimes disparagingly call 'scribbling', is good preparation for the very fine movements needed to produce alphabetic letters.

COMMENTARY: ACTIVITY p. 12, TEXT 1:8

In abbreviating the description of the house, you will have omitted many of the vowels (except where a vowel starts a word) but retained many of the consonants. This approach is at the basis of other examples of abbreviation, such as in 'T-line' shorthand. However, some words have such a distinctive profile, or are used so often in abbreviated form, that we come to understand them even when given only the first part of the word, especially when we see them used in a particular context – for example, the estate agent's material could have had 'beaut', '19thC', 'rec', 'sep', 'ext' and 'incl'. Some phrases are often abbreviated to initial letters (called initialisms) where this occurs on a regular basis: for example, GCH regularly means 'gas central heating', and ONO 'or nearest offer'. The latter examples are not very different from the child's strategy of initial-letter use; this same technique is also used regularly in personal ads (where GSOH in lonely hearts' columns means 'good sense of humour' and WLTM means 'would like to meet'), and in road signs – such as P for 'Parking' and H for 'hospital'. Acronyms also feature single letters, but they are then pronounced as whole words, whether recognised as a collection of letters, as in NATO, or not, as in laser – 'light amplification by the stimulated emission of radiation'.

COMMENTARY: ACTIVITY p. 13, TEXTS 1:9, 1:10

Omar (age 5) enhances his story with a picture where a ghostly figure makes 'ooooo' sounds, in an attempt to provide something of an atmospheric soundtrack. This also occurs within the text itself: the reader knows that the words 'The Spirit, The Spirit' need to be pronounced in a 'spooky' way, as a result of their having wobbly lines round them. It's difficult to say exactly where this convention is from, but likely contenders could be comics and those science-fiction films where the screen 'dissolves' as the narrator goes back in time to remember 'when it all began'. Note the very logical sound-based spelling, 'ones a pone tieem' for 'once upon a time'.

Lauren (age 7) uses a range of devices to suggest features of spoken language. The enlargement of letters and the darker print in the words 'gone' and 'help?' suggest increased volume – in the first word, as a result of shock, and in the second, to signal a voice calling out. The question mark on 'help' indicates a speaker's raised voice when asking another character whether that is the right word to use. While the characters work to build their word out of pebbles, there is a soundtrack: 'Hi ho, hi ho, it's off to work we go'. This is particularly appropriate, as in *Snow White and the Seven Dwarfs,* from which the soundtrack comes, the dwarfs sing this as they go off stone-breaking in the mines. The sense of time passing, as the characters go through a laborious routine of repetitive work, is therefore achieved.

Towards the end, there is a clever use of full-stops to indicate that the letters in the word 'h.e.l.p.' are written (in pebbles, of course) rather than spoken.

COMMENTARY: ACTIVITY p. 16, TEXT 1:12

David Crystal's *The Cambridge Encyclopedia of the English Language* (1995) lists four main functions for punctuation: grammar, where features such as full stops and commas mark out grammatical units; prosody, where such symbols as speech marks, question marks and exclamation marks indicate that someone is speaking, where some forms of punctuation – most notably colons and semicolons – map out aspects of argument or explanation (as in this paragraph); and semantic nuance, where features of emphasis such as quotation marks suggest a particular attitude to a word or phrase being 'marked out'.

Anne Tyler uses punctuation to mark out grammatical units in the same way as writers of many other types of text. There are two examples of the rhetorical function listed above: these are a colon in line 72, which points forward to the explanation that follows it, and the semi-colon in line 66 which balances the **sentences** either side of the punctuation mark, bringing them into more dramatic parallel than a comma would do, and leading up to a rhetorical question (a question posed for effect, rather than one requiring a real answer).

What is noticeable, however, is Tyler's extensive use of the prosodic and the semantic nuance functions. This is hardly surprising, given that these are concerned with constructing a sense of voice, and with establishing attitudes.

- *Examples of the prosodic function*: within the language of the characters themselves – speech marks, lines of dots suggesting a voice trailing off, question marks, exclamation marks, italics to suggest emphasis; within the language used by the narrator – brackets and dashes in lines 23, 63 and 64, and 89 to suggest a change in pace as a result of adding extra information.
- *Examples of the semantic nuance function*: quotation marks in the narrator's report of Delia's thoughts in lines 6 and 7; the same in the narrator's commentary in lines 39 and 59.

Despite these extensive markers, there is still much about the way the characters speak that has to be described by the narrator. Here are some examples: 'she called over her shoulder'; 'he lowered his voice'; 'she murmured through ventriloquist lips'; 'he whispered'; 'he startled her with a sudden burst of laughter'; 'he told her too loudly'; 'Delia echoed faintly'; 'the way he let his voice die reminded her . . .'. These examples illustrate that, in the end, written language cannot do justice to the subtleties of speech. All it can do is to give us some signposts as readers, via devices such as punctuation marks, to help us create the idea of speech in our heads.

COMMENTARY: ACTIVITY p. 21, TEXT 1:13

Types of activity

Dodie's site emphasises activity and interactivity. She offers various sections for the visitor to explore, and invites them to play games and give her feedback. Her own language is interactive, asking visitors questions - whether they like the site, whether they know what to do. There is a sense that she really wants to communicate with her readers, and is concerned that they should feel at home: for example, she welcomes them twice, uses the greeting 'hello', tells them not to worry, uses 'please', and invites them to give her suggestions for improvement (quite a risky offer!). She wants to know how popular her site is, and whether visitors have enjoyed it.

Types of content

Dodie uses certain objects and images to signify her identity: for example, the silver 'shooting star' icon, which has connotations of celebrity and fame. The idea of stardom is also picked up in the phrase 'the show must go on'. The fact that the shooting star is jewellery enhances the idea of showiness and glitz.

A further image on Dodie's front page is the cartoon graphic representing a girl busy at the computer – perhaps a representation of herself, and/or an image of who she thinks might be interested in her page. This figure is quite different from the idea of the 'star', wearing a baseball cap and working clothes rather than items for display and show.

The two very different representations described above are equally valid notions of Dodie's identity: online authors can express multiple identities or voices (as can offline authors).

Types of structure

Dodie's page contains written text, graphics (including animated emoticons), sound, interconnected pages with 'cool links', an access counter, a guestbook, and a chat page. She has constructed a multimodal site incorporating music, colour and movement as well as conventional writing. The site shows how many different kinds of representation are now available to young writers in this new online context. The skills required are those of a designer, a 'bricoleur' – keyboard skills and a sense of how texts need to be organised, rather than the paper-based skills of manual handwriting and linear composition.

Satellite texts

The following satellite texts look in detail at ideas covered in this unit:

The Language of Advertising looks at the use of semiotic signs to help sell products.

Language Change looks at how the use of signs in texts has developed over time.

The Language of Children looks at how children acquire linguistic and cultural knowledge.

The Language of Comics looks at a genre which makes extensive use of multimodal systems.

The Language of Drama and *The Language of Fiction* look at literary representations of talk.

Language and Gender looks at how signs are used to represent social groups.

The Language of ICT and *The Language of Websites* look at aspects of computer mediated communication.

The Language of Magazines, The Language of Newspapers and *The Language of Television* look at signs in media texts.

The Language of Sport and *The Language of War* look at the use of signs in particular contexts.

Unit two

Sounds

Aims of this unit

The aims of this unit are to explore the relationship between sounds and texts, to introduce the concepts of phonetics and phonology, and to apply some skills in phonetics and phonology to a selection of texts.

Why learn about phonetics?

A text is a piece of language written down, so why in a book about texts, might we be interested in knowing about sound? Sounds, after all, form the basis of speech, but they do not form the basis of writing. However, there is a relationship between spoken and written language: writing can be seen as a representation of the spoken language. You might also encounter texts which use symbols designed specifically to represent the sounds of language, the symbols of the International Phonetic Alphabet (IPA).

So the spelling system that we use every day to read and write is a representation of the sounds that we use in language. However, there is not a one to one relationship between the letters that we use to write our language down and the sounds that we make. Although it is a bit of a simplification, there are forty-four sounds in English and yet there are only twenty-six letters that we can use to represent them. It is immediately obvious that twenty-six letters can't individually represent forty-four sounds – there simply are not enough letters in the alphabet for that. However, that's not to say that we can't use combinations of more than one letter to represent a particular sound. This happens in English (mostly!), but the reality is that the history of English means that we have ended up with a huge vocabulary containing words that come from lots of other languages. Without going into the history of spelling and all its complexities, here is a rather extreme example of the mismatch between sound and spelling in English:

> A rough-coated, dough-faced, thoughtful ploughman strode
> through the streets of Scarborough; after falling into a slough,
> he coughed and hiccoughed.

If we compare the pronunciation of all of the sounds that are represented by the string of letters 'ough' here, we find that they are not the same; they don't rhyme. Even if we just look at the first four, they're all different.

rough
dough
thoughtful
ploughman

Activity

Look at the combinations of letters below and decide what sounds they represent. Are they consistent, or can you think of any examples where they represent another sound?

ch
th
ci

Commentary

Note: Angled brackets like this < > can be used around letters of the alphabet. This helps to distinguish the way words are spelled from the phonetic alphabet which will be introduced later.

<ch> can be pronounced as in 'cheap' and 'beach', but it is pronounced differently in 'machismo' and differently again in 'machine'. <th> can be

pronounced as in 'the' and 'breathe', but also differently in 'teeth' and 'thimble'. <ci> can be pronounced as in 'pencil' and 'cinema', but also differently in 'delicious'.

As you can see, looking at spelling is not a reliable guide for pronunciation, and that is before we even begin to take into account the differences between speakers. It is also rather clumsy trying to describe these sound differences without using the special symbols that are used for representing the sounds of English, or the terminology that we use to describe sound. For example, it would be difficult to represent children's pronunciation or a regional pronunciation accurately on paper without using something other than conventional spelling.

RECEIVED PRONUNCIATION

Received Pronunciation (RP) is the name of an accent that some speakers of English have. Unlike regional accents, which people speak as a result of what geographical area they are from, RP can be spoken by people from any area. Traditionally, RP was spoken by broadcasters, and as a result it is sometimes called 'BBC English', although nowadays television and radio broadcasters might speak with a regional accent. If someone is speaking RP, it is more likely to tell you something about their education or social class rather than where they are from. People often say that someone speaking RP 'has no accent', meaning that they don't have a *regional* accent. Linguists would say that everyone speaks with an accent, but that some accents do not give clues about regional origin.

The sounds of RP

In the introduction it was mentioned that there are forty-four sounds in English. More specifically this is the number of sounds that it is generally accepted are found in RP. Each of the words below has been chosen to illustrate one of the forty-four sounds.

The function of the IPA symbols used is specifically to represent sound. You will probably have seen some of these symbols before in a dictionary, where they are used to show the standard pronunciation of entries.

The symbols used in the IPA have a much closer relationship to the sounds of speech than spelling does, but it is still important to remember that they are not the sounds themselves; they are a way of representing them. Each symbol has an arbitrary relationship with the sound that it represents. That means that there is no real connection between the sound and the symbol except that we all agree that the symbol ʃ represents the sound that we make at the beginning of the word 'ship' and so on.

In the words below, the symbol represents the sound that has been underlined in the word next to it.

/ɪ/	as in KIT	/p/	as in POT
/e/	as in DRESS	/b/	as in BED
/a/	as in TRAP	/t/	as in TIP
/ɒ/	as in LOT	/d/	as in DID
/ʌ/	as in STRUT	/k/	as in COD
/ʊ/	as in FOOT	/g/	as in GAP
/ɑ/	as in PALM	/m/	as in MAN
/ɜ/	as in NURSE	/n/	as in NEAT
/i/	as in FLEECE	/ŋ/	as in KING
/ɔ/	as in THOUGHT	/l/	as in LOOP
/u/	as in GOOSE	/r/	as in RIP
/ə/	as in LETTER	/f/	as in FIT
/eɪ/	as in FACE	/v/	as in VAT
/əʊ/	as in GOAT	/θ/	as in THANK
/aɪ/	as in PRICE	/ð/	as in THIS
/ɔɪ/	as in CHOICE	/s/	as in SEA
/aʊ/	as in MOUTH	/z/	as in ZOO
/ɪə/	as in NEAR	/ʃ/	as in SHEEP
/ɛə/	as in SQUARE	/ʒ/	as in BEIGE
/ʊə/	as in CURE	/h/	as in HIP
/ʧ/	as in CHIP	/ʤ/	as in GIN
/w/	as in WOOD	/j/	as in YES

Source: Adapted from lexical sets by Wells (1982)

IPA transcriptions appear in either slashed brackets / / or square brackets [ ]. The choice of brackets is significant, and will be explained later in the unit.

Activity

The following words (pronounced with an RP accent) have been transcribed using the IPA symbols listed above. Try to work out what the words are.

/θɪsl/

/bəʊt/

/kaʊtʃ/

/kjʊərɪəs/

/reɪst/

Transcribe the following words using the IPA symbols (try to transcribe the words as they would sound in RP).

rhubarb

three

sugar

sloping

door

custard

yellow

noisy

extensive

The answers for and commentary on this activity are at the end of the unit.

The following text is a transcription of a speaker from Huddersfield telling a story about buying a television stand from a high street retailer. The transcription uses three types of transcription: conventional spellings; representations of the accent using the Roman alphabet, or 'eye dialect'; and some examples of IPA transcription.

Activity

Concentrating on the IPA transcriptions, try to pick out as many features of this accent that are different from RP as possible, and explain how they are different from RP.

Text 2:1

> When we went for t' table you know .hh Currys and Dixons are t' same firm aren't [ðe] .hh and we ad us Dixon [buk] with us (0.8) and we went for t'table .hh an uh (2.0) we looked at it in t' Dixon [buk] (0.8) and wo-worrit either ten or twenty pound cheaper in t'Dixon [buk] than what it were in Currys uh they were chargin anyway we tell them and we showed it 'em .hhh an he says oh we shall ave to match that price then so we gorri- t at Dixon pri he ce eh heh .hh I says ooh I don't know if that were cheekeh .hh cos I says look .hh I says lets get- (.) lets geddit paid fer an never mi:nd she says we're not payin more when we can geddit cheaper at Dixons (0.5) an uh (0.5) so: (.) e says o:h we shall ave to match it then I don't know what- what t'difference is and e [tʊk] us [buk] with im went somewhere to [lʊk] .hh whether we went on t'website to look or what (0.8) o:h do they o:h well this were us table (1.0) an uh (0.3) anyway we goddit cheaper (.) well d-Dixons' price (1.0) we were avin black [glas] at first and then s- (.) it'll show all t' [dʊst ʊp] (0.5) black [glas]

Commentary

The IPA transcriptions show vowel differences between this accent and RP. The first difference is in the word 'they' where this speaker pronounces /eɪ/ as [e] as in DRESS. There are no other examples of this in the transcription, so we assume that 'paying' is pronounced with the FACE vowel, /eɪ/. In 'book', the /ʊ/ as in FOOT is pronounced [u] as in GOOSE. The speaker does this each time she says 'book', so it appears to be a consistent feature in this word, but we can see that the speaker still pronounces the FOOT vowel in words like 'look' and 'took'. However, the speaker uses /ʊ/ as in FOOT in 'took' and 'look' as RP would.

Notice that the speaker also uses the FOOT vowel [ʊ] where RP would have the STRUT vowel, /ʌ/ in 'dust'. Northern English accents are well known to not use the STRUT vowel, and stereotypical representations of them often rely on this to characterise them. Finally, where RP would use the PALM vowel /ɑ/ in 'glass', the transcript indicates the use of the TRAP vowel, [a].

EYE DIALECT

In the previous activity, the transcription contained some representations of speech using unconventional spellings. This technique is called 'eye dialect'.

Activity

Below is a different representation of the Huddersfield text you looked at before. This time eye-dialect only is used to represent regional speech. Try to identify aspects of speech that are being represented using the unconventional spellings and explain what features you think they are intended to represent.

Text 2:2

When we went for t' table you know .hh Currys and Dixons are t' same firm aren't they .hh and we ad us Dixon book with us (0.8) and we went for t'table .hh an uh (2.0) we looked at it in t' Dixon book (0.8) and wo- worrit either ten or twenty pound cheaper in t'Dixon book than what it were in Currys uh they were chargin anyway we tell them and we showed it 'em .hhh an he says oh we shall ave to match that price then so we gorri- t at Dixon pri he ce eh heh .hh I says ooh I don't know if that were cheekeh .hh cos I says look .hh I says lets get- (.) lets geddit paid fer an never mi:nd she says we're not payin more when we can geddit cheaper at Dixons (0.5) an uh (0.5) so: (.) e says o:h we shall ave to match it then I don't know what- what t'difference is and e took us book with im went somewhere to look .hh whether we went on t'website to look or what (0.8) o:h do they o:h well this were us table (1.0) an uh (0.3) anyway we goddit cheaper (.) well d-Dixons' price (1.0) we were avin black glass at first and then s- (.) it'll show all t' doost oop (0.5) black glass

Commentary

t'table

t'same firm

show all t'doost oop

These examples all represent the use of a **glottal stop** as a pronunciation of the word 'the' (a definite determiner) by using the letter <t> with an apostrophe. Conventional punctuation uses an apostrophe to indicate that a letter or string of letters is missing – for example, the way that 'telephone' is sometimes written as 'phone, or 'refrigerator' as 'fridge. Do writers use this convention because they see the northern pronunciation of 'the' as missing some sounds? This is interesting because if we revert to IPA representations, we can see that the RP pronunciation /ðə/ and the Huddersfield speaker's pronunciation [ʔ] are completely different. It is not that one sound has been missed and another retained, but we have no clear way of representing this accurately without using the IPA. A further interesting issue is the way that this eye-dialect representation of northern speech seems to have had the effect of making some people doing impressions of a stereotypical Yorkshire accent use a [t] sound to represent 'the' rather than [ʔ].

ad us Dixon book

we shall ave to match it

e took us book with im

The examples above are quite straightforward in that they imply that initial /h/ sounds have been elided, as the <h> has been missed off the spelling. This representation is easily achieved as the /h/ sound is consistently represented as <h> in English spelling.

Other examples of eye dialect in the text include:

worrit either ten or twenty pound cheaper

cheekeh

geddit cheaper

we goddit cheaper

they were chargin

we're not payin more

show all t'doost oop

Eye dialect is a useful technique in literature, in that it can express features of spoken language on the page, to some extent. Most readers of fiction don't need any more than an indication of pronunciation. However, the IPA offers a more reliable and accurate way of representing speech in writing appropriate for language analysis.

THE VOCAL TRACT

Speech sounds are produced in the vocal tract, using air pushed out from the lungs. Different speech sounds are made by changing the shape of the vocal tract. This can be done by moving the lips and tongue to touch different parts of the vocal tract (place of articulation). Sounds can be further modified by placing the articulators different distances from one another (manner of articulation). We can make an even wider variety of sounds in our vocal tracts by vibrating the vocal folds (voiced sounds) or not vibrating them (voiceless sounds).

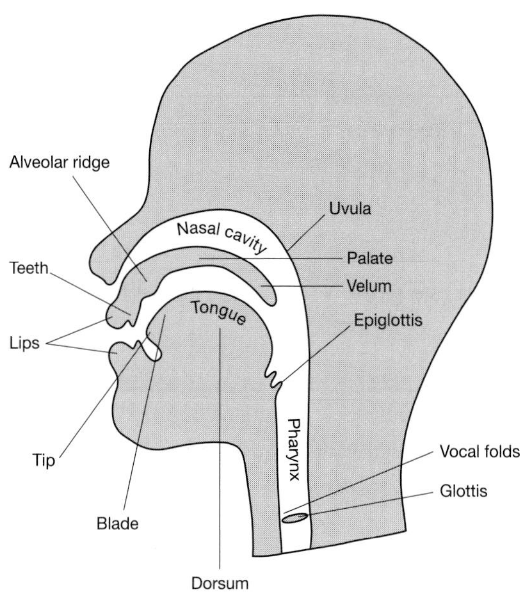

The vocal tract

The articulators are the parts of the vocal tract that are important for speech. Some of the articulators can move (active articulators), such as the tongue and the lips, while others remain still (passive articulators), such as the roof of the mouth. The place of articulation is named after the articulators involved in making the sound. Where one of the articulators is passive, the place of articulation is named after the passive articulator. For example, sounds that are made using the back of the tongue and the velum (for example, [k] and [g]) are called velar sounds.

The following table organises the RP consonants by place and manner of articulation.

Manner of articulation	*Place of articulation*							
	Bilabial	*Labio-dental*	*Dental*	*Alveolar*	*Post-alveolar*	*Palatal*	*Velar*	*Glottal*
Plosive	p b			t d			k g	
Nasal	m			n			ŋ	
Fricative		f v	θ ð	s z	ʃ ʒ			h
Affricate					ʧ ʤ			
Approximant	w				r	j		
Lateral approximant			l					

*The voiced sounds are on the right and the voiceless ones are on the left.

Manner of articulation (how close are the articulators?)

Plosives: /p, b, t, d, k, g/

These sounds are characterised by having the two articulators touching one another – for example the lips touch one another in the sounds /p/ and /b/. Air builds up behind the closed articulators and comes out in a burst.

Nasals: /m, n, ŋ/

These are very similar to plosives in that the articulators are touching, but the air is allowed to escape through the nose.

Fricatives: /f, v, θ, ð, s, z, ʃ, ʒ, h/

These sounds have the articulators almost touching but not quite. The air is allowed to squeeze out of a little space, becoming turbulent, which causes it to make a hissing or buzzing noise.

Affricates: /ʧ, ʤ/

This is an articulation that starts as a plosive and ends as a fricative. /ʧ/ and /ʤ/ are the only affricates in English.

Approximants: /w, r, j/

These sounds are not quite so easy to describe. The feature that ties these sounds together is that that the air is allowed to flow past the articulators without becoming turbulent. The articulators are usually wider apart than for a fricative.

Lateral approximants: /l/

Lateral sounds are characterised by having the air flow down one or both sides of the tongue. In English we have only one of these.

Place of articulation (where are the articulators touching/close to touching?)

Most places of articulation involve the tongue moving towards a static part of the vocal tract, e.g. the teeth or the alveolar ridge. The place of articulation takes its name from the articulator that stays still with the exception of the bilabial and glottal sounds. In these cases, both of the articulators are active – they move towards one another. Which part of the tongue makes contact or near contact with the place of articulation depends on how far back in the vocal tract it is. Places of articulation towards the front of the vocal tract, for example, dental (teeth) and alveolar, tend to involve the tip or blade of the tongue, while places of articulation further back (e.g. velar) involve the back of the tongue. Have a look at the vocal tract diagram to check the names of these different places of articulation.

Voicing (are the vocals vibrating?)

Languages have a tendency to have sounds in voiced and voiceless pairs to make most use of a particular articulation. If you have to learn to make an articulation, it seems sensible to make two distinct sounds using that articulation if possible, for example, /s/ and /z/ are identical except for the fact that for /z/ the vocal folds are vibrating. Try making a /s/ and a /z/ out loud. Notice how your tongue stays in the same place (almost touching the alveolar ridge) but when you make a /z/ you can feel a buzzing in your throat? Gently rest the tips of your fingers on your larynx (commonly known as the 'Adam's Apple') and feel how the buzzing starts and stops as you switch from a /s/ sound to a /z/ sound. The larynx is made of bits of cartilage which protect your vibrating vocal folds. You use your muscles to open them up which gives a voiceless sound, or close them, which results in a voiced sound.

Activity

Each of the following groups of sounds have something in common. What is it? You'll need to look at the grid of symbols above to help you (see p. 46). The first one has been done for you.

/s, v, θ/ These sounds are all fricatives
/t, d, n/
/m, b, p/
/s, f, t, ʃ, h/

There is a commentary on this activity at the end of the unit.

Phonology and phonetics

PHONOLOGY

Phonology is the study of sounds within a particular language and how those sounds function within that language. So, for example, we have seen that English has forty-four sounds. All English words consist of combinations of those forty-four sounds. Hawaiian, on the other hand, has only thirteen, so all their words are made up of combinations of those thirteen sounds. Further phonological observations might include how the forty-four sounds of English can combine together to make words. How many consonants can we have at the start of a word? In English, there are a maximum of three consonant sounds together (two or more consonant sounds together are called a consonant cluster) before the vowel. How many consonants can we have at the end of a word? Are there certain consonants that can go at the beginnings of words but not at the ends and vice versa? These are all phonological issues.

Activity

Come up with three examples of English words that have:

- one consonant sound at the start of the word (e.g. pot)
- two consonant sounds at the start of the word (e.g. tread)
- three consonant sounds at the start of the word (e.g. spring)

Be careful to include words that have three consonants in the pronunciation rather than the spelling – e.g. 'through' has three consonant letters, <thr>, but only two consonant sounds before we get to the vowel, /θr/.

What do you notice about the words that have three consonant sounds at the start?

Commentary

A phonological constraint on English words is that when there are three consonants at the start, the first one is always /s/. In your list of words with three consonant sounds at the beginning, all of them will start with a /s/. There are other constraints on the way that words are formed in a language, such as how many consonants you can have at the end of a word. Four consonants at the end of a word is the maximum that you will find in English, for example, as in <twelfths> /twelfθs/. Notice that there are four sounds, or phonemes, but five letters in the spelling of the consonant cluster. The constraints on the way that a language pronounces its words are particularly interesting when you consider what happens to words when they are borrowed from another language. In Japan, the US sport baseball is very popular and some of the words associated with the game have been adopted by Japanese. Most Japanese words have the structure of a consonant (C) followed by a vowel (V) – this structure of CV can be repeated, so words will be CVCV or CVCVCV and so on. Therefore the Japanese pronunciation of the English baseball related word <strike> is /suturaɪku/. An /u/ vowel is inserted between the consonants /s, t/ and /r/ to make the word more like a Japanese one, and an /u/ vowel is added to the end, so the structure ends up as CVCVCVCV. This phonological process of inserting vowels to separate consonants is called **epenthesis**.

PHONETICS

Phonetics is useful for looking at the detail of how sounds are pronounced. For example, at a general level, what we might think of as the sound 't' can be produced in a number of ways. Perhaps the two most obvious ways are with what we think of as a normal 't' sound, [t], and a glottal stop, [ʔ]* (ignoring for the moment that these two pronunciations may be considered by some people to have different social status).

The glottal stop is not listed as one of the English sounds above, because it is an alternative pronunciation of the sound /t/ rather than a phoneme in its own right. What we have so far been calling a 'sound' must be able to bring about a change of meaning in a word. If we look at the two alternative pronunciations of 'bitter', we have [bɪtə] and [bɪʔə]. We have, it might at first seem, replaced one of the sounds /t/ with another, [ʔ], but yet we still understand the word to mean the same thing (sour tasting), whether the word is pronounced with [t] or [ʔ]. Therefore [ʔ] is considered to be an alternative pronunciation of the sound /t/ rather than a sound in its own right. In the same way, [t] is considered to be a pronunciation of the sound /t/ as well.

However, if we replace the /t/ with a /g/ as in 'bigger' /bɪgə/, we recognise that the meaning of the word has changed.

Two words which are different by only one sound are called a **minimal pair**. So [bɪgə] and [bɪtə] are a minimal pair.

What we have so far been calling 'sounds' are known as 'phonemes' and what we have called 'pronunciations' are known as 'allophones'. Phonemes are transcribed using slashed brackets, / / and allophones are transcribed using square ones [ ].

Activity

Transcribe the following pairs of words using the IPA symbols and decide which ones are minimal pairs, that is, which only differ by one sound (they will have the same number of sounds, too).

cub, cup
cup, pup
pup, pop

*A glottal stop, [ʔ], is often represented as an apostrophe in literature, e.g. bu'er for 'butter'.

pop, pot
pot, spot
spot, spit
spit, spill
spill, spilt

There is a commentary on this activity at the end of the unit.

Uses of phonetics and phonology

An understanding of phonemes and their allophones can be very useful if you are looking at the ways that people from different regions or social groups pronounce their words. In the same way that we can say that RP has a set of sounds that make up its sound system (the list of English sounds on page 40), we can say that each variety of English has a sound system. It might have more phonemes, or fewer phonemes than RP. The same can even be said of different social groups within a particular region. Each might have a slightly different sound system.

You can also use this way of looking at sound to analyse children's speech.

Child speech

Babies aren't able to pronounce any speech sounds when they are first born, but they gradually begin to make speech sounds and put consonants together with vowels during the babbling phase, progressing to more complex combinations of vowels and consonants as they grow. You can use your understanding of phonetics and phonology to investigate which sounds they start producing first and how they are able to use them. Can the child make all the sounds that an adult makes for speech or only a subset of those sounds? If only a subset, which sounds are being produced? Do the consonant sounds they can make have anything in common? Are they only making plosives or can they make fricatives too? Do they pronounce their sounds like adults do, or does the sound that they are attempting sound different in any way?

Activity

Hedy was one year eleven months old at the time she was recorded. Look at the transcriptions of her speech and compare them to the transcriptions provided of how you might expect an adult to pronounce the same word. Square brackets have been used for Hedy's pronunciations of the adult sounds.

Word	*Hedy*	*Adult pronunciation*
sun	[dʌn]	/sʌn/
circle	[dɜkʊ]	/sɜkl/
stripey	[daɪpɪ]	/straɪpɪ/
sky	[gaɪ]	/skaɪ/
drums	[dʌms]	/drʌmz/
green	[gin]	/grin/
fish	[bəs]	/fɪʃ/
phone	[bəʊn]	/fəʊn/
flower	[baʊə]	/flaʊə/
brush	[bəs]	/brʌʃ/
yellow	[jejəʊ]	/jeləʊ/
red	[wed]	/red/

- Does Hedy always pronounce /s/ the same way?
- What are the variants?
- Does there seem to be any pattern which governs when she uses one pronunciation rather than another?
- If you look at the place and manner of articulation can you notice what the similarities and differences are between Hedy's pronunciations of /s/ and the adult pronunciation?

Now have a look at the words that begin with a consonant cluster.

- Does Hedy pronounce both sounds where a word begins with two consonants together in the adult pronunciation?
- Which of the two consonants tends to be pronounced?
- Are there any exceptions to this, and if so, why do you think that is?

Commentary

If you look for the words that the adult pronounces beginning with a /s/, like <sun> and <circle>, you can see that Hedy pronounces these with a [d]. However it seems that she can pronounce [s] at the end of a word. In these cases though, [s] is not the target pronunciation. She pronounces <fish> with the [s] at the end rather than /ʃ/. If we rely on the data provided here as a representative sample of Hedy's speech, she only pronounces /s/ one way – as [d]. Why does Hedy choose [d] as her pronunciation of /s/? If we compare the features of the two sounds we can see that although [d] is a plosive and the target pronunciation [s] is a fricative, they are both made at the same place of articulation, the alveolar ridge. Perhaps then, the child is nearly getting the target pronunciation right. The choice of [d] seems not to be random.

If we compare how Hedy pronounces consonant clusters in comparison to the adult speech, we find that she pronounces only one of the two sounds. In most cases it is the first consonant that is retained, and the second one is elided (missed out). So, in <drums>, the /r/ is not pronounced and it becomes [dʌms]. <Green> is the same. However, in <sky>, neither of the target consonants is pronounced as in the adult speech. Instead, Hedy produces [gaɪ].

We could analyse this as the /s/ being elided, and the target /k/ being pronounced as the voiced equivalent [g]. The same thing seems to be occurring in <stripey>. Children are known to often produce voiced consonants in place of voiceless ones before a vowel, but it is possible that something more complex is happening in this case. Consider the pronunciation of the word <sky>: If you pronounce it normally as [skaɪ] and then try to pronounce it as Hedy does, but with the /s/ – [sgaɪ], you should notice that the two pronunciations sound the same. This is because in English, the difference between voiced and voiceless plosives is neutralised when they follow /s/. So the /p/ in <spot> sounds a bit like a [b] and so on. Is it possible that Hedy hears this slight pronunciation quirk and follows it even though she cannot yet produce /s/ in that environment?

We will now look at some further data from Hedy.

Activity

The following data was collected three months later, when Hedy was two years and two months old.

Word	*Hedy*	*Adult pronunciation*
a fish	[ə fɪs]	/ə fɪʃ/
over	[əʊvə]	/əʊvə/
veg	[beʤ]	/veʤ/
snail	[neɪʊ]	/sneɪl/
spider	[baɪdə]	/spaɪdə/
eyebrows	[aɪbaʊs]	/aɪbraʊz/
princess	[pɪnses]	/prɪnses/
three	[fi]	/θri/
glove	[gʌv]	/glʌv/
butterfly	[bʌtəbaɪ]	/bʌtəflaɪ/
butterfly	[bʌtəfaɪ]	/bʌtəflaɪ/
pussy cat	[pʊkɪ kat]	/pʊsɪ kat/
pussy cat	[pʊsɪ kat]	/pʊsɪ kat/
check	[tek]	/ʧek/
coming	[tʌmɪŋ]	/kʌmɪŋ/
another one	[ənʌdə]	/ənʌðə/
that's not right	[dats]	/ðats/

In those three months, some of her articulations have changed; in some cases, her articulation is closer to the adult form. Notice also that there are some variations in pronunciations, that is, some words are pronounced in more than one way.

Try to answer the following questions:

- Is there evidence that Hedy has acquired some consonants that she couldn't articulate in the first dataset?
- Are these articulations consistent?
- Which phonemes seem to have more than one pronunciation?
- Are there any other articulations that are interesting that we haven't mentioned so far?

Commentary

It is interesting to note that while Hedy has acquired some new sounds, she is not yet able to pronounce them consistently. /f/ was always [b] in the first dataset, but here it is realised as [f] or [b]. These articulations seem to occur even in the same context, for example, see the two pronunciations of <butterfly>. The voiced sound at the same place of articulation, /v/, is also present in between two vowels in <over> and at the end of a word in <glove>, but appears as [b] at the beginning of <veg> (Hedy has a book called 'Meg's Veg'). Although it's unusual for children to develop /v/ as early as Hedy has, there are still some variations in her pronunciation at this stage. Another sound that is realised on more than one way is the /s/ in <pussy cat>. This is articulated as [s] in one instance and as [k] in another.

Some sounds that are present in this data set that we didn't see earlier, are /ð/, which is pronounced as [d] in <another> and <that's>, and /ʧ/, which is pronounced as [t] in <check>. Both of Hedy's pronunciations are close to the adult sounds. While /ð/ is a voiced dental fricative, /d/ is also voiced, and while it's not a fricative, its place of articulation is close to dental – it's an alveolar sound. If you look at the vocal tract diagram on page 45, you will see that the alveolar ridge is the next place of articulation back from the teeth, where dental sounds are made. In <check>, Hedy's [t] pronunciation is close to the /ʧ/ it represents, as /t/ is a voiceless alveolar plosive, and the target sound, /ʧ/, is a voiceless post alveolar affricate.

An affricate is part plosive, part fricative. In this case it seems that Hedy has articulated the first part, the plosive, successfully.

Extension activities

1 Look at the words in 'a rough-coated dough-faced ploughman' and transcribe all of the sounds represented by the 'ough' spelling. How many different pronunciations of 'ough' do you end up with? Is this the sequence of letters with the most variety in pronunciation that we have in English?

2 In the first child speech dataset, Hedy pronounces 'fish' and 'brush' as homophones – they sound the same. Can you go any way towards explaining why this might be?

3 Make a list of the consonant articulations that Hedy uses in the two datasets and compare them to the full set of RP consonants.

- Which ones are missing from Hedy's list?
- What consonant clusters are present in the adult pronunciations, and how does Hedy pronounce each of them?

4 In the commentary on the first dataset, it was suggested that Hedy might be tuning in to some very slight pronunciation differences in the voiceless plosives /p, t/ and /k/ when they follow /s/. In adult speech they sound a bit like their voiced equivalents, /b, d/ and /g/. Hedy's sensitivity to this pronunciation difference was evident in her pronunciation of [gaɪ] for 'sky'. Although Hedy missed off /s/, because she's not yet articulating consonant clusters, she pronounced the /t/ and /k/ just as an adult would pronounce them after /s/. Is there any further evidence in Hedy's speech three months later, which would strengthen the hypothesis that Hedy hears and reproduces the slight pronunciation difference of voiceless plosives after /s/ rather than pronouncing all voiceless plosives as voiced ones?

Commentaries/Answers to activities

COMMENTARY: ACTIVITY p. 41

Answers

thistle
boat
couch
curious
raced

/rubɑb/
/θri/
/ʃʊgə/
/sləʊpɪŋ/
/dɔ/
/kʌstəd/
/jeləʊ/
/nɔɪzɪ/
/ɪkstensɪv/

In RP, /r/ is not pronounced unless it is before a vowel sound. In <rhubarb>, the <r> in the spelling is before a /b/ sound, not a vowel, so it is not pronounced. So, while American accents and Scottish accents would pronounce <rhubarb> as /rubɑrb/, RP pronounces it as /rubɑb/. <door> is affected in the same way. The correct transcription is /dɔ/ rather than /dɔr/.

The difference between the vowels /ʌ/ and /ə/ are often a source of some confusion for learners of the IPA. The 'schwa' vowel is produced with the vocal tract in a very neutral position. If you open your mouth a small way and make a short vowel sound leaving your tongue relaxed, this is the /ə/ vowel. The /ʌ/ has a more open mouthed position and sounds a bit more like /a/.

In words like <noisy> which is pronounced /nɔɪzɪ/, learners often feel that there should be a /j/ sound at the end of the transcribed word. The same issue affects words like <yellow>, where learners often want to use a /w/ sound. Transcription of RP follows a convention which says that the use of the /j/ or /w/ is superfluous at the end of a word.

Speakers of some regional varieties of English have trouble distinguishing between the vowels /ʌ/ and /ʊ/ for very good reasons. Some Northern accents for example don't contain the /ʌ/ vowel, so speakers would pronounce both <tuck> and <took> as /tʊk/, in other words, these two words are **homophones** (they sound the same but have different meanings).

COMMENTARY: ACTIVITY p. 48

/s, v, ð/	These sounds are all fricatives
/t, d, n/	These sounds are all made at the same place of articulation – the alveolar ridge
/m, b, p/	These sounds are all made at the same place of articulation, the lips. That is, they are bilabial sounds.
/s, f, t, ʃ, h/	Most of these sounds are fricatives, but not /t/, which is a plosive. The thing that they a have in common is that they are all voiceless.

COMMENTARY: ACTIVITY pp. 50–1

/kʌb/ /kʌp/	These two are a minimal pair as they are different by only one sound. The /b/ is replaced with a /p/.
/kʌp/ /pʌp/	Again, these are a minimal pair. The /k/ changes to a /p/.
/pʌp/ /pɒp/	These are a minimal pair. This time, the vowel /ʌ/ changes to a /ɒ/.
/pɒp/ /pɒt/	Another minimal pair. The /p/ changes to a /t/.

/pɒt/ /spɒt/	These words are not a minimal pair. The second word has the same sounds as the first plus an additional sound.
/spɒt/ /spɪt/	These are a minimal pair. The /ɒ/ changes to a /ɪ/.
/spɪt/ /spɪl/	These are also a minimal pair. The /t/ changes to a /l/. The spelling <spill> has one more letter than <spit>, but if you did your transcription correctly then they have the same number of sounds.
/spɪl/ /spɪlt/	These are not a minimal pair. The second word has the same sounds as the first word plus an extra sound.

Satellite texts

The following satellite titles in the Intertext Series are also relevant to this unit:

The Language of Children has further examples of how children talk.

The Language of Comics, *The Language of Drama* and *The Language of Fiction* all show examples of how talk can be represented.

The Language of Conversation looks at some social aspects of talk.

The Language of Politics looks at political speeches.

Language and Region looks at regional varieties of spoken English.

The Language of Speech and Writing considers several aspects of spoken language.

Unit three

Words and things

Aims of this unit

Analysis of text often starts at the level of the word. Words are clearly visible units in written text, and distinguishable units in spoken text. However, the task is not always that simple. What is a word? Are simple definitions such as 'the smallest meaningful unit of language' helpful or even accurate? Is there a straightforward one-to one relationship between words and meanings? Where does the vocabulary of English come from in the first place? This unit attempts to address some of these issues, and to look more closely at the way words work within texts.

What is a word?

Like a lot of questions about language, 'What is a word?' seems at first glance a very simple one to answer. Any user of language knows what a word is and how to use one. Professor Dumbledore greets his students to Hogwarts School with 'a few words': 'Nitwit! Blubber! Oddment! Tweak!' However, once the nature of words is looked at more closely, the question can become a more complex one than it first appears.

WHAT ARE WORDS MADE OF?

The question, 'What is a word?' might be answered by looking at ways in which words in the English language are structured. The study of the structure of words is called **morphology**.

Most users of English would assume that words are the smallest units of language to carry meaning. This, however, is not necessarily the case, which makes questions such as 'What is a word?' even more difficult to answer.

Activity

Look at the following sentences:

1 Dog how was children closed
2 The plogs glorped bliply

- What does each sentence mean?
- What do the words in each sentence mean?

Commentary

The answer to the first question is: not a lot.

The answer to the second is a bit different. In sentence 1, each word has a clearly identifiable meaning and can be defined. The sentence, however, remains meaningless. In sentence 2, the words (apart from the first one) appear meaningless. They are units of text that currently have no meaning attached to them, unlike units such as 'dog', 'how' or 'children'.

We will now look again at the second sentence above.

Activity

Answer the following questions relating to sentence 2 above:

1 How many plogs were there? One, or more than one?
2 What were they doing?
3 Were they doing it now or in the past?
4 How, or in what way, were they doing it?

Commentary

Most speakers of English will have very little trouble answering these questions. There was more than one plog, because this word carries the plural marker 's'. 'Glorped' is marked as a verb by the use of the past tense marker 'ed', so the reader knows what the plogs were doing, and the fact that they were doing it in the past. Finally, the reader can tell how or in what manner the plogs were glorping – bliply – because the word carries the adverb marker 'ly'.

Words have specific meaning in the context of other words, and a brief look at text can establish that units smaller than words are carrying meaning. These units are called **morphemes**. Words may be made up of one or more morphemes:

One morpheme:	dog, elephant, establish, child
Two morphemes:	dog s, elephant ine, establish ment, child ish
Three morphemes	dis establish ment, child ish ness.

In theory, there is no limit to the number of morphemes a word can have, but logic and comprehensibility mean that there tends to be an upper limit, and six morphemes is about it for English:

anti dis establish ment arian ism

There are, though, exceptions to be found in highly specialised areas of language, for example, terms used in organic chemistry.

Activity

Identify the individual morphemes in the following word list. Then classify the morphemes into the groups that follow:

> pigs, barked, unlikely, motherhood, salty, cherry, taller, hammer,
>
> displease, hardship, superheroes, player, payee, coffee

- *Independent or free.* These morphemes can stand on their own.
- *Dependent or bound.* These morphemes must be attached to another morpheme.
- *Grammatical.* These give grammatical information and mark the role of the word in the sentence.
- *Creative or derivational.* These form new words.

Commentary

Many morphemes can constitute words by themselves: 'pig', 'bark', 'like', 'mother', 'salt', 'cherry', 'tall', 'please', 'hard', 'super', 'hero', 'play'. These are usually referred to as **free morphemes**.

Others are only ever used as parts of words: 's', 'ed', 'un', 'ly', 'hood', 'y', 'er', 'ship', 'es', 'er', 'ee'. These are usually referred to as **bound morphemes**.

It is easy to confuse some bound morphemes with free morphemes that have an identical sound and structure. For example, English has free morphemes 'hood' (a head covering) and 'ship' (a seagoing vessel). It also has the bound morphemes '-ship' and '-hood', that are both used to form **nouns**. 'Hardship' means a state of deprivation or difficulty, 'hard ship' means something different, a vessel that is difficult to sail, perhaps. 'Motherhood' means the state of being a mother, not the head covering that a mother might wear.

It is also easy to confuse part of a word that is a single morpheme, like 'hammer', or 'coffee' with a bound morpheme, in this case '-er', that is used to create nouns of agency (as in 'play', 'player') or adjectives of comparison or degree ('tall', 'taller'), or used to create a noun meaning a recipient of goods or actions '-ee'. A 'payee' is the recipient of money paid. 'Coffee' is not the recipient of a cough.

Bound morphemes have two functions. One is to act as a grammatical marker, giving information about number, **verb tense**, aspect and other grammatical functions. These are **inflectional morphemes**. Examples in the data are '-s', '-ed', '-er' (comparative), '-es'. The second is to form new words.

These are called **derivational morphemes**. Examples in the data are 'un-', '-ly', '-hood', '-y', 'dis-', '-ship', '-er' (to create a noun of agency).

When is a word not a word?

Overheard in a car park: 'What do red double yellow lines mean?' This speaker is using the phrase 'double yellow lines' as if it were a single word. Some phrases in English are so commonly used that though they are phrases they frequently function like single words.

Activity

Identify the individual words in the highlighted sections of the following pairs of sentences. Can you omit words or substitute different words without changing the meaning?

A Here comes my **big brother** to beat your brains in, creep!
Are you watching **Big Brother** tonight?

B **How do you do** that?
How do you do?

C The **clear blue water** stretched as far as his eye could see
They want to make sure there is **clear blue water** between their policies and those of the Liberal Democrats'.

D **Supercalifragilisticexpialidocious**
Super Cally Go Ballistic Celtic Are Atrocious

Commentary

In each case, the second sentence of the pair presents a problem.

- 'Big Brother' is a phrase that originally comes from George' Orwell's book, *Nineteen Eighty Four* and has become a phrase much used in the English language to signify a state that has become too controlling. It is now also the name of a popular reality TV show. Neither word can be altered or omitted without changing the meaning. It functions like a single word.

- 'How do you do?' is a **phatic** phrase that works as a single unit.
- 'Clear blue water' as it is used in this example is an idiom (see p. 74). When the phrase is used idiomatically, it functions as a single unit.
- 'Super Cally Go Ballistic Celtic Are Atrocious' is clearly seven words, but the football headline carries a meaning that is enhanced by its relationship with the nonsense word from the film Mary Poppins. This headline would be less effective if any words were changed, moved or altered, therefore it has something in common with a single word.

Meaning therefore exists in units of language both smaller and larger than the traditional definition of 'word' allows for. Words are made of units of language called morphemes. Morphemes carry meaning and are smaller than the word. Users of English frequently use the term 'word' when, strictly speaking, they are referring to morphemes. If someone looks a word up in the dictionary, for example 'dogs', they don't look up the plural form, they look up the base morpheme 'dog'. Phrases can also function in the way that single words function. For this reason, and for reasons looked at later in this unit, many linguists prefer the term '**lexeme**' to the term 'word'. Lexeme refers to a unit of meaning that may be smaller or larger than the traditional term 'word' implies. This unit (i.e. Unit 3) could, therefore, be more accurately called 'Lexemes', but 'Word' is used as being more familiar.

Words and meanings

The previous section looked at meaning in units that were both smaller and larger than the traditional definition of 'word' allows. This section looks at the relationship between words and meanings.

In *Alice through the Looking Glass,* Humpty Dumpty says:

> 'When I use a word, it means just what I choose it to mean – neither more nor less.'

At first, Humpty Dumpty's point seems ridiculous. Common sense tells us that each word in the English language has a meaning, and that meaning is well established. Look in any dictionary. Why is it, then, that even the most skilled and experienced users of language can get into trouble, by meaning one thing and saying another? One of the most famous examples comes from radio cricket commentary when the bowler was Michael Holding and the batsman was Peter Willey. The commentator announced: 'The bowler's Holding, the batsman's Willey.'

The satirical magazine *Private Eye* runs a weekly column, 'Colemanballs', devoted to errors made by people whose profession depends on language and meaning: journalists, commentators, politicians. However, lexical ambiguity can be used intentionally to create meaning.

Activity

The examples of text below all depend on the ambiguous relationship that can exist between word and meaning. Try to identify the word(s) where the ambiguity exists, and say why these words can make the meaning unclear.

1 Time flies like an arrow, fruit flies like a banana.

2 Q. What is George W. Bush's position on Roe vs Wade? [Roe vs Wade refers to a famous court judgement in the USA.]
A. He really doesn't care how people get out of New Orleans.

3 I still miss my ex-husband. But my aim is improving.

4 Notice in a field: The farmer allows walkers to cross the field for free, but the bull charges.

5 If you're not part of the solution, you're part of the precipitate.

Commentary

The relationship between individual words and meaning is a complex one. Different words can have similar or identical meanings. Words that sound the same can have different meanings. The same word can change its meaning depending on its context. All of this can affect meaning and lead to ambiguity. Some of the ways in which the relationship between words and meanings can be identified are:

- **Homophone** – words that have the same sound, but different, unrelated meaning. They may be represented by different spellings e.g. roe, Roe, row.
- **Synonym** – words that have the same or similar meanings.
- **Polyseme** – a word that has several related meanings, e.g. fly: a small winged insect; to move through the air; to move very quickly.

If the synonyms aren't closely related in meaning, or if the meaning of the polyseme isn't clear, then the reader or listener may not be able to identify which meaning is intended. There are many kinds of ambiguity, but this section is concerned with lexical ambiguity, which occurs when it is not possible to decide on the intended meaning of a word.

In the activity above, some of the words used in these examples have synonyms, or are polysemes. Some are homophones: they have an identical pronunciation but a different meaning. If the producer of a text intends one meaning, but the context in which a word is used implies another, or if the producer of the text deliberately makes use of the potential for confusion, the text becomes ambiguous.

The English language, therefore, has a broader capacity for meaning than a simple one-to-one word and meaning relationship. Producers of text are aware of this capacity and make deliberate use of it.

The examples above are presumably intentional. However, ambiguity can arise in contexts where it is not intended.

Activity

Look at the following headlines. They are all ambiguous in that there are at least two potential meanings for each one. Try to identify the word(s) that have caused the problem, and say why the problem has arisen:

TROOPS GRILL RUMSFELD OVER IRAQ
(BBC December 2004)

IRAN REMOVES UN'S NUCLEAR SEALS
(BBC 10 August 2005)

US OFFENSIVE IN EUPHRATES REGION
(BBC 4 October 2005)

WATERVOLE SLIDE 'CAN BE HALTED'
(BBC 18 May 2005)

BIRD FLU FOUND IN TURKEY
(*Snowmail*, 13 October 2005)

TOASTING SHAKESPEARE IN ARMENIA
(BBC 1 October 2005)

Note that there is no commentary on this activity.

Certain shops and service providers exploit the potential ambiguity of meanings to create playful names.

Activity

Below is a list of names of various shops, businesses and services. Discuss the ways in which words and meanings are used here. What effects are created by using language in this way?

Hairdressers
- Curl Up and Dye
- Fresh Hair
- Hair Force One
- Look Ahead
- Kuttin' Kru
- Headlines
- Making Waves

Pet shops and services
- Barking Mad
- Paws Here

Fish and Chip shops
- Jolly Frier
- A Salt 'n' Battered
- Chip Inn
- Codfathers
- Manfryday's

Health food shops
- Open Sesame
- In a Nutshell
- Your Nuts
- Grain of Truth

Commentary

All of these names are playing games with language, and exploiting its capacity to produce ambiguous meanings via the use of synonyms and polysemes, and by the use of homophones. The creators of these names are playing on our ability as users of language to create a meaningful link where, strictly speaking, none should exist. The effect of this is to entertain the recipient, and to make the names memorable, whilst using words that give a positive view of the product or service on offer.

Humpty Dumpty may not be right, but the study of words in use demonstrates quickly that the relationship between words and meanings is more complex than it seems at first. This section looked at the ambiguity that can be created (accidentally or deliberately) by the existence of polysemes, synonyms and homophones. The situation is even more complex than this, as the next section will discuss.

Metaphor: 'Life's a beach, and then you fry'

This section looks at the way words can be used to create connections between areas of meaning that may have no direct link, but offer a useful comparison or connection that helps to enhance, clarify, make more vivid or even reinforce existing ideas and concepts.

The existence of metaphor allows for a further expansion of meaning. By linking words or concepts that don't generally have a semantic link, a new meaning can be expressed. Metaphor allows producers of text to make connections in a few words that would take lines of writing, or long stretches of speech, to make in a more literal way. The literal translation of a metaphor rarely produces the same effect as the metaphor. Metaphor can be used to make comments on aspects of human behaviour or society without the writer having to spell out literally the point they are trying to make.

The earliest extant literary writing in English, Old English poetry, is rich in metaphor that expresses a great deal about the way in which these early communities viewed the world. The leader, the ruler, sometimes even God, is the *hlaford*, the 'bread lord', the body is the *banhus*, the 'bone house' and the sea is the *hronrad*, the 'whale road'

Metaphor is often seen as something that is more likely to exist in the domain of literature, and not as something that has a lot to do with everyday life. It isn't unusual for people to associate metaphor with written language, and particularly with written language that is literary or has literary associations. Advertising, for example, is often very creative; tabloid newspapers are known for their inventive ways of using the phonological and lexical levels of language. However, metaphor is much more a part of day-to-day uses of language than you might think.

Activity

Look at the example of dialogue in Text 3:1, from *The Sandman – The Doll's House* by Neil Gaiman, Mike Dringenberg and Malcolm Jones III. A group of serial killers are meeting for a convention! They are casually chatting to each other before proceedings begin.

- Identify any popular phrases or well-known sayings that you recognise. (The first two have been underlined.)
- What is the literal meaning of these?
- Why has the writer used these particular phrases in this context?

Text 3:1

ON ARRIVAL THEY EYE EACH OTHER WARILY, STRIKE UP CAUTIOUS CONVERSATIONS.
SOME ARE ALREADY ACQUAINTED, AND THEY FORM INSTANT KNOTS AND WHORLS IN THE BAR AND THE LOBBY, WAITING TO CHECK IN, OR FOR THE RESTAURANT TO OPEN.
MAN, I BEEN TRAVELLING FOR FIVE DAYS NOW. THE JOURNEY WAS A REAL KILLER BELIEVE ME.
HATE THESE LITTLE HICK TOWNS. WOULDN'T BE SEEN DEAD HERE, IF IT WASN'T FOR THE CONVENTION.
...THAT'S JUST WHAT THEY'LL DO. ONE OF THESE DAYS THESE BOOTS ARE GONNA WALK ALL OVER YOU.
TELL YOU, I COULD MURDER A STEAK. A GOOD, BLOODY STEAK.
SO THAT WAS WHEN HARRY KILLED THE LIGHTS. I COULD'A DIED.
THEY DO THIS CHOCOLATE FUDGE WHIP THAT IS JUST TO DIE FOR.

HAS ANYONE SEEN THE FAMILY MAN?
TEX
REGISTER HERE!
WESTERN RE-CON II
THE DEVIL? UH, WOULD THAT BE THE KENTUCKY DEVIL, OR THE OREGON DEVIL? I GOT BOTH HERE.
YEAH. HE SLAYS ME. YOU HEARD HIM DO THE "I AM JOHN'S COATHANGER" ROUTINE?
HELL, I THOUGHT THE WHOLE ISSUE WAS DEAD AND BURIED IN THE SIXTIES.
EXCUSE ME? CAN YOU ALL GET YOUR BADGES AND REGISTRATION PACKS FROM THE REGISTRATION TABLE IN THE SCARLETT O'HARA ROOM?
KNOTS BECOME GROUPS AND CLUSTERS, ATTRACTING NEW MEMBERS.
THE TV VERSION? THE TV VERSION BUTCHERED IT! BUT I HEAR YOU CAN GET IT UNCUT ON VIDEO IN CANADA.
DON'T FORGET TO CHECK IN, ONCE YOU'VE REGISTERED.
AND, UM, HAS ANYONE SEEN THE FAMILY MAN?

Commentary

A lot of language that is used regularly involves metaphor. It isn't unusual for somebody describing a situation that has embarrassed them to say, 'I could have died,' or to hear someone say, 'It nearly killed me,' when talking about some major effort. This is not meant literally, but gives a clear expression to the strong feelings aroused by, for example, social embarrassment.

This writer has chosen everyday uses of metaphor that relate to death and violence. The examples used are deliberately commonplace – as readers we probably wouldn't notice them except that so many are used. The effect is interesting. It enhances the role of the participants in the narrative. These are people for whom violence is a way of life, but by drawing attention to the sheer 'everydayness' of such language, the writer is enforcing a point he makes further on in the narrative: violence is so much a part of our lives that we almost fail to notice it.

The examples of language in Text 3:2 are all ready-made phrases that are a familiar part of the day-to-day experience of language. They have been classified according to topic.

Activity

What metaphors are used here? What connections are made to enhance meaning? How does the metaphoric use of language here reflect our cultural attitudes?

Text 3:2

Immigrants

- Immigrants are pouring across the borders in record numbers.
- Our communities simply can't successfully absorb newcomers at this rate.
- The UK is already full. We are bursting at the seams.

Countries and places

- States like these constitute an axis of evil.
- Our wish is to defend the nation against attacks by rogue nations.
- The United States and Israel are the closest of friends and allies.
- The rape of Beirut.

Commentary

There is clear metaphoric use of language in these examples. People arriving in the UK and Europe are linked by metaphor with an unstoppable force of nature. Countries and places are treated as people who have emotions and moral intent. They are evil, they are rogues or friends, they suffer as people (rape).

What is more revealing, though, is the connections that are made through these metaphoric uses. Immigrants lose their individual status. 'Water' is a mass noun and is defined in terms of volume. By using this metaphor, people arriving in this country lose their individuality and are defined purely in terms of danger and destruction. Countries, on the other hand, are given the status of individuals who need defending and who are threatened by other dangerous individuals.

Cultural attitudes to particular areas of human activity can often be seen in the choices of metaphor used when that activity is discussed. A useful linguistic concept to be aware of here is that of **semantic field**, sometimes called just field, or field of meaning. Particular topics, trades, concepts are associated in the mind of the user of language with particular groups of words. Texts that belong to a particular area of meaning draw from a range of words that relate specifically to that area of meaning. For example, a text that used the words chop, fry, stir, simmer, season, taste, would almost certainly belong to the semantic field of cooking. However, writers can also draw on semantic fields to create metaphorical effects and associations that can enhance the meaning of the text.

Metaphor, then, is very much a part of the day-to-day language, so much so that its presence is often not even noticed by users of language. It serves to encode and possibly reinforce our attitudes to many aspects of life. Given this, metaphor has the capacity to be a very powerful tool of language.

Activity

Look at the following list of words. They are all from the same text. What topic do you assume the text addresses?

- communities
- victimising
- negative behaviour
- police
- strong community system

It would be reasonable to assume that these words come from a text about society relating to problems within a community.

Now read the opening paragraphs, shown in Text 3:3. What 'community' is referred to here? Are the references to communities noted above metaphoric?

Text 3:3

Gamers don't want any more grief

Players who abuse others in online games may soon be ostracised as virtual communities start to police their own environments

Martin Davies, Thursday June 15, 2006

The gaming community calls them "griefers": people who like nothing better than to kill team-mates or obstruct the game's objectives. Griefers scam, cheat and abuse, often victimising the weakest and newest players. In games that attempt to encourage complex and enduring interactions among thousands of players, "griefing" has evolved from being an isolated nuisance to a social disease.

"The most common 'griefer counter-measure' is to put in place a strong community system," says Stephen Davis of IT GlobalSecure, a firm that specialises in developing security technologies for online games.

"These community services provide clan features, friends lists, reputation stats, and other features both to tie players more closely to the game and create an environment that reduces anonymity for misbehaving players." Increasingly, the solution to griefing is not simply to ban nuisance players, but to encourage the development of virtual societies capable of dealing with their own virtual crimes.

This is becoming essential for titles falling within the genre of massively multi-player online role-playing games (MMORPGs). These complex and persistent worlds are particularly vulnerable to negative behaviour, not only because they offer more rules to break than the average first-person shooter, but also because there is more at stake for players. The gap between virtual worlds and real life is constantly closing, with developers encouraging in-game economies with currencies that translate to real-world pounds and dollars. A player might craft a rare item that can be sold via eBay; if such digital property is stolen, the player is effectively losing real money. . . .

Commentary

The community that the article addresses is people who play computer games online. The extent to which the word 'community' is itself metaphoric in this context is debatable. The article gives the gaming 'community' the status of a real-life community. It is 'policed', it's members are killed, scammed, cheated on and victimised. This community has weaker and stronger members. Interestingly, the metaphor and the reality are blurring. 'Virtual' artefacts can command value in the real world and at least one real murder has been committed over such an item.

Idiomatic language: 'Flogging dead crocodiles' and 'Keeping your feet under water'

The section on metaphor above looked briefly at the daily use of metaphor that is so commonplace that it goes almost unnoticed. A lot of these structures have a fixed and expected form. Some are so fixed that it is not possible to change a word or the structure without losing, or irretrievably changing, the meaning. Such structures are called idioms.

Idioms are units of language with a fixed grammatical and lexical content. Their meaning cannot be worked out from a study of the individual words contained in the idiom, and they frequently operate on a metaphorical level.

Idioms therefore function more like individual words than like phrases or sentences, and can be considered as lexemes according to the discussion at the beginning of this unit.

Activity

Rewrite the idioms below into clear, non-idiomatic English. How helpful would a word-for-word translation be to a non-native speaker?

- brownie points
- pie in the sky
- cock-and-bull story
- fly on the wall
- red herring
- having a free hand
- barking up the wrong tree

Commentary

Idioms present problems for non-native speakers. Direct translation will not help. Possible translations for the above examples are:

- gaining merit for achievement
- an unrealistic prospect of future happiness
- a concocted or incredible story
- an unperceived observer
- something that diverts the attention
- the scope to chose how to act
- wrong or mistaken

Internet translators such as Babelfish http://babelfish.altavista.com give interesting results when they are used to translate idioms. It can be interesting to move the phrase through several languages, translating back into English at each stage. For example:

- Put the idiomatic phrase 'barking up the wrong tree' into the text box.
- Translate from English to German. Babelfish gives *abstreifen herauf den falschen Baum* – 'strip up the wrong tree'.
- Translate the German phrase from German to French. This gives *dépouiller le faux arbre* – 'to strip the false tree'.
- Translate the French phrase into Portuguese. This gives *contar a falsa árvore* – 'to count the false tree'.
- Translate 'to count the false tree' into German. This gives *den falschen Baum zählen.*
- Finally, translate back to English. This gives 'the wrong tree count'.

The phrase undergoes a shift in meaning every time it is translated. At no stage does the actual English meaning emerge.

The activity above doesn't simply demonstrate how unreliable internet and other electronic translators are. It demonstrates that idioms are not susceptible to simple translation and their meaning must be learned both by native speakers and by second language learners as a unit.

Idioms are useful devices. They provide users of language with ready made phrases that communicate a clear, agreed meaning. They add colour and variety to the language. Because of the fixed structure and lexis of most idioms, they function more like words than phrases, and in any discussion or analysis of words and meanings, it is useful to treat idioms as words.

Computer analysis of words

This section explores how computers can help us to study words and frequent patterns of words, particularly by the use of corpora. A corpus (plural corpora) is a collection of texts from various sources. These corpora consist of texts which have been typed or scanned into a computer so that large quantities of information about the English language can be collected and analysed.

Activity

The following activity is adapted from *Reading Concordances* (John Sinclair, 2003).

Look at the following set of words. It is taken from a corpus and has identified the thirty most frequent examples of the phrase 'free hand.' The data set gives the phrase in the context in which it occurred. 'Free hand' can be an idiom but it can also have other uses.

Datafile 04_freehand.doc

```
against allowing Western businesses a   free hand to buy Russia's forests and
regional interests are: to have a       free hand in Lebanon and to regain the
no doubt like to give the military a    free hand but is wary of further
referred to as giving parents a         free hand closing hospitals and
I says, "she thinks she's got a         free hand . After all Claire
this instruction, he gave Stephanie a   free hand in the decoration. Her main aim
and glows with pride in being given a   free hand by the most influential
the army wants to be granted a          free hand to crack down against the
gives President-elect Bill Clinton a    free hand to shape the bank and thrift
is widely rumoured, have been given a   free hand if they don't rock the boat on
boots. She brushed on makeup with a     free hand cheeks like a clown, red mouth,
if financial deregulation gave them a   free hand , bank managers would lend first
on the federal bench a judge has a      free hand . A decade from now it may be
But Quayle denied Channel 9 had a       free hand in nominating telecast
unlikely to give them a completely      free hand in the matter. What Burma
```

```
er You've got a fairly                  free hand ? Yeah. Yeah.
was pointing down the road with her     free hand . look. The train's in. We'll
the rain had stopped. With his          free hand he rolled down the window
resting on her shoulder. He moved his   free hand around to the front of her
he yelled, but he grabbed her with his  free hand , his fingers winding in her
the bottle against the palm of his      free hand . He was a big man in his
at his chest with the thumb of his      free hand . "I don't care about you, I
health club, sir." He extended his      free hand . "A while ago. You'll maybe no"
wrist so tightly, she had only one      free hand . Kelly pulled as hard as she
Nurse!" she shouted as with her one     free hand she closed each window in turn,
allowing nature to have a relatively    free hand . The spring garden, for
and he gives them a relatively          free hand . They often abuse, they often
new broom will be brought in with the   free hand to cut the dividend, clean out
setting. She was given a totally        free hand by her clients to do exactly as
will only need the body brush so your   free hand can be used to steady the horse"
```

1 List the words that come immediately to the left of 'free'. Group them into: words that occur in this position more than once, words that occur only once.
2 Of the words that occur only once, can you group them either by word class or by similarity of meaning?
3 Can you identify a difference between the idiomatic and non-idiomatic uses of the phrase?
4 Is it possible to draw up rules for when a phrase is being used idiomatically, and when it is not?

There is a commentary on this activity at the end of the unit.

The next sequence of data looks at the word 'like'.

Activity

Look up the word 'like' in a good dictionary.

- How many meanings are given?
- Which, in your view, is the most common use?
- Are you aware of any uses of the word 'like' that aren't mentioned in the dictionary?

Commentary

The word 'like' has four entries in the *Oxford English Dictionary* (*OED*) covering a very wide range of uses including noun, adjective, adverb **conjunction** and **verb**. Many of these are rare, archaic or dialectal. The main current uses of the word given in the *OED* are:

- adjectival: carrying the meaning 'resembling' or 'similar', e.g. 'I suppose it's a skill like any other';
- adverbial, acting as a conjunction, e.g. 'He'll do it like a shot'; or colloquially 'And I thought, like wow, this is for me';
- an interjection, e.g. 'We were all over, like';
- a verb: 'to find agreeable' or 'to find attractive', e.g. 'He really likes her'; or 'to feel inclined', e.g. 'I should like to'; or as part of a phrase, e.g. 'if you like'.

The following word list gives the first twenty examples of the word 'like' in the British National Corpus of Spoken English.

1	you gonna say like, when you go on a	**like**	overtake mode, when you' re like that, they
2	cents acc accent if they have one. Ah.	**like**	er Liverpudlian or Get No it I won' t see
3	like a frame what you put in along.	**like**	a venetian blind in a way . Mm. Or a strai
4	be terrific. Yeah that' s alright.	**like**	we' ve got the, quite, similar lot Yeah. Sa
5	minus three plus five, they' re always	**like**	that. Cos they' re what we call complex con
6	your there' s no rush for me Anyone	**like**	I' ll have the fresh ones Anyone like mayon
7	like I' ll have the fresh ones Anyone	**like**	mayonnaise? Oh thank you very much Can' t M
8	ordinary one. what the other ones are	**like**.	Unless you, unless you get the fridge in
9	yeah, I drove up, up there and back,	**like**,	my leg don' t ache, they ached a bit at
10	Well I want something in between,	**like**	the old sports , straight down the bike jo
11	what you doing and Eyeing up the bums	**like**	you. and I said I said to Bob I said
12	there were gonna be a good ride, but	**like**	Andrew' s . He probably got the rough one.
13	No it still makes you very careful.	**Like**	that still unnerves me. A bit of mud on the
14	Well I certainly, yeah, I certainly	**like**	this one. When you say you' ve had what
15	ces but a woman doesn' t scream and cry	**like**	that unless Unless there' s something
16	I know Steven would like . Mm. He' d	**like**	one with a spare bedroom so the children
17	it to the grandchildren. See, Ricky' d	**like**	that I' m sure, little Corgi car I said .
18	Mm mm. That' s true. She' d	**like**	to change the car. I mean she never liked
19	wanna I' d like to know. Mm. I' d	**like**	to know before you know You' ve got to get
20	like that. You tend to sort of I' d	**like**	to book a table for two on Saturday night.

17	it to the grandchildren. See, Ricky' d	**like**	that I' m sure, little Corgi car I said .
18	Mm mm. That' s true. She' d	**like**	to change the car. I mean she never liked
19	wanna I' d like to know. Mm. I' d	**like**	to know before you know You' ve got to get
20	like that. You tend to sort of I' d	**like**	to book a table for two on Saturday night.

Activity

Look at the twenty examples of uses of the word 'like' shown on p. 78. Identify the uses that match the *OED* uses given above. Are there any unaccounted for? Can you describe and define these?

There is a commentary on this activity at the end of the unit.

Denotation and connotation: what are words worth?

This section looks at the way words can carry value judgements with them. Each word will have its straightforward dictionary definition, but a large number of words will also carry extra associations, often personal or emotional, that the use of the word brings to mind. The dictionary definition of a word is its denotation. The denotation of the word 'dog' (noun) is 'carnivorous quadruped of the genus Canis'. The personal or emotional meaning that a word may carry is its **connotation**. The connotations of the word 'dog' will vary from individual to individual and context to context. To one person, 'dog' may connote loyalty, bravery, faithfulness, love; to another person, it may connote noise, nuisance, filth, danger.

Some words carry strong connotations, and those connotations are generally agreed on by users of the language. Such words are often described as 'loaded'. Loaded words have strong negative or positive connotations, and can have a powerful emotional impact.

Activity

Look at the following words. Decide whether they have (a) no particular connotations, (b) strong negative connotations, (c) strong positive connotations.

vehicle, slavery, democracy, was, fascism, photosynthesis,
islamophobia, the, morphophonemics, Arctic Monkeys, building,
vivisection, hovel, a

Compare your analysis of the list with someone else's. Do you agree on which words are loaded, and whether they are positive or negative in their connotations?

Commentary

As discussed above, connotation depends to a certain extent on individual response. However, certain words do tend to evoke similar responses from individuals. Here is an analysis of the list produced by a group of students who did the activity collectively:

no connotations:	vehicle was the morphophonemics building a
negative:	slavery fascism islamophobia hovel vivisection
positive:	democracy Arctic Monkeys

There was some disagreement about fascism, Arctic Monkeys and democracy. The group felt that Arctic Monkeys represented a type of music that could have negative or positive connotations depending on taste, but they also felt that the band represented a form of successful independence that should be seen as positive. They agreed in their response to fascism and democracy, but decided that people with different political beliefs might think differently.

What characterises the words that are not loaded? Grammatical words such as articles and auxiliary verbs are less likely to carry connotations, as their meaning is grammatical rather than lexical. Therefore 'was', 'a', 'the' carry no connotations.

Words that are highly specialised and are restricted to a particular area of meaning are less likely to be loaded. 'Morphophonemics' and 'photosynthesis' are probably too restricted and specialised in their use to carry any emotional loading. The majority of English speakers will not have 'morphophonemics' in their vocabulary, and though 'photosynthesis' is more widely known, it still has a restricted range.

Words that are highly general are also less likely to be loaded. There are a lot of words that have a classification function, in that they are general terms that encompass more specific terms.

'Vehicle' is a general term that encompasses car, bus, bicycle, lorry, truck, van, etc. 'Car' encompasses sports car, saloon, hatchback, and a whole range of specific names such as BMW, Rolls Royce, Lamborghini, that have a wide range of cultural connotations.

Words that have this classification function are called **hypernyms**. Examples of hypernyms are:

fruit, animal, bird, flower

The words with a more specific meaning that can be classified by the hypernyms are called **hyponyms**. Examples of hyponyms are:

apple, orange, banana
dog, cat, buffalo, warthog
robin, vulture, eagle

Hyponyms are more likely to carry strong connotations than hypernyms, though this is not an invariable rule. The word 'animal' can carry negative connotations in metaphors such as 'He behaved like an animal.' However, more specific connotations can be carried by the use of more specific words. 'He ate like a pig.' 'You rat!' 'She's a bitch.'

The section on synonyms above looked at the way the English language often has a range of words that focus around the same area of meaning. There are historical reasons for this that the next section will discuss, but often this wealth of synonyms allows speakers or writers to express an opinion by choosing a synonym that is loaded in a negative or positive way.

Activity

Read the following excerpts (shown in Text 3:4) from the novel *The Forest of Souls*, by Carla Banks. The first extract is an account of a public hanging in the city of Minsk under the Nazi occupation. The second is an account, 60 years after this event, of someone visiting a museum in the city devoted to the atrocities of the Nazi occupation and seeing photographs of the execution.

- How are words used in each extract to identify people and groups?
- How are they used to identify emotions and physical states?
- How are words used differently to describe the hangings in the two extracts? What effects does this create?

Text 3:4

Extract 1

The hangings were brutal. The victims were hanged separately, so those who died last would know what was to come. They were not hooded or blindfolded. The gallows were crude. The victims were given no drop, and the noose was made of thin twine in a simple slip knot. Death was slow.

The first public hanging took place in October. Three people, Kiril Trous, a veteran from the last war, Masha Bruskina, a seventeen year old girl, and Volodia Shcherbatsevich a sixteen year old boy were hanged in front of the gates of a local factory. The Nazis slung a crude sign around the girl's neck: *Wir sind Partisanen und haben auf deutsche Soldaten geschossen. We are partisans and we have fired on German soldiers.* They hanged them one at a time.

Extract 2

A group of uniformed men marched three prisoners, a young boy, a girl and a man through the streets. There was a placard round the girl's neck, crudely lettered in Cyrillic and in Latin symbols: *We are partisans and we have shot at German soldiers.*

Men in uniform crowded round, interested spectators. Now they were at a building that looked faintly industrial. An officer in a peaked cap was placing a noose round the neck of the girl, his face calm and intent. The soldiers watched.

And now she was hanging, her face distorted in agony, and now she was dead, and the officer was noosing the boy whose mouth stretched in a mute plea and whose wrists strained against the bindings, and now the man who had watched the death of the others was noosed. His face was a mask of terror. And then they were dead, left hanging from the gateway.

Jake stood for a while, trying to decipher the words on the card by this cabinet. The 'episode' had occurred in 1941, the 26th October, just three months after the fascist invasion.

Commentary

Extract one, which represents a contemporary account of the hangings, focuses on the victims. At first they are anonymous: victims. Words such as brutal, hanged, gallows and crude are used to emphasise the horror of the executions. As the passage moves on, the specific victims are given their full names and their status: veteran, girl, boy, partisans. The executioners are barely mentioned and when they are, they remain anonymous: Nazis.

The second account tells the same story through the eyes of someone looking at photographs. All the participants are anonymous: uniformed men, prisoners, boy, girl, apart from the observer, Jake. The naming sets up the sense of distance that time creates. The description of the hanging is visually more detailed: distorted, agony, mute plea, strained, noosed, terror, dead. The description is also sequenced: *now, now, now, then* as the observer moves from photograph to photograph.

The term 'word' is, therefore, not as easy to define as it first seems. Any analysis of text that is looking at word level needs to be done with an awareness of the complicated relationship that exists between words and meanings, the patterns words create with other words, how frequently the words occur, whether they are primarily spoken or written, and whether they can be interpreted literally or not.

Words and histories

This section looks at the origins of the English word stock, and the ways in which the language gains new words through the processes of borrowing, changing the use of existing words and creating new words.

THE ORIGINS OF ENGLISH

The origins of the English language lie in the distant past, but the recorded history of English begins in the fifth century with the arrival of the Germanic tribes in Britain. The language they brought with them, later assimilating the Norse languages of the Viking invaders, is the ancestor of modern English and is a major source of many of our most commonly used words.

Activity

For this activity, you will need a dictionary, electronic or printed, that gives **etymological** information (information about the origins of a word). Using the dictionary, look at the origins of the following words:

> the, knee, I, you, and, father, bread, for, of, shirt, in,
>
> daughter, sister, to, hat, egg, heart, on

Divide them into grammatical words , i.e. words that form part of the structure of the language, like auxiliary verbs, prepositions, pronouns, conjunctions, and 'lexical' words that have a clear dictionary meaning or content.

Note that there is no commentary on this activity.

All the words in the above list have their origins in the Old English period. The grammatical words in this list are some of the most commonly used in the English language, both in its spoken and written forms.

Activity

Group the lexical words into semantic fields. Which fields can you identify? Can you comment on why these groups of words have remained in the language from such an early period? Add other words from the same field to each group and look up their origins. Are these from the same or from a later period? Can you say why some semantic fields contain words from the earliest period of the language, and others have a range of words from different periods? Are there other semantic fields where you might expect to find words from very early periods?

Commentary

Words for family relationships, parts of the body, food and items of clothing will have been essential in the language from the start. Immediate family relationship terms haven't changed much over the centuries, even though family systems have become more complicated. Words for more distant relatives – aunt, uncle, grandparents, niece, nephew – come into the language at a slightly later period. Names for parts of the body have remained the same, though developments in biology and medicine mean that in later periods, new words have come into the language.

Words for food and for items of clothing reflect the changes in fashions over the centuries. Basic items of clothing: shirt, shoes, skirt, hat are all early in origin. The origins of bread, butter, milk, honey, meat, egg, fish, beer give an interesting picture of the diet of the Old English period.

Other semantic fields you might have looked at are days of the week, months of the year and counting systems.

BORROWING: GOT ANY SPARE WORDS?

> The problem with defending the purity of the English language is that the English language is as pure as a crib-house whore. It not only borrows words from other languages; it has on occasion chased other languages down dark alley-ways, clubbed them unconscious and rifled their pockets for new vocabulary.
>
> (James Nicoll, 1846–1918)

English has often been described as having a very rich and extensive word stock. For political and historical reasons, it has borrowed from other languages all over the world, and still does. As new cultures and concepts enter society, their influence is seen in the language by, among other things, developments in the English word stock.

Activity

Look up the words in the following lists, and locate them on a world map according to their country and language of origin. Some words may not be located in a specific country, but a more general area such as North America.

List 1 contains words that are comparatively recent additions to the language. You may not be able to find them if your dictionary is not a very recent one, but you should be able to identify the place of origin.

List 1 anime, bada bing, barbie, g-man, honcho, intifada,

jilbab, karaoke, sushi, wok

List 2 contains words that have been in the language for a relatively long time, and therefore should be in any comprehensive dictionary. Try to locate the original source, for example, bonanza is identified as American slang, but its origins are Spanish.

List 2 adobe, algebra, bonanza, carriage, contralto, dilettante, dingo, giraffe, hoosegow, jazz, juggernaut, pariah, tattoo (marking on the skin), tobacco, voyage

Commentary

A short dictionary investigation of this kind shows how widely the English language has borrowed from other languages. The borrowing is worldwide; in fact, there are very few languages English has not borrowed from at one time or another. The reason for this lies in the history of both the language and the country. The earliest borrowed words, or loan words, are from Latin, with a very small number from the original Celtic languages of Britain.

The Viking invasion introduced Scandinavian words. The Norman conquest introduced a massive number of French loan words. Later contact with other European languages through cultural exchange, trade, political contacts and exploration gave the language Portuguese, Dutch, Spanish and Italian loan words. Languages from the Near East – Arabic, Turkish, Persian, Hindustani, Indic, Tamil – came via trade, exploration, colonisation and, sadly, the slave trade.

How long has this pick 'n' mix approach to our lexicon existed? The English language has always borrowed from other languages, so are there any words that are 'truly' English?

This concept, 'truly English', is a difficult one to define. The earliest language spoken in Britain was the ancestor of modern Welsh. The earliest words that are identifiably English come from the Germanic languages from which English developed. It is probably reasonable to say that these earliest words from the Old English period are 'truly English'.

Activity

Look at Text 3:5 below. It is a Mystery Play (a series of dramas representing bible stories) from the York Cycle. The manuscript is dated 1463–77.

- How many words do you recognise?
- How many are familiar but are spelt differently?
- How many are unfamiliar?
- Can you work out the meaning from the context?

Text 3:5

The Crucifixion of Christ

From York
The Pinneres and Painters

Crucifixio Christi.

[The soldiers arrive at Calvary with Jesus.]

1 Soldier. Sir knightis, take heede hydir in hie!
This dede on-dergh we may noght drawe.
Yee wootte youreselffe als wele as I
Howe lordis and leders of owre lawe
Has geven dome that this doote schall die.

2 Soldier. Sir, alle thare counsaile wele we knawe.
Sen we are comen to Calvarie,
Latte ilke man helpe nowe as him awe.

3 Soldier. We are alle redy, loo,
That forward to fullfille.

4 Soldier. Late here howe we schall doo,
And go we tyte thertille.

4 Soldier. It may noght helpe here for to hone
If we schall any worshippe winne.

2 Soldier He muste be dede nedelingis by none.

3 Soldier. Thanne is goode time that we beginne.

4 Soldier.	Late dinge him doune! Than is he done; He schall nought dere us with his dinne . . .
3 Soldier	Sen ilke a thing is right arrayed The wislier now worke may we
4 Soldier	The crosse on grounde is goodely graied And boorede even as it awith to be
1 Soldier	Lookis that the ladde on lengthe be laide And made me thane unto this tree
2 Soldier	For alle his fare, he shall be flaied That on assaye sone schall ye see
Jhesus.	Almighty God, my Fadir free, Late this[e] materes be made in minde: Thou badde that I schulde buxsome be For Adam plight for to be pined. Here to dede I obblisshe me Fro that sinne for to save mankinde, And soverainely beseke I thee That thay for me may favoure finde; ; And fro the fende thame fende, So that ther saules be saffe In welthe withouten ende. I kepe nought ellis to crave.

Commentary

The text is relatively easy for the modern English reader to understand, though there are some words that are no longer used in English: on-dergh (undiligently) , woote (know), doote (fool), ilke (each), thertille (to it), nedelingis (necessarily), graied (prepared). Others look unfamiliar, but are fairly common words that are spelled differently (dede – deed, wele – well, dome – doom, none – noon). Some words look familiar but have a different meaning from the one a modern reader might expect. Hone is a dialect word meaning delay or tarry. Others look unfamiliar, but are still found in current use. Assaye is a test or a trial, used currently (assay) only for metals. Tyte is found in modern

English as 'tight', but the meaning in this text, smart or capable, is marked as obsolete in the *OED*. It is coming back into use as can be seen in this comment posted on an internet message board in summer 2006: 'If U cool den U pop yo collar me and some other of my homies look tight when they pop they collar up.' Buxsome (buxom) in modern English is used to mean plump or well-built. The earlier meaning represented here is obedient or compliant.

However, the majority of the words are still in current use. Some may have changed their meaning slightly, but the greatest change is the spelling. Spelling was not standardised at this time and these spellings reflect the pronunciation of the writer(s). English spelling underwent the process of standardisation in a rather haphazard manner, which means that we are left with spellings that reflect archaic pronunciations. Examples are knee, thought, through, night. Other spellings indicate word endings. Earlier forms of English were morphologically more complex than modern English. Old English used more inflections (the modification of a word, usually by adding an ending) to carry grammatical information than modern English. The word endings indicated in the spellings are the remains of this.

Activity

In the late Middle English period, English was borrowing from a range of languages, especially, Greek, Latin and French. Identify the origins of the following words in the extract above. The first set are from the dialogue given to the soldiers, the second set are from the words given to Christ.

1 assay, counsel deed, each (ilke), flayed, heed, law, leader, lord, worship,

2 almighty, matter, oblige, obligate, plight, sovereign, favour

Commentary

Both the soldiers and Christ use words from Old English. The soldiers use very few from Latin, Greek or French. The ones they do use, counsel and assay both refer to specific matters relating to the legal system. Christ, on the other hand, uses words from Old French, Anglo-Norman and Latin.

In the early ME period, French words were particularly associated with the church, law and chivalry. Loan words from Greek and Latin are even today associated with formality and learning, words from French are often associated with sophistication.

Activity

Text 3:6 is from the fashion pages of the *Observer* and Text 3:7 is an e-mail explaining how to make a particular dish. Look up the origins of the underlined words. How does the origin of these words reflect the function and topic of each text?

There is a commentary on this activity at the end of the unit.

Text 3:6

> Coco Chanel first introduced the androgynous look to womenswear back in 1930s Paris; her pioneering appropriation of masculine tailoring for female attire has since become a staple of the working woman's wardrobe. This summer, city-boy chic looks good in or out of the office, with briefcase or mobile phone as optional accessories.

Text 3:7

> Hi – you wanted that pork casserole recipe from last week. I use belly pork and take the fat off, but you can use pork fillet if you want to be posh. You'll need a couple of pounds. Cut it up and fry it – I render down some of the pork fat, but veg(etable) oil is fine. Then fry the onions (sliced and diced) in the fat in the pan. Put it all in a casserole dish. Add some stock, some sherry and about a tbsp of soy sauce – you should have enough liquid to cover the meat but only just. Then give it a long, slow cook.

Words mean what I want them to mean

The English language doesn't only acquire words by borrowing from other languages, though as the previous section demonstrates, many new words came into the language via that route. Another route is that of semantic change, or a change in the meaning of a word over time. A fairly recent example is the word 'gay', which has a range of meanings in the Oxford English dictionary. It used to have the primary meaning of happy or carefree, but now has the primary meaning of homosexual. It is also used in current slang to mean bad, stupid or unfortunate.

Activity

The following text appears puzzling at first. This is because the underlined words have been used with their original or earlier meaning. Look up the original meanings of the words, and rewrite the text into modern English.

> The girl wore his best frock to the dinner party. He was a healthy young man with a healthy appetite and he was in danger of eating so much he would starve. There was plenty of meat to suit his vegetarian tastes. After the meal, his disease was so bad he had to go and lie down.

Note that there is no commentary on this activity.

This text demonstrates the extent to which the meaning of a word can change. The problem faced by language purists who object to change of this kind is that many of the words that are commonly used have undergone the process they are objecting to, and unless they demand that the language should be subjected to some kind of 'purification' process in which all words were restored to their original meanings, the purists' position is a bit illogical.

There are patterned and recognised ways in which the meanings of words can change.

GENERALISATION AND SPECIALISATION

A very common way for semantic change to occur is where a word either expands its meaning to include a wider range (generalisation) or narrows its meaning to become more specific (specialisation). Examples of this include 'wife', a word that used to mean woman in the general sense. The word gradually specialised to mean 'a woman of humble rank or low employment', giving the language constructions such as ale-wife or fish-wife. The word now means married woman. The word 'novice', on the other hand, has generalised in meaning. It used to have a specific religious context, but now it is used to describe a beginner in any field.

Activity

Look at Text 3:6 again. Say whether the underlined words have generalised or specialised in meaning.

Note that there is no commentary on this activity.

BEWARE OF THE WORD! TABOO AND EUPHEMISM

An important influence in the semantic change of words is the change of meaning brought about by the associations a word may have. There are certain concepts a culture may be uneasy about, and words associated with these concepts may attract censure. When this happens, such words can develop negative connotations. They may then be replaced by other words that are seen as a better or 'nicer' way of expressing the concept. Unfortunately, once the new word becomes associated with the concept, it too begins to attract negative connotations and needs to be replaced in turn. This process is known as deterioration or pejoration. The reverse process, whereby a word acquires a 'better' meaning, is known as amelioration.

Activity

The following words refer to the act of human excretion, and the location where this should take place. Classify the words into groups under the following headings: casual/slang, technical/medical, formal/polite.

pee, piss, urine, shit, crap, faeces, wee, pass water,
urinate, defecate, go to the toilet/lavatory/bathroom,
powder my nose, rest room, comfort station, w.c.,
ladies, gents, loo, lavatory, bog

Which words or phrases would be acceptable in a fairly formal situation?

Commentary

A quick analysis of this word list suggests that excretion is a social minefield in the English-speaking world (or parts of it). A group of students doing this activity decided that in informal, peer-group situations, English is well equipped with words , though there are many groups who would not find these terms acceptable, even in very informal situations.

Interestingly, 'crap', a word that is mildly taboo, is probably a euphemism in origin. Its original meanings were husk, weeds and residue. 'Shit' has not changed its meaning over time, but is described in the *OED* as 'not in decent use'. 'Piss' is also an old form that has become mildly taboo.

Therefore, one word associated with a socially difficult concept began as a euphemism and has become taboo, while words that carry the original meaning have been considered taboo for some time. Presumably, newer euphemisms will also become taboo in turn.

'Piss' and 'shit' also seem to be acquiring new, non-taboo meanings. 'Pissed' is a well-known English slang term for drunkenness, and more recently American English has developed the meaning of belongings, detritus, the rest, etc., for 'shit', as in the following examples: 'It's just where I keep all my shit.' 'You won't get shit if you don't ask.' 'Microsoft won't get their shit together until Mac gets serious.'

Technical and medical terms, urinate and defecate, would appear to be clear and direct in meaning. Urinate has just the meaning to pass urine, but defecate has the original meaning of to purify.

The formal terms are all euphemistic. The group noted that there is no polite way to say what you are going to do. In this context, the use of a technical term will not help. 'I am going to urinate' would not be seen as socially acceptable. There are only polite ways of saying where you are going or asking directions. Even the most apparently direct words for the place are euphemisms.

'Toilet' originally meant a piece of cloth in which clothes were wrapped, then a cloth cover for a dressing table, then the dressing table itself. Its current meaning is fairly recent and is American in origin.

'Lavatory' used to mean a place to wash yourself (compare with current use of bathroom). Both 'toilet' and 'lavatory' have become socially a bit difficult, and the language has acquired a newer range of euphemisms: ladies, gents, powder room, bathroom, rest room, etc.

Semantic change, as with borrowing, is a continuous process, and far more complex than the brief outline above suggests. An awareness of the capacity of words to shift and change their meaning helps the receiver of text to be aware of change as it has occurred, or as it is occurring.

GET YOUR NEW WORDS HERE! CREATING NEW WORDS

A third way in which English acquires new words is by word creation, either through invention following existing word patterns, or through the direct creation of new words. As with semantic change, this is a massive area, and this section will only address aspects of it.

Activity

Look again at Text 3:3. Identify words that are likely to be recent additions to English.

- Have you seen or heard them before?
- Why have these words appeared?
- Are they in the dictionary?
- Are they likely to remain in the language?

Commentary

The words 'online', 'virtual', 'griefers', 'griefing', 'scam', 'stats', 'MMORPGS', are all relatively recent additions to English. 'Griefers' and 'griefing' are both developed from the existing word 'grief', 'MMORPGS' is an acronym, 'scam' was first recorded in English in 1963. It's origins are not known. 'Stats' is a shortening of statistics, recorded as early as 1942. It is only recently that the full stop to mark an abbreviation has disappeared. 'Virtual' is from Latin and has been recorded in English since 1398. Its recent meaning of 'not physically existing but appearing to exist' has been used as a specialist term in computer science since the 1950s. More recently it has moved into general use.

Activity

The following words have recently been added to the *OED*. Write a definition for each word and suggest an etymology. Now look the word up and see if your ideas match the official entry. (Note: you may need access to the *OED* online to find these words.)

- bada bing
- bling
- celebutante
- drive by
- GIF
- heightist
- ho
- meat space
- 0800 number
- 24–7
- 4WD

There is a commentary on this activity at the end of the unit.

Activity

The following words were not in the *OED* at the time of writing (October 2006). Can you suggest a reason why?

- i-pod
- podcast
- Taliban
- 9/11 (or nine-eleven)

Commentary

There is no clear reason why some words that are in wide use are included in a specific dictionary and some are not, or not yet. Different dictionaries have different requirements. Language will always be ahead of the most up to date dictionaries, and lack of resources may mean that even a dictionary like the *OED* will lag behind the language in use.

Online dictionaries such as www.urbandictionary.com can be more up to date, but definitions may be arbitrary and citations are not necessarily checked. Users add words and definitions, and so several competing definitions for a specific entry may be given. Use Urban Dictionary to look up the words listed above that are not yet included in the *OED*. How many definitions are offered? Do you agree with them? What definition would you give? How many variant spellings can you find?

Social and technological change is moving very fast in the twenty-first century, and these have their influence on the word stock of a language. The need for fast communication has led to changes in the English word stock via SMS language or texting and via the language of other electronic forms – e-mail and chat rooms for example. For a fairly comprehensive outline of features of computer mediated communication – CMC – see www.netlingo.com.

Change continues: multicultural London English

A living language is never static and English is undergoing changes constantly. It is now a global language with a range of distinct varieties around the world. Even in the UK, it continues to change.

Recent research into the language of London teenagers carried out at Lancaster University has identified a dialect that is developing in the capital that is not associated with one ethnic group, but draws from the influences of West African English, Caribbean English, Bangladeshi English and South American English. It has been referred to in newspapers as Jafaikan, but researchers refer to it as multicultural London English. This variety isn't confined to any specific ethnic group and is found among young people in Birmingham, Manchester and Bristol.

The accent of this variety is distinct, but like all dialects it is also developing its own distinctive vocabulary:

creps	*meaning*	trainers
yard		home
ends		area/neighbourhood (as in 'what ends you from?')
low batties		jeans/trousers that hang low on the hips or below
nang		good
sick		good ('wow, that's really sick!')
bare		used as an intensifier meaning 'really' ('I'm bare hungry')

hype	hype things up/increase status ('it's all about the hype')
jamming/cotching	hanging around
begging	chatting rubbish
yute	baby/child
blud/bredren/bruv	mate (blood brother)
mandem	people

(Taken from J. Cheshire, S. Fox, P. Kerswill and E. Torgersen, *Linguistic Innovators: The English of adolescents in London*, project funded by ESRC RES-000-23-0680. Further information about this research can be found at www.lancs.ac.uk/fss/projects/linguistics/innovators/index.htm.)

The English language is over a thousand years old. Its word stock is wide and varied, with immense capacity for expressing subtle shades and wide ranges of meaning. As a living language, English will continue to develop and expand its word stock in response to social change and development, technological change, changes in cultural and religious beliefs, and all those other factors that operate to make a language a tool that its users need.

Extension activities

1 Collect examples of names of shops and services that exploit the capacity of words to create ambiguous meanings.

2 Invent names for the following: an undertaker, a baker, a greengrocer, a pest controller, a solicitor.

3 Check in a local Yellow Pages directory. What names do these shops and services use? Which ones do, and which ones don't, play meaning games with language? Why might this be the case?

4 Use Babelfish to translate 'Red herring' from English to German, German to French, French back to English. Find other idioms and translate them through several languages. How useful are these programmes in identifying the meanings of idiomatic language?

5 Collect examples from written language including electronic and digital forms. How is the word 'like' used in these contexts?

6 Observe the language spoken by teenagers and young people in your area. Are there any uses of this form of English? What variety is spoken, and how does it differ from the standard?

Commentaries/Answers to activities

COMMENTARY: ACTIVITY p. 76

- There are 14 uses of 'a', 6 of 'his', 2 of 'relatively', 2 of 'one'. 'Her', 'your', 'completely', 'fairly', 'totally', 'the', all occur once.
- 'Her', 'your' and 'his' are all possessive pronouns and can be grouped together.
- 'Relatively', 'completely', 'fairly', 'totally' are all the same word class and can be grouped together.
- 'The' is an article and can be grouped with 'a'.

A clear pattern emerges. Where a possessive pronoun is used with the phrase 'free hand', the meaning is literal, not idiomatic. Similarly, the word 'one' indicates a literal usage. In example 25, 'one' is preceded by a possessive pronoun.

Where adverbial forms ('relatively', 'totally', etc.) precede the phrase, the use is idiomatic, but in each case, the word 'a' precedes the adverbial. What would happen if a possessive pronoun preceded this? Is 'Her relatively free hand' idiomatic or not? Without a context, it is impossible to tell, but 'free' is an adjective that can't usually be graded. Something is either free or not. Uses such as 'relatively free', 'slightly free' are unusual and more likely to occur in an idiomatic usage.

The indefinite article 'a' precedes an idiomatic use in every case except for 28. This example reads rather oddly to a native speaker and may be a simple error.

COMMENTARY: ACTIVITY p. 79

'Like' as an interjection has expanded its use beyond that given in the dictionary and is currently widely used. There are three examples above: 1. 'a like overtake mode'; 4. 'Yeah that's alright. like we've got the, quite, similar lot'; 9. 'I drove up, up there and back, like, my leg don't ache'. There is also one example of a verbal use that the dictionary doesn't cover: 'like' as a reporting verb to mean 'said': 'Anyone like I'll have the fresh ones'.

COMMENTARY: ACTIVITY p. 90, TEXTS 3:6, 3:7

Many of the underlined words, words relating to the specialism of fashion, are loan words from French. Most of these are very much part of the day-to-day vocabulary. 'Fashion', 'attire', 'tailoring' may all be from a specialist field, but cause no problems to the reader.

As noted above, as early as the eleventh century, French words became associated with sophistication, and it is interesting that new words for artifacts that have clear connotations of 'style' to the modern reader have been taken from French. For example, why 'mobile' (French) phone, rather than 'portable' (Latin) phone? Computers, which are seen as utilitarian are 'hand-held' (Old English). Continued borrowing from French means that we tend to go to the French language when a word for a fashion concept is needed. 'Chic', for example, has its first recorded usage in 1856. Its status as a more recent arrival can be identified by its pronunciation, which has not become anglicised: /ʃik/ rather than /ʧik/.

French words started appearing in relation to food from the time of the Norman conquest. English began to differentiate between the animal and the meat: 'pig' (probably Old English) vs 'pork' (French). These words are so deeply rooted in the language, that a reference to the animal in relation to most food would seem odd and distasteful: *'pig sausages', *'pig casserole', *'pig chops' are all forms that are not used. Words relating to foodstuffs and to methods of cooking are largely French in origin. Only 'fat', 'stock', 'belly' and 'cook' are from Old English. There are also more recent additions: 'sherry' (Spanish) and 'soy' (Japanese).

COMMENTARY: ACTIVITY p. 95

Words are still coming into English via the same routes (the dates mark the inclusion of the word in the dictionary, not the first recorded use):

- **Borrowing**
  - 'Bada bing' (2006): The origin of this word is uncertain, It's possibly imitative of the sound of a drum roll, or it may be from the Italian *bada bene*, 'mark well'. It was almost certainly popularised in the UK by the TV drama *The Sopranos*;
  - 'ho' (2001): from African American, a respelling of 'whore' to match the pronunciation.
- **Blending or combining of existing forms**
  - 'celebutante', 'drive by', 'heightist' (all 2006);
  - 'meat space' (the real world as opposed to virtual space) (2001).

- **Onomatopoeic or imitative words**
  - 'bling' (2006) has its origins in rap and hip hop.
- **Acronyms**
  - 'GIF' (2006) from Graphics Interchange Format.
- - '0800 number', '24-7', '4WD' (2003): these represent a relatively new form. Numbers are used, sometimes combined with letters to create new words.

Satellite texts

The following satellite texts look in detail at ideas covered in this unit:

The Language of Advertising looks at the use of words in advertising.

Language Change looks at how new words are formed and old words change meaning.

The Language of Humour looks at how words are manipulated for comic effect.

Unit four

Sentences and structures

Aims of this unit

The main aim of this unit is to introduce you to some of the most significant patterns of English grammar. It is, of course, impossible to introduce all the patterns, but those selected here are generally likely to be significant in the organisation of texts. Knowing about these patterns and understanding how they function will help you to see how meanings are made in texts and can provide a basis for interpreting what the texts mean to you.

About this unit

Grammar is only one level of linguistic analysis, and interpreting the use of grammar in the text is not the same as interpreting the text. To do this we need to consider other patterns of language too, such as vocabulary, phonology and discourse. But grammar is a central resource for making and communicating meaning, and the more you understand how it works the more systematically you can work with texts that interest you.

Many students are frightened of grammar and of the terminology used to discuss it. Some consider that its study is no more than a mechanical exercise. The aim in this unit is to show how useful grammatical knowledge can be if it is applied to how it works in different texts and contexts of use, rather than being just the naming of parts out of context. To do this we need some language to talk about grammar, and part of that language will involve words and terms that may be new.

Grammar and patterns

The following sentence does not make sense. It is not grammatical. Put all the words in an order so that it does make sense overall. Then ask yourself how you did it.

weekend going am to I next disco the.

One way to do it is to look for groups of words which belong together in a pattern and then to put all the groups of words together. For example:

going am I = I am going (or am I going?)

the to disco = to the disco

weekend next = next weekend

Sentences are made up of individual groups of words which form *patterns* with other groups of words. The patterns can be fixed; that is, they must follow a certain order. Or the patterns can follow different orders , though if they do, the meaning is normally changed.

For example, 'to the disco' is a fixed pattern; but 'I am going' can also be formed as 'Am I going?', which turns a statement into a question. 'I am going to the disco next weekend' can also be written as 'Next weekend I am going to the disco', which, by putting the reference to the time at the beginning, stresses 'next weekend'.

Nouns and patterns

In this section we will examine **nouns** and patterns involving nouns. Nouns are one of the most prominent of forms in a language. In fact, quite a few texts can be made up just of nouns; for example, 'London' is a noun and can stand quite meaningfully on its own on a signpost, or in answer to a question. or on a train or air ticket. or as the title to a book. 'School' is a noun and can stand on its own on a road sign, for example. 'Apples' is a noun and can stand quite independently on a shop ticket or shop sign. Take any word from the first sentence in this paragraph and try to make a meaningful text. You will see that it is difficult to make a meaningful list with words like 'we' or 'this' or 'in' or 'involving' when they occur on their own.

Activity

Write out a shopping list for shopping for your family at your local supermarket. List the ten items which you think your family would judge to be the most essential items. Look at the list you have produced and consider what the words have in common. The words will be mostly consumable or usable items but try to identify what they have in common as words. What does the list look like on the page?

Commentary

The shopping list you wrote probably consisted of nouns such as

- milk
- bread
- tea bags
- oven-ready chips.

As you can see, nouns are not just single words; they can form patterns with other words to make **noun phrases**. Again such phrases can stand on their own: for example, as titles to a book or story such as 'The Man with a Scar', or on a menu in a phrase such as 'Home-made celery soup', or on a shopfront name such as 'The Body Shop' or 'The Vegetarian Restaurant', or on a shopping list such as 'oven-ready chips' or 'semi-skimmed milk'. Writers of all kinds of different texts regularly make creative and communicative use of nouns and noun patterns. A good example is the poem 'Off Course' (1966) by Edwin Morgan.

Activity

1 Why do you think the writer has laid out the text as shown in Text 4:1 on p. 104?

2 Why are there no punctuation marks used in the poem?

Text 4:1

'Off Course'

the golden flood the weightless seat
the cabin song the pitch black
the growing beard the floating crumb
the shining rendezvous the orbit wisecrack
the hot spacesuit the smuggled mouth-organ
the imaginary somersault the visionary sunrise
the turning continents the space debris
the golden lifeline the space walk
the crawling deltas the camera moon
the pitch velvet the rough sleep
the crackling headphone the space silence
the turning earth the lifeline continents
the cabin sunrise the hot flood
the shining spacesuit the growing moon
    the crackling somersault the smuggled orbit
    the rough moon the visionary rendezvous
    the weightless headphone the cabin debris
    the floating lifeline the pitch sleep
    the crawling camera the turning silence
    the space crumb the crackling beard
    the orbit mouth-organ the floating song

Edwin Morgan

Commentary

The most striking feature of the poem is its layout. The arrangement of the words on the page, or what is termed the **graphology** of the poem, is especially distinctive and leaves the reader a little uncertain as to how it is to be read. For example, you could read across the page, which is the more conventional 'direction'; but you could also read down the page, reading the two columns one after the other almost as if the words were part of some inventory or list, rather like the shopping list which you created above. The layout of the lines is unusual and disorientating. The second column does not have the clear order and pattern of the first column, and at line 15 it looks as if a new paragraph begins. The lines move in a different direction and, as in the title of the poem perhaps, appear to go 'off course'.

The new direction appears to be a disturbing one for there is no obvious structure or ending to it. The movement of the second column of words is even more markedly laid out to suggest disorder, and this suggestion is reinforced by the fact that the poem has no real punctuation. There are no commas or colons or semi-colons or capital letters anywhere in the text. And the absence of full stops, especially at line 21, suggests that there is no ending to the text; it remains free-floating, searching for a pattern rather then clearly following an already existing one.

Yet closer inspection of the poem reveals that there are patterns. There are patterns of grammar across the whole text which are remarkably consistent and unchanging. Most striking is the pattern of noun phrases. In each case the structure is that of *d m n,* where *d* = definite article, *m* = modifier and *n* = noun. In fact, this structure is repeated in every line in the poem.

The most basic examples of this *d m n* pattern are in lines such as the following:

> the hot flood

where 'the' is the definite article (*d*), 'hot' the modifier (*m*) and 'flood' is the noun (*n*) Or:

> the weightless headphone

where 'the' is the definite article, 'weightless' the modifier and 'headphone' is the noun.

One reason why the term 'modifier' is preferred here to the more usual term 'adjective' is that 'modifier' is more inclusive. For example, nouns can be modified by other nouns as in 'the space silence' and the 'orbit wise-crack', where 'space' and 'orbit', which are both nouns, fill in these noun phrases the position of modifier, defining more precisely the nouns to which they are attached.

Activity

As we have seen, a basic structural pattern pervades the whole poem, and repetition of this pattern is a key feature of the poem. But there are variations within the repeated patterns. Take a basic pattern such as

> the *pitch* black (2)
>
> the *pitch* velvet (10)
>
> the *pitch* sleep (18)

and then find similar patterns in the poem in which a word is repeated with various partners. List as many of these patterns as you can. Why are there so many repetitions and what is suggested by the constant changes and variations?

There is a commentary on this activity at the end of the unit.

Subject, object and verb

We can now consider other patterns which might go along with the noun phrases. For example, if we were to put the following nouns in a **sentence**, would you be able to make sense of the sentence?

> the tall man the black dog

What other words would you need to add to the sentence in order to make it make sense? Take the verbs out of the following sentences. What are the results? Do the sentences make sense without the verbs?

> The girl kissed the boy.
> They lost the match 4–1.
> My friend's daughter has broken another vase.
> Paris is the capital of France.

There are no main **verbs** in 'Off Course'. One effect of this omission of main verbs is that no clear relation seems to exist between the objects referred to in the noun phrases. Objects either seem not to act upon one another or have no particular 'action' of their own. Verbs create links. The links are usually between a grammatical 'subject' and a grammatical 'object'. In this example the subject 'tall man' is linked by a main verb 'walked' to the object 'dog':

The tall man walked the dog

If the main verb is taken away, then the relationship between the noun 'man' and the noun 'dog' is no longer clear. Similarly, in the sentence

My friend's daughter has broken another vase
SUBJECT VERB OBJECT

if the verb phrase 'has broken' is removed, we are left with 'My friend's daughter another vase', where we cannot work out the precise relationship between 'My friend's daughter' and the 'vase'.

So it is with the noun phrases in 'Off Course'. Verbs generally work to connect things, and so in this case the main effect is that of normal relations being suspended and disconnected. The poet has suspended the normal rules of grammar to create a world in which everything is turned upside down and suspended. In one sense this is appropriate to the conditions of outer space in which there is no gravity, but it may also suggest a space journey in which actions and events have become disturbingly abnormal.

The absence of main verbs in a text also removes any sense of time. Verbs are normally marked when something is taking place or took place. Thus, 'walked' tells you that the action is completed and is in the past tense. If there are no verbs in a text then there is no **tense**, and if there is no tense it is difficult to work out within what timescale things are happening. The poem 'Off Course' has as a result a certain timeless quality, as if normal temporal relations are suspended too.

However, it is not true to say that there are no verbs in the poem. There *are* verbs in the poem. For example, there is another distinct pattern in the text formed from the following groups of words:

the floating song
the growing beard
the shining rendezvous
the turning continents
the crackling headphone
the crawling deltas

and so on. The words ending in '-ing' are all what are termed **present participles**. The differences between the two verbal items in the following sentences

the world turns
the turning world

underline that present participles function to create a sense of continuing, if suspended, action. In the poem they convey a feeling of things continuing endlessly or, at least, without any clear end. It may not be inappropriate, therefore, that the final line of the poem contains the group of words

> the floating song

which, with an absence of punctuation, possibly reinforces the idea of an endlessly drifting journey without a conclusion.

Notice, too, how many film titles contain present participles: for example, *Leaving Las Vegas, Boxing Helena, Being There, No Turning Back*. There are many more similar titles to check out in a local video shop, but consider why such forms are so common. Also consider the increasing number of institutional branding slogans which use present participles, ranging from schools and hospitals through to multinational companies. 'Aiming High' might be a school slogan, ' Treating you well' a hospital slogan.

Pronouns and patterns

Although we interpreted the poem 'Off Course' as being about a space journey which involved the lives of astronauts, there are, in fact, no actual references in the poem to people. The nouns refer to actions which we take to involve humans but the poem does *not* contain lines such as

> His rough sleep
>
> His growing beard
>
> Your hot spacesuit
>
> Her cabin song
>
> Our floating lifeline

Words such as 'you', 'my', 'your', 'his', 'her' are **pronouns**. The main personal pronouns are: 'I', 'you', 'he', 'she', 'it', 'we', 'they'. They are the main means of identifying speakers, addressees and others. The main possessive pronouns are: 'my', 'your', 'her', 'his', 'their', 'our'. They indicate ownership. (Other types and functions of pronouns are explored in Unit 5.) One possible effect of the absence of pronouns from 'Off Course' is to make the poem a little impersonal and cold, almost as if we are hearing a list of facts.

Activity

Text 4:2 also presents a number of facts but does it in a different way. Find all the pronouns in this text and list them.

- To whom do they refer?
- Why are so many pronouns used in the text?

There is a commentary on this activity at the end of the unit.

Text 4:2

Waitrose

Professor R Carter
11 Sutton Drive
Nottingham
NG45 1DF

19841/0052089/0008936

31st May 2006

Dear Professor Carter

Put award-winning Ocado to the test this month.

I'm just writing to make sure you know about Ocado, the online grocery service, which is now delivering in your area - and one which could make your life a whole lot easier.

Ocado has been combining the convenience and value of online shopping with the kind of quality and service you'd expect from the John Lewis Partnership, and has been awarded 'Best Online Supermarket 2005' by The Grocer magazine at their Gold Awards. This is fantastic news and wonderful recognition of their continued commitment to customer service.

With their groceries delivered directly from their warehouse, ensuring excellent levels of freshness and accuracy of delivery, all delivered in convenient one-hour slots, Ocado really does operate a unique and dedicated service.

Get 15% off your first shop.

Of course the only way to see how good the service really is, is to experience it. That's why Ocado is offering you 15% off your first shop over £90. Have a look at the enclosed leaflet to see how easy it is.

So this letter brings news not only of a great award-winning service but of great offers too. I'm sure you'll be delighted with this fantastic shopping experience.

Yours sincerely

Christian Cull
Marketing Director

PS If you would like to contact Ocado, please write to: Ocado Limited, Freepost 13498, PO Box 362, Hatfield, AL9 7BR

Or call on: 0845 399 1122

Food shops of the John Lewis Partnership

One very obvious grammatical difference between Text 4:2 and Text 4:1 is that the letter is written in complete sentences and makes use of much more familiar and conventional patterns of paragraphing and punctuation. The use of upper-case (capital) letters at the beginning and end of the message also emphasises the personal and individual nature of the relationship between the marketing director and the customer.

Activity

Read Text 4:2 again and see how many noun phrases you can find which have the same *d m n* pattern as those in 'Off Course'. If they are the same, consider why they are the same and, if the patterns are different, consider how and why they are different. It may help to list all the nouns that you can find in the text and then all the modifiers which occur in front of these nouns. Here are two examples to start you off:

- great award-winning service
- best online supermarket

There is a commentary on this activity at the end of the unit.

Normally, the more nouns which are used in a **pre-modifying** position the more technical or specialised the reference will be. You can often identify writing in science and engineering by the amount and density of this kind of pre-modification. For example, here are some terms from a car maintenance manual:

metal hub-bearing outer race

low-friction disc brakes

aluminium precision dial gauge.

Although the letter from the company director to potential customers is designed to be a personal letter, it nonetheless suggests that it is from a company which is in some way also specialised and efficient.

Verbs and patterns

One of the most striking features of the poem 'Off Course' (see p. 104) is the absence of a main verb. In that poem one of the effects created by the omission of a main verb is a sense of suspension and disorientation as it becomes increasingly difficult to work out, grammatically, what are the objects and what are the subjects in the text. Readers find it difficult to know where they are.

Activity

Text 4:3 shows the opening four paragraphs from Charles Dickens's novel *Bleak House.* Dickens is one of the major English nineteenth-century novelists who saw the legal system of the country as a source of corruption and as a major obstacle to progress. Here the 'Lord Chancellor' is the head of the legal system.

One of the most striking features of Dickens's use of the language is that the opening three paragraphs do not contain a single main verb. Is the effect which is created for the reader the same as that created in the poem 'Off Course'?

Text 4:3

London. Michaelmas Terms lately over, and the Lord Chancellor sitting in Lincoln's Inn Hall. Implacable November weather. As much mud in the streets, as if the waters had but newly retired from the face of the earth, and it would not be wonderful to meet a Megalosaurus, forty feet long or so, waddling like an elephantine lizard up Holborn Hill. Smoke lowering down from chimney-pots, making a soft black drizzle, with flakes of soot in it as big as full-grown snowflakes – gone into mourning, one might imagine, for the death of the sun. Dogs, undistinguishable in the mire. Horses, scarcely better; splashed to their very blinkers. Foot passengers, jostling one another's umbrellas, in a general infection of ill-temper, and losing their foot-hold at street-corners, where tens of thousands of other foot passengers have been slipping and sliding since the day broke (if this day ever broke), adding new deposits to the crust upon crust of mud, sticking at those points tenaciously to the pavement, and accumulating at compound interest.

Fog everywhere. Fog up the river, where it flows among green aits and meadows; fog down the river, where it rolls defiled among the tiers of shipping, and the waterside pollution of a great (and dirty) city. Fog on the Essex Marshes, fog on the Kentish heights. Fog creeping into the cabooses of collier-brigs; fog lying out on the yards, and hovering in the rigging of great ships; fog drooping on the gunwales of barges and small boats. Fog in the eyes and throats of ancient Greenwich pensioners, wheezing by the firesides of their wards; fog in the stem and bowl of the afternoon pipe of the wrathful skipper, down in his close cabin; fog cruelly pinching the toes and fingers of his shivering little 'prentice boy on deck. Chance of people on the bridges peeping over the parapets into a nether sky of fog, with fog all round them, as if they were up in a balloon, and hanging in the misty clouds.

Gas looming through the fog in divers places in the street, much as the sun may, from the spongey fields, be soon to loom by husbandman and ploughboy. Most of the shops lighted two hours before their time – as the gas seems to know, for it has a haggard and unwilling look.

The raw afternoon is rawest, and the dense fog is densest, and the muddy streets are muddiest, near that leaden-headed old obstruction, appropriate ornament for the threshold of leaden-headed old corporation: Temple Bar. And hard by Temple Bar, in Lincoln's Inn Hall, at the very heart of the fog, sits the Lord High Chancellor in his High Court of Chancery.

Commentary

There are, of course, verbs in this opening to the novel. It is, in fact, difficult to construct a text without verbs and this passage is no exception. In the opening paragraph alone there are verbs such as 'retired', 'waddling', 'splashed', 'jostling', 'slipping', 'sliding', and so on. The verbs all serve to create an atmosphere of constant action and movement in the big city. Yet there are no **finite verbs** in main **clauses** in the text. There is thus a difference between the following two sentences, the first of which (1) contains a main finite verb, the second of which (2) does not:

(1) Foot passengers jostled one another's umbrellas and lost their foothold at street corners.
(2) Foot passengers jostling one another's umbrellas and losing their foothold at street corners.

Main finite verbs provide, as it were, a kind of anchor for the action. You know clearly when something took place and that the action was completed. In the second sentence above you are left suspended, knowing that the action is ongoing, but awaiting a main verb to give you your bearings. A sentence such as the following provides that kind of 'anchor' for the action in the verb 'arrived', which is the finite verb in the sentence:

> Foot passengers jostling one another's umbrellas and losing their foothold at street corners *arrived* at the bank.

A finite verb is thus a verb which tells you when something happened (past or present), how many were/are involved (singular or plural) and who the participants are ('you'/'we'/'I', etc.). By contrast, when a **non-finite** '-ing' form is used the verb can be referring to any number, or tense, or first, second or third person. For example:

> She is singing.
>
> They have been singing.
>
> You might be singing.

In these examples, 'singing', 'been' and 'be' are the non-finite forms; 'is', 'have' and 'might' are the finite forms.

Sentence (2) above is a kind of model for many of the sentences in the first three paragraphs. Sentences such as the following therefore serve to create a sense of both disorientation and dislocation. We feel that all the activity of

London is confused and directionless; and we do not know what timescale we are in. The present participles in particular convey a feeling of continuous action which could almost be timeless.

> London.
>
> Implacable November weather.
>
> Smoke lowering down from chimney pots . . .
>
> Dogs, undistinguishable in the mire.
>
> Foot passengers, jostling one another's umbrellas
>
> Fog in the eyes and throats of ancient Greenwich pensioners,
>
> wheezing by the firesides . . .
>
> Gas looming through the fog in divers places . . .

Given the timeless character which is imparted to these descriptions it is perhaps not surprising that Dickens can suggest that London has an almost prehistoric feel to it – 'and it would not be wonderful to meet a Megalosaurus, forty feet long or so, waddling like an elephantine lizard up Holborn Hill'.

In the final paragraph of this opening to *Bleak House* main finite verbs are restored to the sentences of the text. In particular the main verb 'to be' is repeated: 'The raw afternoon is rawest, and the dense fog is densest, and the muddy streets are muddiest . . .'. The presence of a main verb is most noticeable in the final sentence:

> And hard by Temple Bar, in Lincoln's Inn Hall, at the very heart of the fog, sits the Lord High Chancellor in his High Court of Chancery.

Here the main finite verb is 'sits'. The action and location of the Lord High Chancellor is thus clearly situated. Indeed, the sentence is structured so that the location of the main subject of the sentence ('the Lord High Chancellor') comes first in the sentence.

> [He sits] hard by Temple Bar in Lincoln's Inn Hall at the very heart of the fog.

Structured differently, the sentence might have read:

> The Lord High Chancellor sits hard by Temple Bar in Lincoln's Inn Hall at the very heart of the fog.

This structure would be more normal and would follow the conventional word order for sentences in English in which the subject ('The Lord High Chancellor') occurs first and is then followed by a main finite verb ('sits').

One of Dickens's purposes may be to delay the subject so that it has more impact as a result of its occurrence in an unusual position. It also has a very particular impact as a result of being in the simple present tense ('sits') when readers of a novel or of any kind of narrative might expect verbs to be in the simple past tense ('sat').

'Sits' suggests, however, that the Lord High Chancellor always sits there and is a permanent landmark in this landscape. The simple present tense in English carries this sense of a permanent, general, unchanging truth, as in scientific statements such as:

Oil floats on water.

Mice have long tails.

Two and two make four.

In this final paragraph one of the main effects which Dickens creates may be to imply that the legal system of the country is in a state of permanent confusion or creates states of confusion which cannot be changed. And both in these opening paragraphs and in the novel as a whole 'fog' assumes symbolic importance, reinforcing a sense both of general confusion and of not being able to see clearly. The Lord High Chancellor is always 'at the very heart of the fog' and nothing will alter this position. For this reason perhaps choices of language and of the structure of the sentence position 'the Lord High Chancellor' and 'the heart of the fog' together.

Modals and modality

Text 4:4 communicates information; in this case the information concerns an interruption to the water supply and is on behalf of a water company. Whenever instructions are given, a **modality** enters the relationship between the writer and reader of a text. Modality takes a number of different forms in English but the presence of **modal verbs** is particularly significant. Here are some of the main modal verbs in English:

can, could, will, would, must, should, shall, may

Activity

1 What is the function of modal verbs in Text 4:4?
2 What other verb forms work, in particular, to establish a relationship between the water company and the customers to whom it has distributed this notice?

Text 4:4

Severn Trent Water

Dear Customer

Warning of interruption to your water supply

We will be undertaking essential planned work on the water supplies in your area. This means that the water supply to your property is likely to be interrupted. Please see reverse of this leaflet for the date and time of the interruption.

We will endeavour to carry out this work with the minimum of disruption and I apologise for any inconvenience that may be caused.

If you have particular concerns arising from the foregoing work or have any special needs which you feel we should know about, please contact our 24 hour Operational Contact Centre on 0800 783 4444.

Yours sincerely

Fraser Pithie
Customer Contact Manager (Operations)
Severn Trent Water Ltd

Handy hints

- On restoration of your supply you may suffer some discolouration to your water.
- On most occasions, running your tap for a short period of time will clear the water.
- If you suffer poor pressure on restoration of your water supply, please check and operate your internal stop tap making sure it is fully open.
- If we fail to deliver this notice 48 hours in advance of the interruption and/or if we fail to restore your water supply by the time we have stated, please complete the details opposite.

(For details of date and time of interruption please see reverse)

Commentary

This text operates in a mixed mode. The water company has to inform its customers that repairs are unavoidable. It has to give its customers instructions that they need to follow in their own interests. At the same time the company needs to reassure its customers that a more or less normal service is still available, that, in spite of the interruption to supply, the company still provides a good service and, above all, that there are no safety or health risks involved for its customers as long as they comply with the guidelines and instructions issued with the notice. It is important therefore that the company is clearly seen to be in control. This 'mixed mode' is inscribed in the different modal verbs in the text along the following general lines:

Mode of reassurance/possibility:

- *may* cause some discoloration
- *may* persist for a short time
- they *may* need your help
- flooding *may* result
- any inconvenience that *may* be caused.

Mode of control:

- we *will* be undertaking essential planned work
- which you feel we *should* know about
- *will* clear the water
- the water supply *is likely to be* interrupted ('likely' is an adjective but carries the modal force of a verb such as 'could').

'Control' is also established through an extensive use of imperative forms of the verb which unambiguously inform us what to do and what not to do ('*check* and *operate* your internal stop tap'). At the same time the personal and interactive use of the personal pronoun 'you' allows the company to communicate in a direct and friendly way with customers.

Activity

Collect examples of further texts in which you would expect modal verbs to be used quite extensively. For example:

- horoscopes
- weather forecasts
- problem pages
- school notices
- recipes
- legal texts.

What other examples can you find? Why are modal verbs concentrated in some texts but not others?

Note that there is no commentary on this activity.

Sentences and patterns

In this section we explore the role of grammatical patterns within larger patterns of language. We will consider the role of individual grammatical words and phrases but will focus on complete sentences.

Activity

Read Text 4:5, an advertisement for making a will. Make a list of the main patterns you can find in the text. For example, the patterns can consist of repeated words and phrases, grammatical patterns (same type of pronoun or verb or noun phrase) as well as typographic and other patterns of layout. What do you think are the main effects produced on the reader by the patterns you have noticed?

Note that there is no commentary on this activity.

Text 4:5

Will your only legacy be upset, confusion and paperwork?

Without a Will, your wishes could count for nothing.

Without a Will, the State could take everything.

Without a Will, your family could lose out.

Without a Will, the taxman could easily benefit.

Without a Will, you can't remember your friends.

Without a Will, you can't remember Christian Aid.

Without a Will, life may be difficult for those closest to you.

Without a Will, life may be impossible for those far away.

If you would like to find out how easy it is to make a Will, send for our free new booklet 'A Will to Care' to Christian Aid, Freepost, London SE1 7YY or phone Glenn McWatt 071-620 4444 ext 2226.

Name Mr./Mrs./Ms./Miss ______________________

Address ______________________

Postcode ____________

Activity

Text 4:6 shows the poem 'This is a Photograph of Me' and is by the Canadian writer Margaret Atwood. As you read the poem and start to work out what it means to you, you might think about the following questions:

1 Who is the 'me' in the poem? Who is being shown the photograph?
2 Can you take the words of the poem literally?
3 Why is the speaker only 'just under the surface', if s/he has drowned the day before? Why can we 'eventually' see the subject of the poem if we 'look long enough'?

Text 4:6

'This is a Photograph of Me'

It was taken some time ago.
At first it seems to be
a smeared
print: blurred lines and grey flecks
blended with the paper;

then, as you scan
it, you see in the left-hand corner
a thing that is like a branch: part of a tree
(balsam or spruce) emerging
and, to the right, halfway up
what ought to be a gentle
slope, a small frame house.

In the background there is a lake,
And beyond that, some low hills.
(The photograph was taken
the day after I drowned.

I am in the lake, in the center
of the picture, just under the surface.

It is difficult to say where
precisely, or to say
how large or small I am:
the effect of water
on light is a distortion
but if you look long enough,
eventually
you will be able to see me.)

Commentary

The title to this poem is intriguing. You might consider that its meaning is quite straightforward. You might consider that the line is spoken by somebody who is showing somebody else a photograph. You might consider that the poem is the photograph. Answers to these questions seem to be basic to our understanding of the poem. But it is not impossible that all the references in the poem to things being vague '(balsam or spruce)', 'a thing that is like a branch', and to outlines and shapes being 'blurred' and 'smeared' and 'blended' are deliberate, that everything is not as it at first seems and that we should perhaps not always assume that everything we see is obvious.

And in this connection you might also think about the word 'drown'. Has the speaker literally drowned or are we invited to think of other meanings for the word drown? For example, we can drown in a sea of paperwork, or letters to be written, or we can drown in unsolved problems. However we choose to interpret the poem we cannot ignore such words; and we are likely to remain intrigued, in particular, by a word like such as 'this', which is ambiguous. 'This' is a **deictic**. Words such as 'this', 'that', 'those', 'here', 'there' are all deictics. Deictics are directing or pointing words in so far as they direct our attention to particular points of reference. In this poem 'this' points to something which is near to us, maybe even to what is in front of our eyes, but it is not clear exactly what it refers to.

Several grammatical choices made in the poem by the writer also underline a tone of uncertainty and lack of clarity. For example, the poem refers twice to when the photograph 'was taken'. The choice of voice is that of the passive voice; and the subject, that is, *who* took the photograph, is not declared. In English a passive sentence allows actions to be described without the main agent of those actions needing to be mentioned; and sometimes the omission of the agent can be deliberate because we may not know the agent or because we choose not to mention by whom or by what means something is done. The use of the passive voice here in the sentences

> It was taken some time ago.
> The photograph was taken the day after I drowned

adds to the apparent vagueness and indefiniteness of the experiences described.

References to time are also vague and not entirely logical and consistent. The tense of the poem, although mostly in the present, alternates between past and present. For example, 'the day after I drowned' contrasts with 'I am in the lake'. The reader is consequently not sure of the temporal order or dimension in which they are placed by the poem.

Likewise, what is certain and what is less certain is written into contrasts in modality in the poem. Modality in language underlines our subjective assessments of things; for example, adverbs such as 'probably', 'perhaps', 'generally', 'apparently', 'definitely' and phrases such as 'it is certain', 'I am sure' or 'I don't know', verbs such as 'it seems' or 'it appears' or the use of the present tense (e.g. 'Oil floats on water') encode different degrees of subjective response in the viewpoint of a speaker or writer. More specifically too there are modal verbs and modal expressions such as 'must', 'will', 'can', 'ought to', 'should', 'be bound to'.

In 'This is a photograph of me' there are contrasts between a viewpoint in which everything is definite ('. . . you *will be* able to see me'; '. . . there *is* a lake') and a way of seeing where there is greater vagueness and a lack of clarity ('. . . it seems to be'; 'It is difficult to say where precisely'). The speaker in the poem knows what 'ought to be' but things do not seem straightforward.

A note of strangeness and uncertainty is also created by the poet by putting the conclusion to the poem in brackets. And after the definiteness and confidence of the short penultimate sentence

> I am in the lake, in the center of the picture, just under the surface.

the final sentence is in distinct contrast. It is longer, more complex in structure and mixes subordinate and main clauses (the 'if' conditional clause is a subordinate clause), so that the grammar meanders as if 'it is difficult to say' where things are going and what they might mean.

We perhaps need to ask why the poet is making so much of uncertainty of viewpoint and the difficulty and unreliability of seeing clearly. (Notice, by the way, the number of times that there are references to 'seeing' – 'see', 'scan', 'look'.) We also perhaps need to ask who the speaker is and who is being spoken to. And in so doing we need to accept the seemingly improbable situation of someone who has already drowned showing us a picture of him/herself.

A basic interpretation of this poem might begin by saying that the 'I' in the poem is appealing for help and, in particular, for another person who will take the trouble to look closely at his/her situation. To do this requires another person prepared to see beneath the material surface of things and to adopt a more spiritual perspective. Only then might the identity and problems of the 'I' emerge more clearly.

The above analysis should not suggest, of course, that there are no other significant patterns or that they do not have a part to play. What is, however, evident is that a skilful and careful use of grammatical patterns is a key starting point for recognising significant meanings in the poem and that such analysis can provide a basis for further exploration and interpretation.

Activity

We have observed above that there are several means open to us in language to register certainty and uncertainty, definiteness and indefiniteness. Now read the extract below from a conversation between university students, and underline all those words and phrases which allow the speakers to sound deliberately vague, tentative and 'politely' indefinite. The students are discussing how they've changed since coming to university.

> *A*: But you don't notice so much in yourself, do you? I don't think so, on the whole.
> *B*: I don't know, I definitely feel different from the first year. I don't think I look any different or anything.
> *A*: You're bound to keep changing, really, all your whole life hopefully.
> *B*: I don't know, I think it's probably a change coming away, I suppose . . .

Note that there is no commentary on this activity.

Activity

Read Text 4:7 (p. 124), which shows a page taken from a booklet about bio-diversity produced by the environmental organisation, *Friends of the Earth*.

- Using selected information from this page write a campaign leaflet **of not more than fifty words** inviting people to join this environmental group.

- When you have completed this campaign leaflet, write a short paragraph saying what choices of grammar you have made.

For example, you may like to comment on some or all of these features: present tense; noun phrases; present participles; modal verbs; pronouns.

Note that there is no commentary on this activity.

Text 4:7

Why biodiversity matters

Food, fresh air, clean water, medicines, a stable climate – life on Earth provides the essentials of daily living for everyone. Wildlife inspires and fascinates us, and our open spaces are there to enjoy. Not only are species and habitats valuable in their own right, it's in our own interests to take care of them. That's because our future is bound up with a healthy, thriving natural world in all its diversity.

But we are in danger of losing the range and variety of life on Earth. One in four mammal species, one in eight species of birds and potentially millions of smaller species could face extinction. Wildlife habitats are disappearing at an alarming rate. This loss is already a problem for millions of people around the world, particularly if they depend on the land for a living. But a damaged environment will hurt us all.

So what's behind the destruction? Friends of the Earth believes the answers lie in the way economies work and who controls them. Richer countries and powerful companies are using more than their fair share of resources, and they're not doing enough to protect our world.

But we can make a difference. Individuals and communities in the UK and across the world have shown again and again that there are practical solutions to the threats facing the web of life.

This booklet is about biodiversity and why it is so important. It explains Friends of the Earth's unique approach to tackling the problems now facing our global wildlife and habitats and what you can do to help. Please also visit www.foe.co.uk/campaigns/biodiversity

Contents

Global biodiversity is the richness of life on Earth. It is the web of all living things and ecosystems – everything from whales to warblers and forests to coral reefs.

Scientists estimate that there are about 14 million species on Earth. To date fewer than 2 million of them have even been named.

Living nature works for us for free: cleaning the air and water; recycling nutrients and making soils; stabilising the climate, slowing floods and calming storms; pollinating crops, supplying genetic resources of agriculture and chemicals for medicines; and inspiring us with its beauty and richness. In 1997, the value of these services was estimated to be £18 trillion per year.

Adam Bradbury/Friends of the Earth

One kind of text which requires a very careful selection of words and sentence patterns is the reader for young children.

Activity

Read Text 4:8 and consider the accompanying illustration. Have you read this kind of text before? If so, where? What is the connection between the text and the illustration? What do you notice about the sentence patterns in this text?

There is a commentary on this activity at the end of the unit.

Text 4:8

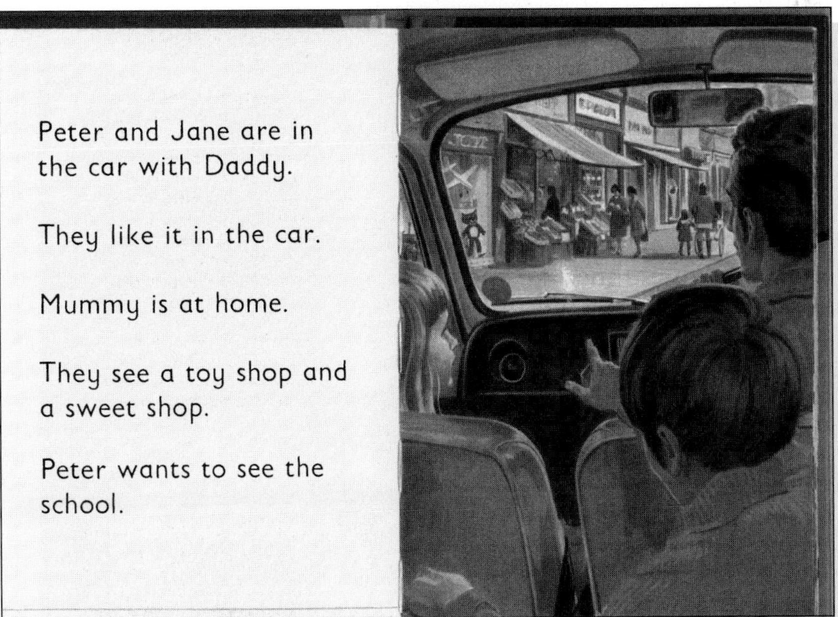

Peter and Jane are in the car with Daddy.

They like it in the car.

Mummy is at home.

They see a toy shop and a sweet shop.

Peter wants to see the school.

Activity

Now compare the previous Text with that for the promotion of a health drink, Yakult (Text 4:9). How many of the clauses in this Text are similar to Text 4:8? If the clause structure is different in Text 4:9, why is it different?

There is a commentary on this activity at the end of the unit.

Text 4:9

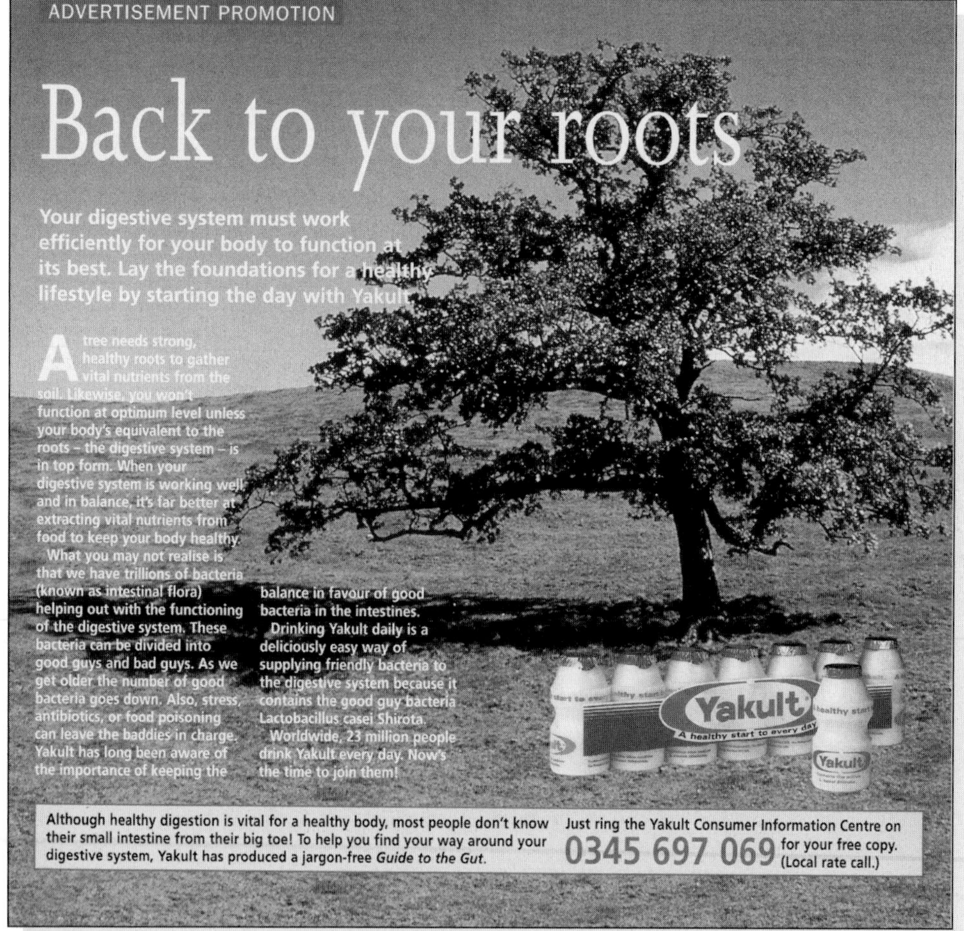

Please note this is not a current advertisement.

Formality

The next activity links sentence structure to aspects of **formality**. Formality is important in making sure that the 'correct' relationship is established between the producer of a text and the receiver of a text, whether it be written or spoken. Getting the formality wrong, as will be seen in the next unit, Unit 5, can lead to problems with communication.

Activity

Look at Text 4:10.

1 How is the memo chatty and informal?
2 Rewrite the memo as a formal letter from Mark Tatchell as if he did not know the recipient of the memo. What have you changed? Are the structures of subject, verb, object any different? Are your clauses different? If so, why. If not, why not?

Text 4:10

Internal Memo

From: Mark Tatchell, Smith Electronics
To: Alison Paulus, Customer Services
cc: Dan Ellis, Smith Electronics

Subject: Computer Purchase

5/5/1999

Hi, We're on our way to Caswell. The battery on the laptop's a bit low so we've stopped at a pub which is letting us use their fax. Just met Richard Haynes (MD at Wulfson) and, because he is spending so much with us on the refitting, agreed with him that we'd also supply a laptop.

He wants at least 6 Gb hard disk and 64 Mb RAM plus a portable printer. He'd prefer a machine which came with a nice carrying case.

Could you set this up with Kyle Barber and come up with a quote. Either Toshiba or Compaq. Fax back his quote to the hotel in Caswell. I'll be able to pick up e-mails there, I hope. Call the mobile, if I've missed something.

P.S. Tell David. Great deal. Worth the laptop. More in the pipeline.

Commentary

The memo is written in an informal style. Here the sender and receiver know each other well and can use informal vocabulary choices such as 'Hi' and abbreviations such as 'quote' (for 'quotation'). Grammatically, there is a balance between main and subordinate clauses with subordinate clauses used as the writer elaborates, amplifies or qualifies information in more detail (for example, 'if I've missed something'; 'because he is spending so much with us on the refitting').

However, the clearest grammatical marker of informality is the use of **ellipsis**. Ellipsis is a grammatical structure in which key grammatical words are left out or are left for the reader or listener to fill in. Examples of ellipsis are 'Good deal' for 'It was a good deal'; 'Either Toshiba or Compaq' for 'It must be either Toshiba or Compaq'; 'Just met Richard Haynes' for 'I've just met Richard Haynes'. In formal letters and memoranda ellipsis would not normally be appropriate. Ellipsis is very common in spoken language and is a key feature of spoken grammar. It occurs when it is obvious or when it can be taken for granted what speakers are referring to and there is no need to elaborate.

Further guidance on the analysis of ellipsis is given in Unit 5.

Actives, passives and meanings

Sentences often express actions, and there are two main ways in which actions can be viewed. What are the contrasts in the way in which the action is expressed in the following sentences?

> Two players chased the referee.
> The referee was chased by two players.

The first sentence uses the **active voice**; the second sentence uses the **passive voice**, which is not as frequent overall. Crystal (1995: 225) describes the following steps in making the basic form of the passive voice:

1 Move the subject of the active verb to the end of the sentence, making it the passive agent. Add 'by'.
2 Move the object of the active verb to the front of the sentence, making it the passive subject.
3 Replace the active verb phrase by a passive one – usually a form of the auxiliary verb 'be' followed by the '-ed' participle.

Activity

Which of the following sentences are passive and which are active?

1 The dog attacked the intruder.
2 The intruder was attacked by the dog.
3 The test tube was heated and the solution was prepared.
4 I was informed by the police.
5 The police informed me.
6 The two substances are mixed in equal proportions.
7 We can obtain both these books from the library.
8 Both these books can be obtained from the library.
9 It is accepted that there is no proper evidence.
10 It has been decided.

The answers for and commentary on this activity are at the end of the unit.

Note that implications of the use of active and passive verb constructions are discussed in the next unit, Unit 5.

COMPUTERS, PASSIVES AND MEANINGS

In the previous unit we looked at lists of frequently spoken and written words using evidence from a corpus – a computer-stored collection of texts which can be read by a concordance. A concordance is a computer program which enables you to work on texts, checking for which words are frequent, how words fit together and in some cases what patterns of words go together in what different kinds of text.

You can also study grammatical patterns using a computer corpus. An interesting pattern to study is the passive voice. As we have seen, in grammar the passive voice contrasts with the active voice.

Another form of the passive voice is the *get-passive*. As with many structures involving the word 'get', the get-passive is a structure which is more common in spoken English than in written English. Examples of this form of the passive are:

I got attacked by a wild dog

which can be chosen in preference to

> I was attacked by a wild dog.

Or

> He got suspended from school three times

which can be chosen instead of

> He was suspended from school three times.

Activity

Now look at Text 4:11 taken from an analysis using a concordance of the get-passive as it occurs in texts in the CIC corpus. What do you notice about the grammatical patterns of the get-passive? Which words appear to the left of the key structure and which words appear to the right of the key structure? Do they have anything in common?

Text 4:11

```
 1  . He couldn't turn the water on. And he got badly burned. And it happened in Mar
 2  you heard of anybody any neighbours who got broken into recently? I know somebod
 3  ken any extra precautions since the car got broken into last time? Er well I cha
 4  d he jilted her at the altar. So so she got brought up by her grandmother not he
 5   she's been a bit nervous ever since we got burgled and and dark nights. Mm. Sin
 6  ou know of? They they got burgled. They got burgled once Yeah. that was a while
 7  ed by crime that you know of? They they got burgled. They got burgled once Yeah.
 8  ave done that so I suppose I could have got caned. Yeah. And as you've gone thro
 9   fool for being honest. Mm. You know he got called an idiot for being honest. An
10  know it didn't seem much point. No. All got deported I think. Every one of them
11   Yeah. Yeah. +to the machines. They all got deported in the end didn't they. Sen
12   road. Mm. And this chap actually he he got done for either the drugs. Cos it wa
13  p on that should have been white but it got dyed grey in the wash and my hair wa
14  ghs Yeah. Anyway tell us about when you got er picked up. About the hitchhiking.
15  randmother not her real mother then she got jilted at the altar by this fellow t
16  cently and she was saying that she they got kerb crawled her and her friend were
17  om the Social from the Job Centre. Em I got led up the garden path a fair few ti
18  I suppose and some do it you know. Em I got offered a job about three weeks befo
19  d then all of a sudden they em got they got raided by the police. Mm. And we wer
20   shop and told you about them. Mm. tuts Got ripped off didn't I. laughs laughs T
21   er say yes you are my daughter. She em got robbed in the will when she died. Em
22  entioned in October when your neighbour got robbed. Could you tell me what happe
23  y good like I just got there and I just got seen straight away. But then I think
24  eah. As did all the housewives who then got slapped in the face for it Mm. becau
25  ho's van got stolen. What about ? a van got stolen. Yeah. Where? My cousin . Yea
26   the on the the picture. Dear dear. And got sued by the owners because of it. Th
27  ve been there I don't know but we never got told about it you know. So. But trut
```

Commentary

The lines from the corpus show:

- the get-passive is commonly used with personal pronouns. That is, we use it to describe things which have happened to us personally. It is not used much to describe what is done to impersonal things. For example:

  The Ministry of Finance was attacked by leading journalists at a meeting in London yesterday

  is more common than

  The Ministry of Finance got criticised by leading journalists at a meeting in London yesterday

- When the get-passive is used, it is often used without reference to an agent. That is, the agent or source of responsibility for the action done to you is not mentioned. (In the sentence 'I was attacked by a wild dog' the agent is 'wild dog'.) An example here is 'A van got stolen.'

- The get-passive form is more emotive. It seems to convey feelings about the action more directly than the standard passive found in most written texts.

- The words to the right of this passive structure frequently suggest things which are problematic or which describe adverse circumstances. For example,

  got burgled
  got deported
  got led up the garden path
  got ripped off
  got robbed
  got sued

The get-passive can, of course, be chosen to describe positive things. For example, 'She got promoted', 'He got made captain'. However, the standard passive is more commonly used to describe circumstances which are positive as well as negative, is more neutral overall and makes a speaker or (more normally) a writer appear a bit more detached.

So a computer can help us to analyse patterns which we may not otherwise notice. The patterns can be significant for understanding how we choose to express meanings. We can see differences between spoken and written words. And we can see that certain grammatical choices entail certain vocabulary choices. Although we have looked at grammar and vocabulary separately so far, it is worth underlining that grammatical patterns and lexical patterns are more closely interrelated than is often assumed.

One way in which you can continue to explore for yourself how words are used, using a very large number of words as your database, is to obtain the sampler disk for the BNC (the British National Corpus). The BNC is a collection of 100 million words (90 million written and 10 million spoken). The sampler CD disk contains 1 million words from spoken texts and 1 million words from written texts. The CD comes with customised software systems which can be used to do different kinds of analysis, including frequency analysis, word counts, collocations (which words commonly keep company with one another) and concordances of lexico-grammatical patterns of the kind we have just examined in the above activity. The CD can be obtained from the Humanities Computing Unit of Oxford University, Oxford, England.

More information, including details of an online free browse facility is available from http://info.ox.ac.uk/bnc. For further analysis of the use of the passive voice in texts see Unit 5. For further analysis of concordance lines see Schmitt (2000) to whom we are indebted for the above lines.

Extension activities

1 Collect branding slogans which use the present participle, such as 'Aiming High'. Try to see how widespread the use of this grammatical feature is, and how it is often linked to more than one meaning.

2 Write a brief advertisement. You may choose the product for which you wish to write the advertisement but your text should make particular use of personal pronouns and of premodified noun phrases. Your choices of language should be appropriate to the product you wish to advertise.

3 Write a page for a book which is designed to be read by children who are learning to read in the very early years of primary school. Your text should have the topic of family and family life. Twenty to thirty words should be sufficient.

After you have written a page consider what kinds of words you have selected? What are your most typical sentence patterns? Did you repeat these words and sentence patterns?

4 If you were writing an advertisement for a product, which products might you choose to promote using these very basic grammatical structures and why? Using the Text 4:8 as a model, write an advert in the same style for one of the following products.

a mobile phone
a soap
organic food
a convertible car

5 Collect two written texts which exhibit what are in your view different degrees of formality. One text should be more 'spoken' and informal and one should be a formal text with little or no elements of typical spokenness and informality. Make notes on the grammatical properties of the texts with particular reference to use of pronouns; modality; sentence structure and clause patterns; ellipsis.

6 Look at the following concordance lines for the verbs 'cause' and 'provide'. What do you notice about the patterns of meaning they create? Are the patterns similar? Are they different? If so, how?

have searched for a single	cause of aging – a critical gene, hor
s in property lending will	cause a a serious credit crunch – compa
lit second nobody moves?	Cause we're looking at the dolly-bird
ith in the fas lane is no	cause for driving without due care and
ion so far available gives	cause for concern about the circumstan
of 70–90 mph expected to	cause structural damage. The forecaste
aming. If untreated it can	cause permanent damage to heart. "
urder came not from any	cause worth the name but from the very
e in prison without good	cause, he says. The Foreign Office has
es of martyrdom in a noble	cause. He said they had been granted "
South West Water] did not	cause the problem is no defence at all
obviously bleeding, could	cause blood to seep from veins and art
justice is the Palestinian	cause and the right of the Palestinian
d the relevant details may	cause an underpayment and perhaps resu
onous toxins which could	cause kidneys to fail. This could happ
e of information liable to	cause serious injury to the nation wi
ity and its strength gives	cause for optimism for the prospects
ng legislation which could	cause considerable problems for compan
t in a situation likely to	cause unnecessary suffering, and permi
on of schools is likely to	cause ministers more problems than it
ffice staff, said the main	cause of recruitment problems was low
inspectors as the biggest	cause of poor reading standards. "Some
mmit criminal damage, and	cause public disorder, yesterday were
dence in you is total. Our	cause is just. Now you must be the thu
in 1987 for conspiracy to	cause explosions, was yesterday refuse

e opportunity, rather than	provide it. The House of Lords amended
and Outdoor World might	provide the breath of fresh air that i
t horrendous, a swap can	provide a route into areas where there
and the venues which can	provide such facilities will not doubt
major car-hire companies	provide cars with mounted phones. Amer
ed out. The motion was to	provide an access gate into the city
show is being prepared to	provide training throughout England an
he said. The bill aims to	provide the first coherent framework
said: "What we earn and	provide for ourselves is only one part
er international action to	provide places of safety for refugees
BARCLAYS Bank is to	provide a year's paid materinity leave,
s to encourage people to	provide their own pensions, by offerin
Plans to	provide power for the south-west of
mming pool operations, to	provide lifeguards or any other
any occasion declined to	provide the resources that are require
st time in British history	provide statutory guarantees for the
tish Constitution does not	provide for an Act of War to be approv
0 vehicles. We have had to	provide a site for them. It has just
a litre would be needed to	provide enormous killing power."
oops, the specialists will	provide support to medical and nursing
ns are run by BR staff to	provide tourist trips and do not compe
hedules will be cleared to	provide continuous news coverage for
(1,770–2,017m), which can	provide skiing from December until ear
says. The Government will	provide extra hostel beds if necessary
million every two years to	provide safe storage facilities for th

Commentaries/Answers to activities

COMMENTARY: ACTIVITY p. 106

Here are some of the main patterns:

the floating *crumb* (3)
the space *crumb* (20)
the space *debris* (7)
the cabin *debris* (17)
the *space* debris (7)
the *space* walk (8)
the hot *spacesuit* (5)
the *space* silence (11)
the *space* crumb (20)

These are fairly straightforward repetitions, involving the same word classes in each case (for example 'crumb' is a noun and is still a noun when it is repeated with a different partner word). But some of the words are in different patterns when they are repeated. For example:

> the *orbit* wisecrack (4)
> the *smuggled* orbit (15)

– where 'orbit' is both a noun (15) and a modifier (4). But we can notice how the repetitions are in effect no simple repetitions. The repetition of words helps to tell a story. The 'space debris' referred to in line 7 has become the 'cabin debris' in line 17. Bits and pieces floating in outer space are relatively normal but the presence of debris in a cabin works to suggest a kind of narrative in which events may have taken a turn for the worse.

In other words, the basic grammatical pattern provides a structural frame within and across which there are changing partnerships of words which in turn cumulatively create patterns of meaning. An increasingly prominent pattern is one in which there are suggestions of disaster or at least suggestions of things going seriously 'off course'. For example, headphones that crackle because of decreasing reception as the spacecraft moves further away from earth appear to become detached:

> the *crackling* headphone (11)
> the *weightless* headphone (17)

A 'beard' which was 'growing' normally (3) now collocates with 'crackling' in an unusual and disturbing formation (20), possibly suggesting the movement of the hairs of a beard on the face of a dead body or on a body which has been subjected to electrical shocks or freezing air. The changing words within the same basic grammatical pattern enable the poet, Edwin Morgan, to embody changes to events and to perceptions of what is happening.

COMMENTARY: ACTIVITY p. 109, TEXT 4:2

The strategy of Waitrose here is to address the customer directly and to show their sensitivity to their customers as individuals. In this message personal pronouns such as 'I', and in particular, 'you' and 'your' are extensively employed. A key sentence is the opening line:

> I'm just writing to make sure you know about Ocado, the online grocery service which is now delivering in your area – and one which could make your life a whole lot easier.

The message manages to describe the delivery of groceries to customers as if it were designed primarily to be a service ('a dedicated service') rather than a commercial venture with the fundamental aim of making everything convenient and requiring no effort on the part of the customer. There is a strong emphasis on words like 'convenient' and on providing reassurance that the food will be fresh because the delivery is direct and accurate and is based on a background of winning Gold Awards for grocery service (notice the two seals in the top left-hand corner of the letter which underline the company's appointments for service to the royal family). One aim is to personalise the relationship with 'you', the customer. Although the letter is laid out in a formal structure and the customer is addressed by a title, the voice in the text is relaxed with the use of words such as 'just' and 'a whole lot' ('I'm just writing'; '. . . make your life a whole lot easier'), together with informal words like 'fantastic' and 'wonderful'.

COMMENTARY: ACTIVITY p. 110

In 'Off Course' the noun phrases are written, as we have seen, in the same pattern of *d* (definite article), *m* (modifier) and *n* (noun); in the 'Online Grocery service' text the pattern is more complex. Here are some more examples:

> Fantastic shopping experience
> Excellent levels of freshness
> Convenient one-hour slots
> The convenience and value of online shopping

These examples illustrate the much wider range of noun phrases which are possible in English, and they also illustrate that modifiers can occur after the main noun as well as in front of the main noun. The modifiers which occur before a main noun are called **pre-modifiers,** while the modifiers which occur after a main noun are called **post-modifiers**. In these examples 'of freshness' and 'of online shopping' are post-modifiers. On the surface they help to make the text a little more dense and complex to read than 'Off Course'.

Compared with 'Off Course' the 'Online Grocery Service' also employs more premodifiers in front of the main noun. This feature allows description to be a little more detailed and precise. Several of these pre-modifiers are also themselves nouns; and we should note that the pre-modifying nouns cluster in phrases which describe organisations or which provide a more technical definition of actions or entities (for example, 'a great award-winning service', 'convenient one-hour slots').

COMMENTARY: ACTIVITY p. 125, TEXT 4:8

Texts similar to this are often found in schools as part of reading schemes for children who are learning to read. Such texts are basic 'readers' with 'key words' which will help most in the early stages of learning to read.

This text is also laid out in a traditional typeface associated with many such readers, such as those produced in the Ladybird series (which can be found in the children's section of most libraries). Such texts also promote basic values with children often shown, as in the illustration here, as part of happy (usually white) families engaged with their parents, brothers and sisters, and often their pets, in simple and basic everyday pursuits such as gardening, picking and storing fruit, sailing toy boats, helping to build a rabbit pen (for Peter) and helping with the cooking (for Jane) or, as here, on a shopping trip and a visit to their new school.

The sentence structure is also very basic and is built on five sentences in which the same type of main clause is repeated. The sentence in each case is short and simple and readable. In each case the subject (S) comes first followed by a verb (V) and an object (O) or a phrase (here all the phrases are prepositional phrases – 'in the car', 'at home', 'in the car with Daddy'). Basic structures reinforce basic values.

This very basic structure can be varied (for example, an alternative pattern is to put an object first: 'Wine I like but I prefer beer', where the first clause here is OSV) but it is a fundamental sentence pattern in English and it is reinforced here by the repetition.

COMMENTARY: ACTIVITY p. 126, TEXT 4:9

This text contains a greater variety of clauses. The patterns include both main clauses and subordinate clauses. A subordinate clause relies grammatically on the main clause to which it is attached, usually in a dependent relationship so that the information in the subordinate or dependent clause contains information which is in the background compared to the main clause. Examples from this text are (the subordinate clause is underlined):

> <u>As we get older</u>, the number of good bacteria goes down.
>
> <u>Although healthy digestion is vital for a healthy body</u>, most people don't know their small intestine from their big toe!
>
> Drinking Yakult daily is a deliciously easy way of supplying friendly bacteria to the digestive system <u>because it contains the good guy bacteria</u> . . .

The text has a scientific character and seeks to impress the reader with references to research and by using technical vocabulary. The advertisement provides the reader with a lot of information and scientific explanation and the subordinate clauses, in particular, are used to elaborate the information contained in the main clause. The clauses are linked by conjunctions which signal the way in which the information in the main clause is elaborated. (The main conjunctions are 'as', 'although', 'because'.) Thus:

AS introduces reference to a process.

ALTHOUGH introduces a concession.

BECAUSE introduces a reason.

Text 4:10 is explored further in Unit 5, with particular reference to its metaphorical structure.

COMMENTARY: ACTIVITY p. 129

Answers

1	Active	6	Passive
2	Passive	7	Active
3	Passive	8	Passive
4	Passive	9	Passive
5	Active	10	Passive

Crystal (1995: 225) describes the following steps in making the basic form of the passive voice:

1 Move the subject of the active verb to the end of the sentence, making it the passive agent. Add 'by'.

2 Move the object of the active verb to the front of the sentence, making it the passive subject.

3 Replace the active verb phrase by a passive one – usually a form of the auxiliary verb 'be' followed by the '-ed' participle.

Satellite texts

The following satellite texts look in detail at ideas covered in this unit:

The Language of Advertising looks at the use of language to help sell products.

The Language of ICT and *The Language of Websites* look at aspects of computer mediated communication.

The Language of Poetry looks at other poems and how they use language.

The Language of War looks at how grammar can be used to apportion or blame or deny responsibility.

Unit five

Text and context

Written discourse

Aim of this unit

The aim of this unit is to explore some of the language devices which enable whole written texts to work.

Discourse analysis

In linguistics, the phrase **discourse analysis** is used to refer to the analysis of both spoken and written texts. In each case, the aim is to analyse the way texts work across the boundaries of single sentences or utterances to form whole stretches of language.

This sounds very simple, but actually the word 'discourse' has had quite a long and complicated history. The situation now is that it means slightly different things inside and outside the academic world; it can also mean different things in different academic subject areas. For these reasons, it's worth spending a bit of time thinking about its variant meanings.

The basic meaning of 'discourse', in modern ordinary usage, is 'talk'. Originally, the term 'discourse' came from Latin, *discursus,* meaning 'to run', 'to run on', 'to run to and fro'. Historically, it has been applied more to rehearsed forms of spoken language – like speeches, where people 'run on' about a topic – than to spontaneous speech. The modern meaning of 'discourse' as encompassing all forms of talk has evolved because conversations, like formal speeches, 'run'. This means that speakers make an effort to give their interactions shape and coherence – not consciously, but as an integral part of co-operating with another speaker to make meaning. So when people refer to *talk as discourse* they are drawing attention to *the way talk is a crafted medium*. While it has long been understood that this was true of speeches and other aspects of formal oratory, it has only recently been recognised that casual conversation is subtly and skilfully fashioned by speakers as they go along, often at rapid speed. The way different types of talk work will be explored in Unit 6.

Another way of looking at talk-as-discourse is to use the metaphor of weaving. In fact, we use this metaphor very often in our own talk about talk: for example, we talk about 'losing the thread of the conversation', 'cottoning on' to what people mean when they 'spin us a yarn'; teachers often close their lessons by referring to 'tying up loose ends'. We clearly see speakers as engaged together in discourse in the way a group of weavers would be to create a pattern in some fabric.

But it's not only spoken language that 'runs' or gets woven into patterns. This is also true of written language; and the modern use of the word 'discourse' can also be used to refer to aspects of written texts. This tends to be used much more within the academic world than outside it.

The word 'text' itself originally meant 'something woven' (Latin *texere, textum* – 'to weave'), and you can see a relationship between text, textile ('capable of being woven') and texture ('having the quality of woven cloth'). Written language is also often referred to as 'material'.

Like speakers, then, writers manipulate different aspects of language in order to weave their texts and give their material 'texture'. So to talk about discourse in written texts is to focus on the way written texts are constructed. This is what this unit is all about.

Picking up the threads

Activity

Our constant and powerful need to understand what's around us leads us to try to make sense of anything that's presented to us as a text. To illustrate this idea, read through Text 5:1.

1 Can you read Text 5:1 in any way that works and makes sense? If you can, that proves that you were already looking for patterns within the text.

2 In fact, Text 5:1 you have just read contains statements in random order from three completely different sources. With your knowledge of this, use any strategies you have in order to put the original texts back together.
3 Then, within each text, arrange the statements in order, so that they read naturally.
4 When you have finished your sorting, check your answers by turning to the end of this unit.
    - Where you got the order right, how did you know what the sequence should be?
    - Look also at where you didn't get the order right. Can you see what led you astray?

Answers for this activity are given at the end of the unit.

Text 5:1

Allow the fruit to steam in its own juice for a further 15 minutes.

So she hated it when that infuriating Keith Scott seemed to go out of his way to suggest that her heart wasn't in the affair.

That's why we created 'Portfolio', a brand new concept in saving.

Put them into a fireproof dish with the water, and a tablespoon of the sugar.

She knew that he loved her – in a calm settled way rather than any grand passion – and that he would make her a good, kind husband. Ensuring that the lid is tightly sealed, put the dish into a preheated oven, Gas Regulo 6.

So that way, you can have your cake and eat it too.

Pour over the top, and serve with double cream.

Melodie Neil and Jed Martin were old friends.

Mix juice with the brandy, mulled wine, and rest of the sugar.

We do, too.

Wash and core the apples, taking care to remove all pips.

In short, when she became engaged to him she knew exactly what she was doing.

Spoon out the cooked apples and arrange them attractively in rounds on a serving plate.

Do you feel that you never get a fair slice of the capital cake?

Slice finely.

Portfolio is a high interest investment account that makes your money work for you, while still giving you instant access to your capital.

Reduce temperature to 3 after 10 minutes.

The following section aims to show you some of the linguistic strategies you have just been using in working with texts.

Tracing the patterns: cohesion

If a speaker or hearer of English hears or reads a passage of the language which is more than one sentence in length, he or she can normally decide without difficulty whether it forms a unified whole or is just a collection of unrelated sentences. **Cohesion** (or its absence) is what makes the difference between the two.

> Cohesion is what gives a text texture.
>
> (Halliday and Hasan, 1976)

LEXICAL COHESION

One of the strategies you used in the activity above was your understanding of words and phrases in the English language – the vocabulary system. In particular, you used your awareness of *relationships between words*: this is called **lexical cohesion.** There are many different kinds of relationship that could be involved.

In Text 5:2 below, some of the links that are commonly used between words are outlined, with an example in each case from the sorting exercise you did previously (Text 5:1). Can you see how the relationships illustrated below helped you to order the statements correctly?

Text 5:2

Direct repetition (exactly the same word repeated):

Text C: juice . . . juice

Synonyms, or near-synonyms (use of words with similar meanings):

Text B: saving . . . investment

Superordination (where one word encompasses another in meaning):

Text C: fruit . . . apples

Antonyms (opposites):

Text A: loved . . . hated
Text C: put [them] into . . .

Specific-general reference (words referring to the same thing or person, but where one has more details than the other):

Text C: a fireproof dish . . . the dish
Text C (going from general to specific): . . . cooked apples

Ordered series (word that we know as a series – for example, the days of the week, months of the year, or the seasons):

Text C: Regulo 6 . . . 3; 10 minutes . . . 15 minutes

Whole-part (where one term names a part of an item that the other word describes in full):

Text C: apples . . . pips

A much more general aspect of lexical cohesion is the use by writers of particular semantic fields (see Unit 3): this means referring to a specific area of experience or knowledge. The clearest examples of semantic fields occur in the specialist language of occupations.

Activity

Read through Text 5:3, which contains the language of ten different occupations. Try to work out what the occupations are, and which particular words and phrases helped you to pinpoint them.

Answers for this activity are given at the end of the unit.

Text 5:3

The vehicle was seen proceeding down the main street in a westerly direction leading to a spacious and well-appointed residence with considerable potential. She went to work, mixing up the six-ten with two parts of 425, and dabbing the mixture through 6 ezimeshes. 'This one has a fine shaggy nose and a fruity bouquet with a flowery head', she said. He managed to get into a good position, just kissing the cushion. He said 'Just pop up onto the couch and we'll see what we can do'. She pulled down the menu, chose the command by using the cursor, then quit. She said to knead well, roll into a ball and leave overnight to rise. Instead, he mulched well, turned over and left the beds to settle. Good progress made, but concentration sometimes rather poor; more effort required if success is to be expected in the important months ahead.

However, semantic fields do not have to contain specialist technical language, or occupational terms. It may be simply that a text uses several words that all refer to the same subject matter, activity or experience: for example, the romantic fiction text in the sorting exercise at the beginning of this unit contained many words associated with love.

Sometimes, writers deliberately weave together different semantic fields for particular reasons. One way of bringing different fields together is to use metaphor: this is where one thing is described as if it were another. Because metaphor invites us to see one thing as another, it is a powerful factor in positioning the reader and framing a particular viewpoint.

Activity

Text 5:4 is a fundraising advert for the Prostate Cancer Charity, asking prospective marathon runners to collect for that charity. The text relies on a kind of metaphor for its interpretation. Can you explain how?

There is a commentary on this activity at the end of the unit.

Text 5:4

Another important aspect of lexical cohesion is the level of formality in vocabulary (see also Unit 4).

We talk about language being more or less formal as a way of describing how we vary our language according to the context we are in: for example, we will all use a relatively informal type of language when we are in the pub, relaxing with friends, compared with the more formal style we are likely to produce in a court of law or in an interview for a job. Formality can also be a reflection of social-group membership, particularly occupation, where some types of occupational language have retained specialist words which can sound very formal in everyday discourse: for example, a financial consultant or solicitor might use the word 'remuneration' where the rest of us would use 'salary' or just 'wages'. Calling a type of language formal or informal refers to more than simply vocabulary, but vocabulary will be an important contributory factor in a reader's impression of the formality of a text. For example, although the words 'home', 'house', 'residence' and 'domicile' might refer to exactly the same building, they vary a great deal in formality and therefore to replace one with another in a text will create a very different effect.

Activity

To enable you to see what formality of vocabulary might mean in practical terms, read through Texts 5:5, below. In each text, the level of formality has been disrupted at various points by the insertion of inappropriate vocabulary. Can you pinpoint where this happens, and suggest some vocabulary in each case which would be more in keeping with the style of the passage?

Note that there is no commentary on this activity.

Text 5:5

Letter from a bank manager to a customer

Dear Ms Allen,

Thank you for your letter of 1st September, requesting overdraft facilities of £500. In order that this overdraft facility can be granted we would first need sight of your contract of employment. Would you therefore kindly inform us of the School at which you will now be earning your daily crust.

Yours sincerely,
A. Curtis

Teacher's report

James needs to realise that success is the result of hard work and consistent effort. At present, he is being a real pain because he is so bone idle in class. If he wishes to do well in the examination, and achieve a grade which will do justice to his considerable ability, he must pull his socks up – and sharpish.

Memo from a university professor to his staff

Can I remind you that travel claims must be submitted *promptly*. Other departments, I learn, are not paying claims which are more than two months late. In particular, please remember that the financial year-end is now 31st July. Claims not submitted by 15th August will be substantially delayed by year-end procedures, and screw up our budgeting. Please get your claims in ON TIME.

Biology exam paper

Q1 As they pass from testis to oviduct during and after mating, mammalian sperms will pass through each of the following structures except the:

(a) urethra
(b) vas deferens
(c) vagina
(d) bottom

Q2 When the water in which a certain species of frog is living contains 5cm^3 of dissolved oxygen per litre the frogs remain totally submerged, but when the oxygen content falls to 3cm^3 per litre they go up to the top for a breather.

As a result of reading the information above, do you have any inkling about how frogs breathe in water?

Extract from a hotel brochure:

Reception of Guests
The Hotel endeavours to have rooms ready to receive guests by noon, and it is hoped that departing guests will courteously assist in making this possible by getting a move on and not hanging about in bedrooms on the day of departure.

The texts in the previous activity come from genres of writing which tend to have a particular level of formality associated with them, although changes in levels of formality can occur as part of the process of language change.

But the operation of formality is actually more complex and subtle than that: for example, a writer, group of writers or members of an occupational group may write about the same subject in different ways, according to the audience they are aiming at, and the purpose of their text.

To complicate matters even further, writers sometimes deliberately manipulate formal and informal styles within the same text, in order to achieve certain effects.

Activity

Text 5:6, *Oranges Are Not the Only Fruit* (1987), is an extract from the novel by Jeanette Winterson. In it, the narrator is talking about her experiences as a child in a Lancashire primary school in the 1950s – particularly, the way that the boys and girls taunted and bullied each other.

Can you see how the writer interweaves more and less formal vocabulary in order to suggest two different voices – that of the adult narrator, and that of the child she originally was?

Pick out examples of language features which help to construct each voice.

There is a commentary on this activity at the end of the unit.

Text 5:6

> Country dancing was thirty-three rickety kids in black plimsolls and green knickers trying to keep up with Miss who always danced with Sir anyway and never looked at anybody else. They got engaged soon after, but it didn't do us any good because they started going in for ballroom competitions, which meant they spent all our lessons practising their footwork while we shuffled up and down to the recorded instructions on the gramophone. The threats were the worst; being forced to hold hands with somebody you hated. We flapped along twisting each others' fingers off and promising untold horrors as soon as the lesson was over. Tired of being bullied, I became adept at inventing the most fundamental tortures under the guise of sweet sainthood.
>
> 'What me Miss? No Miss. Oh *Miss,* I never did.' But I did, I always did. The most frightening for the girls was the offer of total immersion in the cesspit round the back of Rathbone's Wrought Iron. For the boys, anything that involved their willies. And so, three terms later, I squatted down in the shoebags and got depressed. The shoebag room was dark and smelly, it was always smelly, even at the beginning of terms.

GRAMMATICAL COHESION

You used your lexical knowledge – your knowledge of vocabulary – as a strategy to help you reorganise the jumbled-up texts in the first part of this unit. The way lexical items are woven together through a text was referred to as lexical cohesion.

But in working on those texts, you also used your understanding of grammatical structures, and this forms the focus for what follows. The way that grammatical features are woven together across sentence boundaries is called **grammatical cohesion**.

Anyone who can speak and/or write a language knows grammar, as these structural patterns are learnt very early in life as an integral part of learning language; knowing grammar is different from knowing how to label parts of sentences, however. The knowledge you were using in the early part of this unit was your knowledge of grammar in use, and that was all the equipment you needed to do the tasks. But in order to see what you did, this part of the unit will need to go into a bit of detail about some of the structures you were using and matching. This will mean labelling some of the most commonly used grammatical principles and patterns. You may well be looking again at some of the aspects of grammar you studied in Unit 4; the focus here, however, is how grammar works across sentences rather than within them.

Reference

The Penguin *Concise English Dictionary* defines 'to refer' as 'to send for information', 'to seek information'. The principle of **reference** within texts is exactly that: it tells the reader that they can only make complete sense of the word or structure they are looking at if they look elsewhere in the text to get a fuller picture.

There are particular words that are often used for reference purposes. Some details are given below.

Personal pronoun reference

Personal pronouns are words that can substitute for nouns, and are as follows:

> I; you (singular); he; she; it; one; we; you (plural); they

Note that some of these pronouns can occur in different forms, depending on the role of the word in a particular sentence. Below are the possible variants:

> me; him; her; us; them

When one of these pronouns occurs in a text, readers expect to have to link it with something – either an item that has already been mentioned or something that's coming up. The fact that these pronouns are called personal pronouns gives an indication of their reference function – they will mainly be referring to people; however, the words 'it' and 'they'/ 'them' can also be used to refer to non-human animates, inanimate objects and abstract ideas.

If the pronoun is referring back to something, this is called **anaphoric reference**; if the pronoun is referring to something coming later, this is called **cataphoric reference**. Here is an example of each:

> *Tom* said that *he* was going home (anaphoric reference)
>
> I couldn't believe *it – the house was a complete wreck* (cataphoric reference)

Although as writers we are often at pains to make sure any pronoun references are clear, there are some circumstances where it's quite useful for them to be rather vague. For example, what does the word 'it' refer to in the Coke slogan 'Coke is it', or in the Nike slogan 'Just do it'? In these cases, the fact that the 'it' is unspecified means that every reader (or listener) can give the word a reference point that relates to their own life. That is a very useful outcome, from the point of view of the advertiser – the reader is in effect doing all the work of customising the advert to their own specifications.

Literary writers, like advertisers, sometimes manipulate pronoun reference in order to create particular effects.

Activity

Text 5:7, 'A Haunted House', is the opening of a short story by Virginia Woolf, published in 1921. How does Woolf's use of personal pronouns help to create a mysterious atmosphere?

There is a commentary on this activity at the end of the unit.

Text 5:7

Whatever hour you woke there was a door shutting. From room to room they went, hand in hand, lifting here, opening there, making sure – a ghostly couple.

'Here we left it,' she said. And he added, 'Oh, but there too!'

It's upstairs,' she murmured.

'And in the garden,' he whispered.

'Quietly,' they said, 'or we shall wake them.'

But it wasn't you that woke us. Oh, no. 'They're looking for it; they're drawing the curtain,' one might say, and so read on a page or two. 'Now they've found it,' one would be certain, stopping the pencil on the margin. And then, tired of reading, one might rise and see for oneself, the house all empty, the doors standing open, only the wood pigeons bubbling with content and the hum of the threshing machine sounding from the farm. 'What did I come in here for? What did I want to find?' My hands were empty. 'Perhaps it's upstairs then?' The apples were in the loft. And so down again, the garden still as ever, only the book had slipped into the grass.

Activity

Text 5:8 is a poem by Stevie Smith, called 'Not Waving But Drowning' (1957). In it, she uses a range of pronouns to refer to a number of different people, and to create specific effects. Map out how these pronouns work, thinking particularly about the following:

- Who are the various people in this poem?
- Why did Stevie Smith choose to use pronouns to refer to people rather than their names?

There is a commentary on this activity at the end of the unit.

Text 5:8

'Not Waving But Drowning'

Nobody heard him, the dead man,
But still he lay moaning:
I was much further out than you thought
And not waving but drowning.

Poor chap, he always loved larking
And now he's dead
It must have been too cold for him his heart gave way,
They said.

Oh no, no, no, it was too cold always
(Still the dead one lay moaning)
I was much too far out all my life
And not waving but drowning.

Activity

Text 5:9 is from Lewis Carroll's *Alice in Wonderland.* The text is delivered as a speech by the Rabbit to the court, and is referred to in the book as a set of 'mysterious verses'.

How does Carroll use pronoun reference in order to create an air of mystery?

Note that there is no commentary on this activity.

Text 5:9

They told me you had been to her,
And mentioned me to him:
She gave me a good character,
But said I could not swim.

He sent them word I had not gone
(We know it to be true):
If she should push the matter on,
What would become of you?

I gave her one, they gave him two,
You gave us three or more:
They all returned from him to you,
Though they were mine before.

If I or she should chance to be
Involved in this affair,
He trusts to you to set them free,
Exactly as we were.

My notion was that you had been
(Before she had this fit)
An obstacle that came between
Him, and ourselves, and it.

Don't let them know she liked them best,
For this must ever be
A secret, kept from all the rest,
Between yourself and me.

Stepping out of the text

At the beginning of this sub-section on grammatical cohesion, the idea of reference was defined as 'seeking information from elsewhere'.

Up to now, the focus has been on the reader searching various parts of the text for that information. But reference, particularly involving certain of the personal pronouns, can also involve moving outside the text to find the appropriate locus of information.

For example, the use of 'you' in a text as a direct address to the reader tells that reader to use himself/herself as the reference point; the use of 'I' in a text tells the reader that the writer (or the narrator) is being self-referential. In both these cases, the pronouns are functioning as signposts leading out of the text and making us focus on the human agents who are producing and receiving the text.

Where a reference item moves us outside a text, so that we can only make full sense of the text by referring to its context, this is called an **exophoric reference**; where we stay within the text, not needing any support from outside, this is called **endophoric reference**.

Activity

Go back to the texts you worked on in the first part of this unit, and find as many examples as you can of exophoric reference. Are there particular types or 'genres' of text that rely heavily on exophoric reference as part of their written conventions?

Commentary

There are certain types of text that are characterised by their use of exophoric references via the personal pronoun system: for example, many advertisements address the reader directly, using 'you', and companies refer to themselves as 'we'. An example of these pronouns can be seen in the 'Portfolio' advert you reassembled .

Address forms which take us outside the text are also very characteristic of literature, particularly some types of prose fiction. For example, nineteenth-century novelists often addressed the reader directly: at the end of Charlotte Bronte's *Jane Eyre,* the narrator, Jane, talking of her relationship with Mr Rochester, says: 'Reader, I married him'.

The attraction of referring outside a text is that this can leave plenty of room for manoeuvre, as it is unclear who 'you', 'I' and 'we' actually are.

While this could suggest confusion, in fact there is much creative potential in not pinning down exactly who the creators and receivers of a text are, because that then means that readers have to construct their own versions of these figures: for writers of literature and adverts alike (and any other texts that try to work in an interactive way), it means that many possible 'readings' can occur.

Because the type of communication that's described above is potentially very complex, it can be useful to represent diagrammatically how these layers of reference might work.

Look back at the Yakult advert in Unit 5.

In this, the copywriters are the real writers of the advert, but there is an implied writer/speaker constructed through the language that's used to address the reader. The real readers are us, but there are some implied readers, too: ideas about what we might think of as important, ideas about how we live, what we know and the attitudes we have are all embedded in the text, constructing 'us' as certain types of people, and not necessarily the people we really are.

All this goes to show how a text can create a particular relationship between the real writer and the real reader by constructing a piece of fictional discourse between implied versions of themselves:

real writer –	implied writer –	TEXT –	implied reader –	real reader
advertising copywriter	narrator		assumptions made about us in the text	the real person

Activity

Look at Text 5:10, which uses references to 'you'. Try to identify what assumptions are being made about the figure(s) being referred to by the term 'you' in the text. In your analysis, don't forget the work that you did on signs and symbols in the first unit of this book.

There is a commentary on this activity at the end of the unit.

Text 5:10

Important

We need to turn your water off

To help us improve the water mains in your area, we need to turn off your water supply during these times

ਤੁਹਾਡੇ ਇਲਾਕੇ ਦੇ ਪਾਣੀ ਦੇ ਮੁੱਖ ਸਪਲਾਈ ਦੇ ਪਾਈਪਾਂ ਵਿਚ ਸੁਧਾਰ ਲਿਆਉਣ ਲਈ. ਅੱਗੇ ਲਿਖਿਆਂ ਸਮਿਆਂ ਦੌਰਾਨ ਅਸੀ ਤੁਹਾਡੇ ਪਾਣੀ ਨੂੰ ਬੰਦ ਕਰਾਂਗੇ।

為了幫助我們改良你區內的主要供水，
這段時間內我們需要關閉你的供水設備。

আপনার এলাকার পানি সরবরাহ উন্নত করতে হলে কিছু সময় আপনার পানি সাপ্লাই বন্ধ রাখার প্রয়োজন হবে।

آپ کے علاقے میں پانی کی فراہمی کو بہتر کرنے کے لئے ہمیں ان اوقات کے دوران پانی بند کرنے کی ضرورت ہے۔

आपके एरिये में पानी के मुख्य सप्लाई के पाइपों में सुधार लाने के लिये हमें निम्नलिखित समय पर पानी की सप्लाई बंद करनी पड़ेगी।

આપના વિસ્તારમાં પાણીનાં મુખ્ય પાઇપોમાં સુધારા-વધારા કરવા માટે અમારે નીચે જણાવેલ અમુક સમય દરમિયાન આપના પાણીનો પુરવઠો બંધ કરવો પડશે.

Day	Date	Water Off	Water On	Work Order No.	Int I.D.
FRI MON TUES	31/8/01 3/9/01 4/9/01	8AM	4PM		

The water may go on and off more than once between these times but you should not try to use it. We are sorry for any problems this causes.

Please keep this card safe and handy until we have finished our work. It has some useful information for you.

For further information please phone **08457 462200**

Demonstrative reference (deictics)

Another type of reference which acts as a cohesive tie is carried by the following terms:

> the, this, that, these, those, here, there.

These terms demonstrate where something is; they are deictic terms – they are 'verbal pointers'.

As with personal pronouns, demonstrative reference can work backwards (anaphoric) or forwards (cataphoric). Here is an example of each:

> I went to *Italy* last year, and I want to go *there* again soon
> *(anaphoric)*
>
> But the problem is *this*: *how can I afford it?*
> *(cataphoric)*

The terms above can be categorised according to how they position the writer and reader (or speaker and listener, since the terms are used frequently in speech, too). 'This', 'these' and 'here' all mean 'near the writer/speaker', while 'that', 'those' and 'there' all mean 'away from the writer/speaker'.

While in speech these terms are often used to refer to physical items in the environment, in writing physical proximity can stand metaphorically for attitude as well. Advertisers, literary authors and writers of all kinds can use our knowledge of demonstrative terms to signal relationships and point of view.

Activity

Look at Text 5:11, Ovaltine. What part do demonstrative and personal pronoun reference play in positioning the readers of the text?

It may be useful to know that Ovaltine was originally classified as a medical product, being sold in chemists' shops, rather than as a general foodstuff.

There is a commentary on this activity at the end of the unit.

Text 5:11

An open letter to Mothers of fast-growing children

THOSE children of yours are growing so rapidly. The great concern of every mother must be that the growth shall be normal and regular, and that body, mind and muscle shall develop at the same rate.

Many children show a tendency to outgrow their strength. They become listless and disinclined for play. Their appetites are capricious and they are often weak and ailing.

Healthy and normal development depends almost entirely on correct diet and proper nourishment. Every particle of the material used in creating energy and building up the brain and body is obtained from food.

Growing children need more nourishment than ordinary food supplies. That is why "Ovaltine" should be their daily beverage. This delicious food-drink supplies, in a concentrated, correctly balanced and easily digested form, all the nourishing elements and vitamins that are essential for healthy growth.

"Ovaltine" is prepared from creamy milk, malt extract, and eggs from our own and selected farms. These are Nature's best foods. Eggs supply organic phosphorus—an essential element for building up brain and nerves.

The addition of "Ovaltine" removes the objection many children have to plain milk. "Ovaltine" renders milk more digestible, and therefore more beneficial. The nourishing value of all ordinary foods is increased when "Ovaltine" is the daily beverage.

Give your children "Ovaltine" instead of tea, coffee, etc. They will grow up strong and healthy—with sturdy bodies, sound nerves and alert minds.

"OVALTINE" BUILDS UP BRAIN, NERVE AND BODY

Prices in Gt. Britain and Northern Ireland, 1/3, 2/- and 3/9 per tin. P677

Activity

Text 5:12 shows a fold-out leaflet. How does it play with ideas about location, via its use of 'here, there and everywhere'?

There is a commentary on this activity at the end of the unit.

Text 5:12

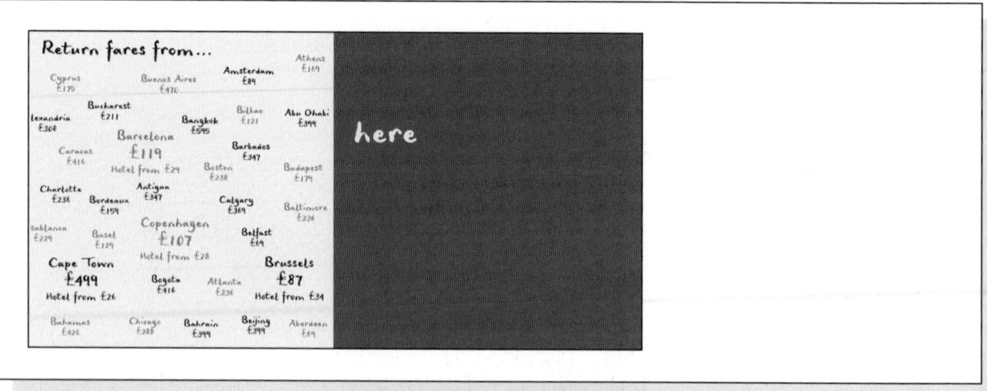

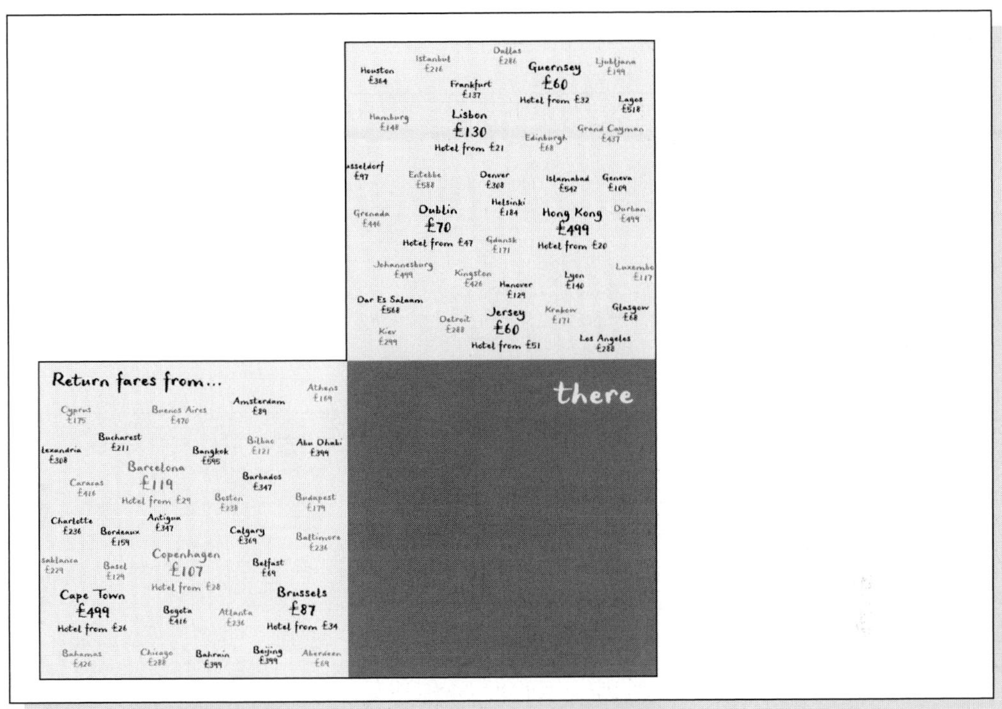
Houston £364
Istanbul £216
Dallas £286
Guernsey £60
Hotel from £32
Ljubljana £199
Frankfurt £137
Lagos £518
Hamburg £148
Lisbon £130
Hotel from £21
Edinburgh £68
Grand Cayman £437
Entebbe £588
Denver £308
Islamabad £542
Geneva £109
Grenada £446
Dublin £70
Hotel from £47
Helsinki £184
Hong Kong £499
Hotel from £20
Durban £499
Gdansk £171
Johannesburg £499
Kingston £426
Hanover £129
Lyon £140
Dar Es Salaam £568
Detroit £288
Jersey £60
Hotel from £51
Krakow £171
Glasgow £68
Kiev £299
Los Angeles £288
Return fares from...
Amsterdam £89
Athens £169
Cyprus £175
Buenos Aires £470
Bucharest £211
Bilbao £121
Abu Dhabi £399
Bangkok £595
Barcelona £119
Hotel from £29
Barbados £347
Caracas £416
Boston £238
Budapest £179
Charlotte £236
Bordeaux £159
Antigua £347
Calgary £369
Baltimore £236
Basel £129
Copenhagen £107
Hotel from £28
Belfast £69
Cape Town £499
Hotel from £26
Bogota £416
Atlanta £236
Brussels £87
Hotel from £34
Bahamas £426
Chicago £288
Bahrain £399
Beijing £399
Aberdeen £69
there

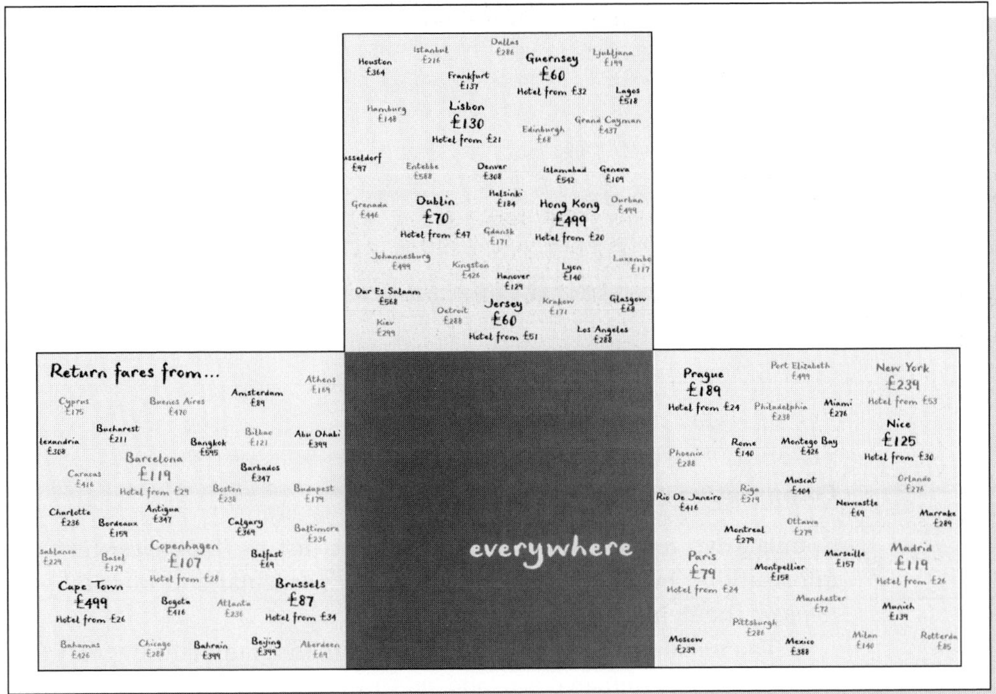
Prague £189
Hotel from £24
Port Elizabeth £499
New York £239
Hotel from £53
Philadelphia £238
Miami £276
Nice £125
Hotel from £30
Phoenix £288
Rome £140
Montego Bay £426
Muscat £404
Orlando £276
Rio De Janeiro £416
Riga £219
Newcastle £69
Montreal £279
Ottawa £279
Paris £79
Hotel from £24
Montpellier £158
Marseille £157
Madrid £119
Hotel from £26
Manchester £72
Pittsburgh £286
Munich £139
Moscow £239
Mexico £388
Milan £140
everywhere

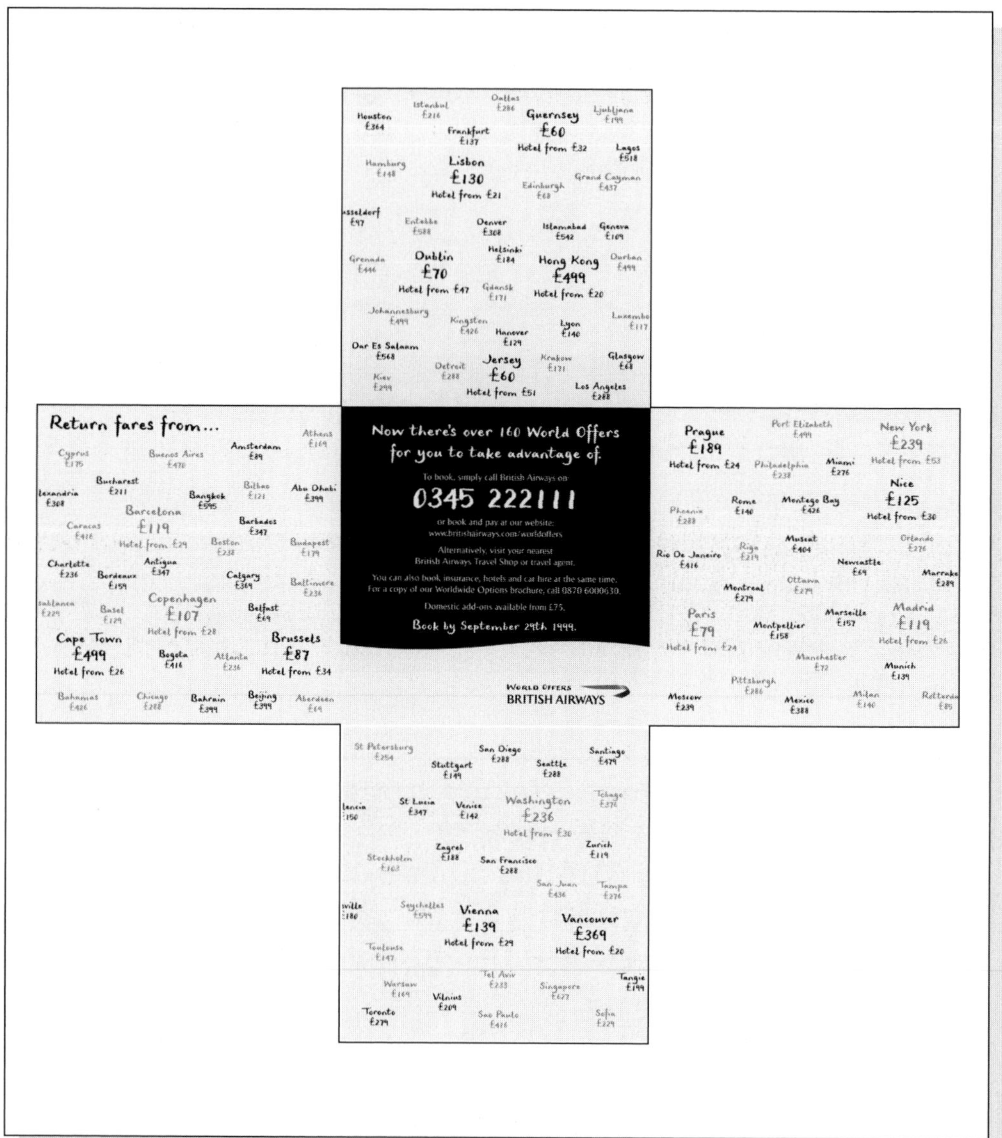

Comparative reference

Comparative reference tells the reader not just to 'look elsewhere for information', but to look elsewhere with a particular aim in mind – to *compare* the items that are being linked.

The most common way in English to mark grammatically that two items are being compared is to add 'er' to an adjective: for example, taller, nicer, healthier. It's also possible to suggest comparison with more than one item, by adding 'est': for example, tallest, nicest, healthiest.

Comparison can involve ideas about quantity and number: these meanings are carried by words like 'more', 'fewer', 'less', 'another'.

In many cases, we are given the reference point for the comparison being made, for example:

Annie is taller than Sue.
This sweater is nicer than that one.
Salad is healthier than fried bread.

But it is also possible to omit the reference point – leaving out the aspect that the mentioned item is being compared with.

Activity

Look at Text 5:13, which is a list of slogans taken from advertising texts. In each case, the comparative reference is incomplete. Try to explain in each case what the effect is of not completing the reference.

There is no commentary on this activity.

Text 5:13

MORE CATS PREFER IT	A CLEANER FUEL – FOR CLEANER AIR
GET YOUR CLOTHES WHITER	KINDER TO THE ENVIRONMENT
THE MILDER TOBACCO	McVITIES BAKE A BETTER BISCUIT
FOR A TASTIER MEAL	MORE POKE, LESS SMOKE: MOBIL DIESEL PLUS
BE HEALTHIER – LIVE LONGER	

Activity

Now look at a whole text that uses comparative reference. How does Text 5:14 work? Can you identify more than one possible reading?

There is a commentary on this activity at the end of the unit.

Text 5:14

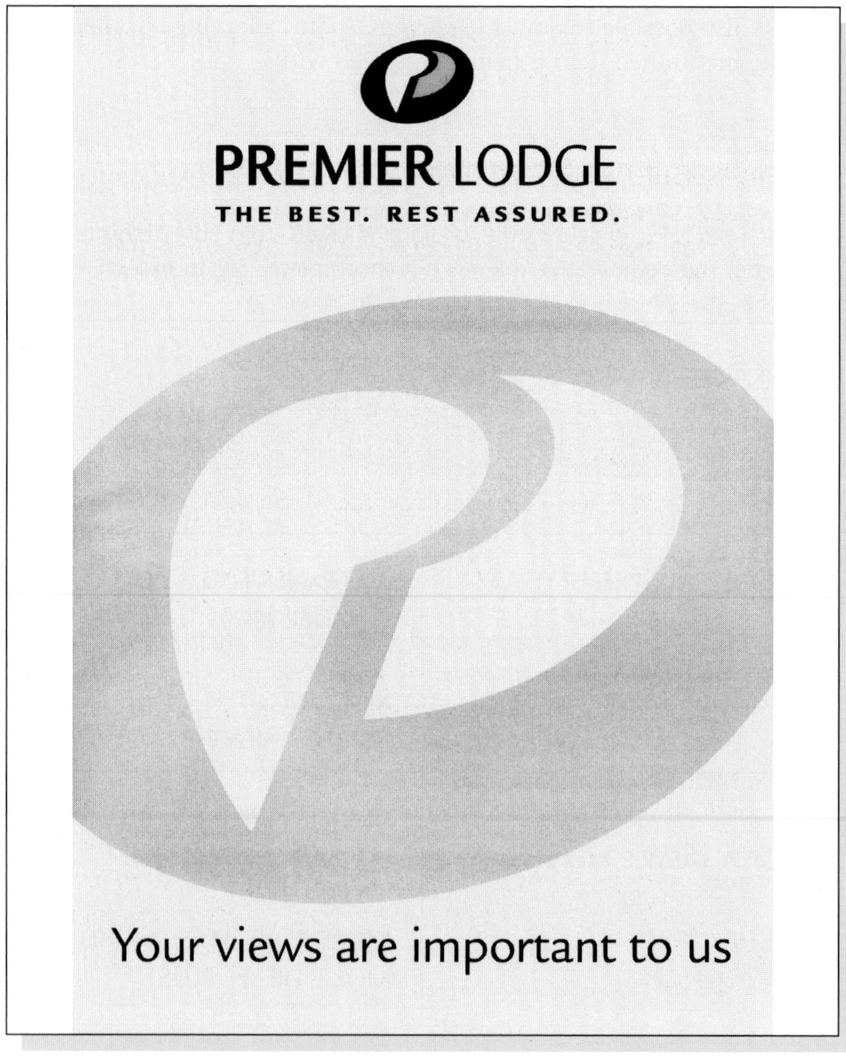

Substitution and ellipsis

Alongside reference, substitution and ellipsis are also both powerful ingredients in textual cohesion.

Substitution means what it suggests – the writer or speaker has substituted one item for another in the text. This can often involve long phrases, replaced by useful smaller items such as the single words 'do' or 'so', and is very characteristic of spontaneous spoken discourse. One important function of this type of substitution is to make texts more economic by avoiding tedious repetition. The examples below show how, while 'do' is used to replace verbs, 'so' is more often used as a substitute for whole clauses. In each case, the phrase that is being substituted by 'do' or 'so' is in italics. The dialogue is between two friends, and they are discussing A's intended house sale.

A: Has the agent for your house *put it in the local paper*?
B: I think he must have *done*, because Terry saw it advertised around his chips from the chip shop.
A: *That must have been a bit of a shock* if you hadn't told him.
B: I think *so*.

Substitution can also involve nouns, and here we often make a substitution in order to redefine the original item. For example:

He looked at the potatoes, and picked out *the large ones*.

Please read through the contracts, and sign *the duplicate one*.

While substitution is about swapping elements, ellipsis involves omitting elements altogether. Speakers who know each other well often use ellipsis because they have many shared meanings and references that do not need stating explicitly. As a result, when measured against writing, speech can appear to have gaps and incompleteness: for example, minor sentences (sentences without a verb) are very common in speech.

In some types of written texts, ellipsis can be used deliberately in order to create an illusion of closeness between writer and reader. The reader is forced to adopt the same position towards the writer that a speaker would adopt to a close friend in conversation. Rather than obscuring meaning or loosening the cohesion in a text, ellipsis is a binding factor because ties between writer and reader are strengthened through the work that the reader has to do to fill the gaps.

Activity

Look at Text 5:15, and identify places where there are omissions – ideas left incompletely stated, apparent gaps in sense or structure.

- To what extent does ellipsis contribute to the feel of this text as spoken language?
- What advantage do you think there might be for the advertiser in creating this illusion?

There is a commentary on this activity at the end of the unit.

Text 5:15

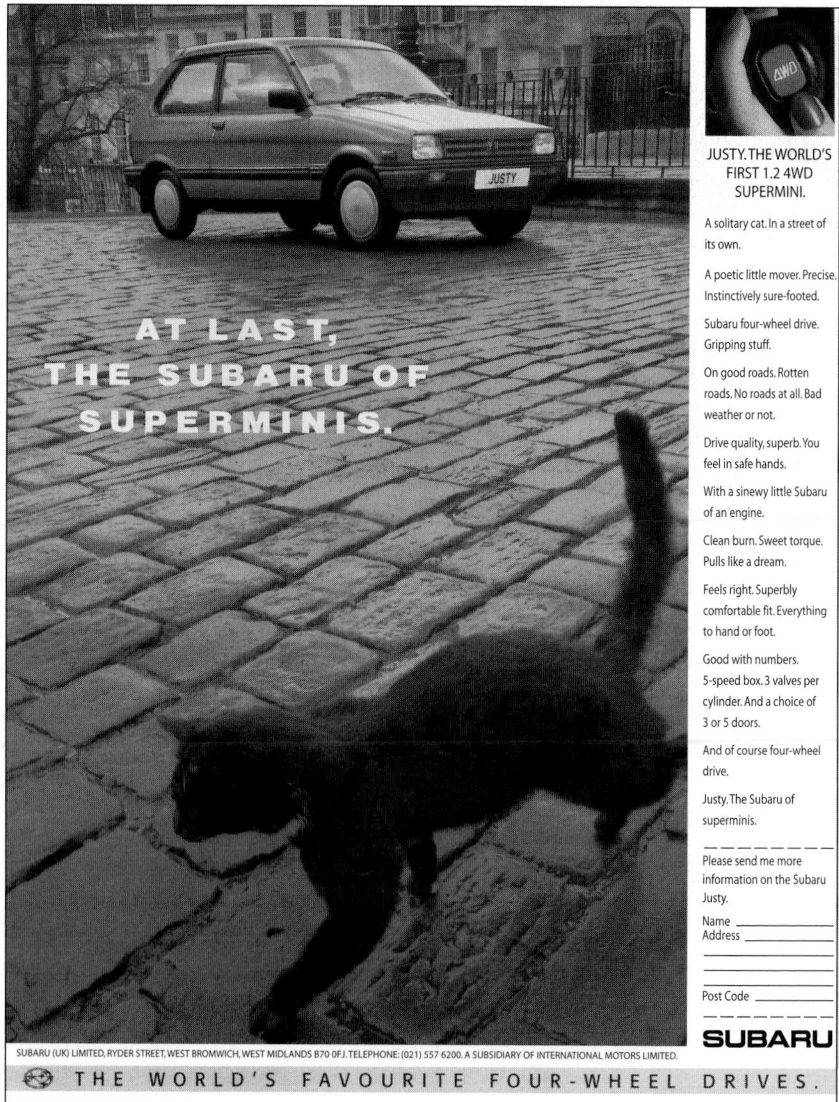

Conjunction

The term **conjunction** means 'joining'.

In a sense, all the aspects of cohesion are about joining or linking items together, but conjunction refers specifically to words and phrases which express *how* items should be linked. An example from the sentence you have just read is the word 'but': this tells the reader that what is to follow will revise, limit or re-focus the first part of the sentence.

Different types of writing tend to use different types of connecting word. This is not just about conventions that have developed – it is often very much to do with the purpose of the piece of writing (see also 'Information structure', later in this unit). So, for example, a story may well concentrate on the way one event followed another in time. If this is so, then conjunctions such as 'first', 'then', 'after that', 'in the end' are likely to appear. On the other hand, an information text may be more interested in showing how an idea or theme is made up of different interrelating elements, and phrases such as 'on the other hand' may be more relevant here (as at the beginning of this sentence).

Activity

To look at this idea more practically, read through Text 5:16, which is the front page of an information leaflet on conservation areas from the High Peak Borough Council.

- In the text, the conjunctions have been underlined for you. Decide how they link together the various parts of the text – what instructions do they give the reader on how to put elements of the text together?
- When you have finished, look for any more cohesive links, based on the types you have covered so far: for example, uses of 'this' and 'these'.

Note that there is no commentary on this activity.

Text 5:16

HIGH PEAK BOROUGH COUNCIL

CONSERVATION AREAS

Hayfield

This leaflet is one of a series which forms additional guidance to the statutory planning policies contained in the High Peak Local Plan.

The purpose of this leaflet is to give guidance upon the aims and policies of High Peak Borough Council for the control of development within Conservation Areas.

WHAT IS A CONSERVATION AREA?

Planning legislation requires the Borough Council to determine whether any parts of their area are "areas of special architectural or historic interest, the character or appearance of which it is desirable to preserve or enhance".

These areas, which are then designated as Conservation Areas derive their special qualities from the buildings, their traditional details, materials, scale and form. Equally important, however, is the way in which buildings and spaces relate to each other, the historic form and layout of street patterns, views, open spaces, trees and other landscape features.

Conservation Area status does not rule out the need for new development, which is sometimes necessary to maintain an area's economic and social vitality. Rather, it aims to direct any changes so that the existing historic and architectural character is respected and the new can sit sympathetically alongside the old. It follows that there will be a strong presumption in favour of retaining existing buildings wherever possible. The Borough Council aims to encourage careful maintenance and improvements to the buildings and their surroundings using traditional techniques and materials.

Activity

Here are some more conjunctions, with a brief explanation for each group of what they are telling the reader to do. (Note that some conjunctions can occur in more than one category.)

Read through the notes, add any further examples you can think of, then specify the types of text (e.g. stories) that tend to use the various types of conjunction.

Note that there is no commentary on this activity.

Type of conjunction	**Meaning**	**Examples**
additives/ alternatives	add/give an alternative	and, or, furthermore, in addition, likewise, in other words
adversative	contradict, concede	but, yet, though, however, on the contrary
causal	one idea/event causes another	so, then, for this reason, consequently, it follows that, as a result
temporal	one event follows another in time	one day, then, finally, up to now, the next day
continuatives	please continue to follow the text	well, now, of course, anyway, surely, after all

INFORMATION STRUCTURE

So far, attention has been focused on the way vocabulary and certain grammatical structures act as binding agents in texts. This sub-section looks at further aspects of both these areas, but with a focus on how particular types of text are connected with the internal ordering of information within them.

Different texts follow different rules which dictate to a certain extent the shape of the text produced: to return to the metaphor of weaving, you could say that texts come in different shapes in the same way that fabric is made into different garments.

But texts also have internal patterns in the same way that fabric has particular designs. The equivalent of a fabric design for a text is the pattern which results from how information and ideas are organised. For example, in Text 5:16, there are certain features that mark it out as belonging to the genre we might call 'information text', and some of these are to do with its directly visual shape: the title, in upper-case letters, the illustration, the boxed nature of the text, the way the text is broken up into spatially distinct sections. This is the equivalent of recognising a garment as a shirt or a dress. But there are also features of a more narrowly linguistic kind that relate to the way the text chooses to present its information and to foreground certain parts of it: this is more like the designs we see printed on a piece of material. These features are also part of the way we recognise and typify a genre, and they form the focus for the work that follows.

Sentence functions

Different sentences can perform very different functions, and, for this reason, the kind of sentence chosen often relates directly to what the text is trying to do.

Here are the four main functions sentences in English can perform:

- *Questioning*:
  Question sentences ask the reader to look for information.
- *Stating*:
  Statement sentences offer the reader a description of the state of things.
- *Commanding*:
  Command sentences (sometimes called 'imperatives') tell the reader to do something.
- *Exclaiming*:
  Exclamations express emotion directly.

To illustrate the differences in these functions, look at the High Peak Borough Council leaflet again (see p. 168, Text 5:16).

The writers of this leaflet have chosen to use a question-answer format as a way of presenting information, so they have a question sentence as the heading:

> WHAT IS A CONSERVATION AREA?

The effect of this is to justify the text that follows, in the sense that the text 'pretends' the reader has asked this question in the first place, so the writer is therefore doing the reader a favour by answering it. This in turn makes the text seem less authoritative than if the question had been a statement sentence:

> CONSERVATION AREAS EXPLAINED

The other possible sentence functions – command and exclamation – would have had different effects again: a command sentence would increase the distance between writer and reader by giving the reader an order to be carried out:

> FIND OUT ABOUT CONSERVATION AREAS – READ THIS LEAFLET

while an exclamation would have suggested that the whole subject of conservation was highly emotive and controversial (which it may well be, but the council is unlikely to want to suggest this):

> CONSERVATION AREAS!

To summarise: information texts are known to be difficult texts to read because they demand a lot of information-processing skills from the reader. They are also likely to seem remote and authoritative, since explaining something to someone suggests that the giver of information is more powerful (because more knowledgeable) than the receiver. In this particular leaflet, the writer has tried to remove this distance by using a question sentence to introduce the information.

Activity

Go back again to the texts you reassembled in the initial part of this unit (see Text 5:1, p. 143).

- Do the different genres of the texts use different kinds of sentences?
- What are the effects of the different kinds of sentence they use?

Note that there is no commentary on this activity.

Verbs

Another way we learn to recognise different genres of writing is by looking at the verbs used, particularly **tense** and **voice** (see also Unit 4). Tense refers to the way verbs are used to signal time: for example, a verb can be marked to show that an action happened in the past. This is done mainly by adding 'ed', but a minority of verbs change their internal structure. Here is an example of each type of marking: talk → talked (regular verb); speak → spoke (irregular verb). Certain types of writing tend to use particular verb tenses as part of their convention, and this in turn is related to what the text is trying to do. As an illustration of possible differences in what texts are concerned with, it is useful to think in terms of broad categories – for example, prose fiction compared with non-fiction information texts. Because information texts are intended to tell the reader about 'the nature of things' or 'how things are', these types of text tend to use present tense verb forms couched in statements about present 'reality'.

While prose fiction may equally give messages about the nature of the world, it tends to do this by looking back and giving an account of a series of events that happened to a set of fictional characters. It is therefore more likely that prose fiction will employ past-tense verb forms. Note that these statements are referring to norms or tendencies, not absolutes – so exceptions are always possible. In particular, it can be a very useful scene-setting strategy in fiction to 'stop the clock' and give a description of a place or person which uses present-tense verbs to convey the idea 'this is how things usually are in this place/with this person'.

Activity

Compare the verb tenses in Text 5:16 (p. 168) with those in Text 5:17 *K is for Killer,* which is from a detective novel by Sue Grafton. How far do the verb tenses bear out the picture given above?

Note that there is no commentary on this activity.

Text 5:17

K is for Killer

I drove east along Cabana, the wide boulevard that parallels the beach. When the moon is full, the darkness has the quality of a film scene shot day for night. The landscape is so highly illuminated that the trees actually cast shadows. Tonight the moon was in its final quarter, rising low in the sky. From the road I couldn't see the ocean, but I could hear the reverberating rumble of the tide rolling in. There was just enough wind to set the palm trees in motion, shaggy heads nodding together in some secret communication. A car passed me, going in the opposite direction, but there were no pedestrians in sight. I'm not often out at such an hour, and it was curiously exhilarating.

By day, Santa Teresa seems like any small southern California town. Churches and businesses hug the ground against the threat of earthquakes. The rooflines are low, and the architectural influence is largely Spanish. There's something solid and reassuring about all the white adobe and the red tile roofs. Lawns are manicured, and the shrubs are crisply trimmed. By night the same features seem stark and dramatic, full of black and white contrasts that lend intensity to the landscape. The sky at night isn't really black at all. It's a soft charcoal gray, nearly chalky with light pollution, the trees like ink stains on a darkened carpet. Even the wind has a different feel to it, as light as a feather quilt against the skin.

The real name for CC's is the Caliente Cafe, a low rent establishment housed in an abandoned service station near the railroad tracks. The original gasoline pumps and the storage tanks below had been removed years before, and the contaminated soil had been paved over with asphalt. Now, on hot days the blacktop tends to soften and a toxic syrup seeps out, a tarry liquid quickly converted into wisps of smoke, suggesting that the tarmac is on the verge of bursting into flames. Winters, the pavement cracks from dry cold, and a sulfurous smell wafts across the parking lot. CC's is not the kind of place to encourage bare feet.

I parked out in front beneath a sizzling red neon sign. Outside, the air smelled like corn tortillas fried in lard; inside, like salsa and recirculated cigarette smoke. I could hear the high-pitched whine of a blender working overtime, whipping ice and tequila into the margarita mix.

Verb voice is also something that tends to vary according to the genre of the writing. Voice refers to the way different emphases can be given to sentences (see also Unit 4).

There are two types of voice: active and passive.

If a verb takes an object (a thing or person affected by the action of the verb) as well as a subject (the thing or person doing the action) then it can be changed from active to passive. In the sentences below, the elements in italics form the object of the verb in each case:

> She sold *the car.*
> He kept *the pictures.*

These sentences are in an active form at present. Each can be expressed in a different way, however:

> The car was sold by her.
> The pictures were kept by him.

Now the sentences are passive: the object of the previously active sentence has moved to the front, to subject position; the verb has changed its form (to the form that it would take with 'have') and has added the verb 'to be'; the previous subject has moved to the end of the sentence, becoming a phrase (called the 'agent phrase'). In fact, this phrase could be left out altogether:

> The car was sold.
> The pictures were kept.

The fact that this phrase could be left out is a crucial factor in why the passive construction is favoured in some types of writing. Passives are often a way of depersonalising a text, because in removing agent phrases, the people and forces behind actions can be downplayed, leaving the process itself as the major focus – above, the selling of the car, the keeping of the pictures. It follows that any written genre wanting to highlight, for example, institutional procedures rather than individual concerns – such as legal documents or scientific reports – will tend to choose passive structures rather than active ones. In the High Peak Borough Council leaflet (see Text 5:16, p. 168), the italicised parts of the text below are passives:

> These areas, which *are* then *designated* as Conservation areas . . . Rather, it aims to direct any changes so that the existing historic and architectural character *is respected* . . .

Passives are not simply an alternative form of expression, however. The fact that the agent behind the process can be removed from a passive construction can also mean that a text can appear to have a veneer of neutrality, scientific 'truth' or newsworthy 'fact' when, expressed in another way, it seems to be nothing more than personal dogma or ideological bias.

Activity

Text 5:18 shows three brief texts written entirely in the active voice.

1 Turn them into the passive throughout, leaving out, wherever possible, the agent phrases.

2 When you have finished changing the texts around, think about the following:

- What differences in meaning or emphasis have resulted from your rewriting?
- What advantages might there be for writers, in using the passive voice?
- What types of text, in your experience, are likely to use passive structures?
- Are there valid reasons for using passives, as well as dubious reasons?

Possible rewrites are given at the end of this unit, although there is no commentary on this activity.

Text 5:18

They drove the car quickly away from the scene of the crime. They had blown open the safe, shot the security guard and left him for dead. A bystander called the emergency services and a passing motorist comforted the guard until they arrived.	I took a group of 40 people and surveyed their attitudes to alcohol. I found that most of the people surveyed drank more alcohol per week than the level that the government recommends.	If you take out a mortgage, the building society will repossess your house if you do not keep up the monthly payments. You must let the building society know if you are going to make late or reduced payments at any time.

Theme

Another important aspect of textual cohesion is the way in which the feature we call **theme** works across sentence boundaries.

Theme refers to the first part of a sentence, which is where the subject matter of the sentence is usually laid out for the reader. It covers all the material before the main verb. When sentences are woven tightly together, the end of one sentence (called the 'focus') can become the theme of the next. But themes have to have some continuity across sentences, otherwise a text that *looks* tightly knit can make complete nonsense.

Activity

Text 5:19 shows a text that is tightly knit in that the end of each sentence (focus) is linked with the start of the next (theme). But there are no links between themes (which have been italicised). As a result, the text reads somewhat bizarrely.

Do a short piece of writing like the one in Text 5:19, where there is no thematic continuity, but where the end of each sentence links with the start of the next.

Note that there is no commentary on this activity.

Text 5:19

I got up early and fed my cat. *Cats* like cream. *Cream* is a popular colour for paint. *Famous painters* include Michelangelo, who painted the Sistine Chapel in the Vatican. *The Vatican* is where the Pope lives.

Activity

Although the text you have just written for the Activity above would be considered faulty if judged by the rules of normal discourse, you might be able to find a text written in this way in some types of prose fiction – particularly where the writer is trying to imitate a kind of free-wheeling consciousness, where a character's thought process is being presented. Such texts are often described as using a 'stream of consciousness' technique. Text 5:20 shows an example of this.

- Can you see any cohesion in this text, or is it composed of entirely random sentences?

There is of course no right answer here.

Note that there is no commentary on this activity.

Text 5:20

> Must take the dog for a walk this morning. Washing waving about. Wonder what he might think of me if I don't phone. Blue sky, blue sky. Helen never said, did she? Bloke over there, sitting on the wall. Where's my coat? Thought I left it somewhere else. Funny how old towns speak about their past. To swim, or not to swim, that is the question. Nicer on a Greek beach, body brown and oily, cheap novels in abundance. Don't need many clothes in some parts of the world. On then.
>
> *Deborah Freeman*

Activity

Text 5:21 is an extract from the novel *The Shepherd* by Frederick Forsyth. The extract shows how sentence themes can be controlled very carefully in order to give the reader a sense of place and time. Read it through and plot the way in which the themes construct a particular spatial and temporal orientation for the reader as the text proceeds.

There is a commentary on this activity at the end of the unit.

Text 5:21

The Shepherd

For a brief moment, while waiting for the control tower to clear me for takeoff, I glanced out through the Perspex cockpit canopy at the surrounding German countryside. It lay white and crisp beneath the crackling December moon.

Behind me lay the boundary fence of the Royal Air Force base, and beyond the fence, as I had seen while swinging my little fighter into line with the takeoff runway, the sheet of snow covering the flat farmland stretched away to the line of the pine trees, two miles distant in the night yet so clear I could almost see the shapes of the trees themselves.

Ahead of me, as I waited for the voice of the controller to come through the headphones, was the runway itself, a slick black ribbon of tarmac, flanked by twin rows of bright-burning lights, illuminating the solid path cut earlier by the snowplows. Behind the lights were the humped banks of the morning's snow, frozen hard once again where the snowplow blades had pushed them. Far away to my right, the airfield tower stood up like a single glowing candle amid the brilliant hangars where the muffled aircraftmen were even now closing down the station for the night.

Inside the control tower, I knew, all was warmth and merriment, the staff waiting only for my departure to close down also, jump into the waiting cars, and head back to the parties in the mess. Within minutes of my going, the lights would die out, leaving only the huddled hangars, seeming hunched against the bitter night, the shrouded fighter planes, the sleeping fuel-bowser trucks, and, above them all, the single flickering station light, brilliant red above the black-and-white airfield, beating out in Morse code the name of the station – CELLE – to an unheeding sky. For tonight there would be no wandering aviators to look down and check their bearings; tonight was Christmas Eve, in the year of grace 1957, and I was a young pilot trying to get home to Blighty for his Christmas leave.

Interpreting the design

The title of this whole unit is 'Text and context'.

So far, the focus has been on how texts work internally, in how they are put together. This section examines another level at which texts operate, in the sense of the context that surrounds them.

The word 'context' contains the word 'text': it refers to the factors that work alongside or with the text to create meaning. 'Con' means 'with', and in Latin, the verb *contexere* means 'to weave together with'; the word 'con' in contemporary Italian and Spanish still means 'with', and you can see its operation in phrases such as the Spanish 'chili con carne' ('chili with meat').

So the context for any text is the larger culture which surrounds it, and the reading of any text results from the interplay of the text itself and the cultural framework that the reader brings to it.

The word 'culture', however, is not a straightforward term to define.

One use of the term refers to being part of an elite group: when we say someone is 'cultured', the suggestion is that they know about such areas of artistic expression as classical literature and music, and that they go to such venues as the theatre or art galleries as part of their social life. This is also what is meant by 'high culture', which was a phrase coined by Matthew Arnold to describe, in his opinion, 'the best that has been thought and said in the world'. In contrast, Arnold would have considered such pastimes as going to football matches, watching TV, viewing mass-circulation films or reading popular fiction or magazines as examples of 'low culture'.

This elitist view of culture, however, is not the whole story.

In sociology, culture has a much wider meaning: it refers to all the factors that bind groups together in all aspects of social life:

> Culture refers to the ways of life of members of a society, or of groups within a society. It includes how they dress, their marriage customs and family life, their patterns of work, religious ceremonies and leisure pursuits. It also covers the goods they create and which become meaningful for them: bows and arrows, ploughs, factories and machines, computers, books, dwellings . . .
>
> (Giddens 1993)

Activity

In the quotation above, culture is defined as *the ways of life of members of a society, or of groups within a society*. Look at Text 5:22. What aspects of culture are embedded in this advertisement? Think about the following:

- What is the role of the black athlete in this text? What does he symbolise (represent, or stand for)?
- What kind of figure do you imagine would normally be sitting in the vacant airline seat?
- Think of other texts where non-white figures were depicted or described. Were they presented in particular ways?

There is a commentary on this activity at the end of the unit.

Text 5:22

Try Iberia's new Intercontinental Business Class and enjoy a world class experience on a world class airline. Outstretching the competition is our business. Iberia gives you 132 cms. of room between your ergonomically designed seat and the one in front. Relax in style and made-to-measure comfort wiling away the time watching films, sports or news on your individual video
www.iberia.com

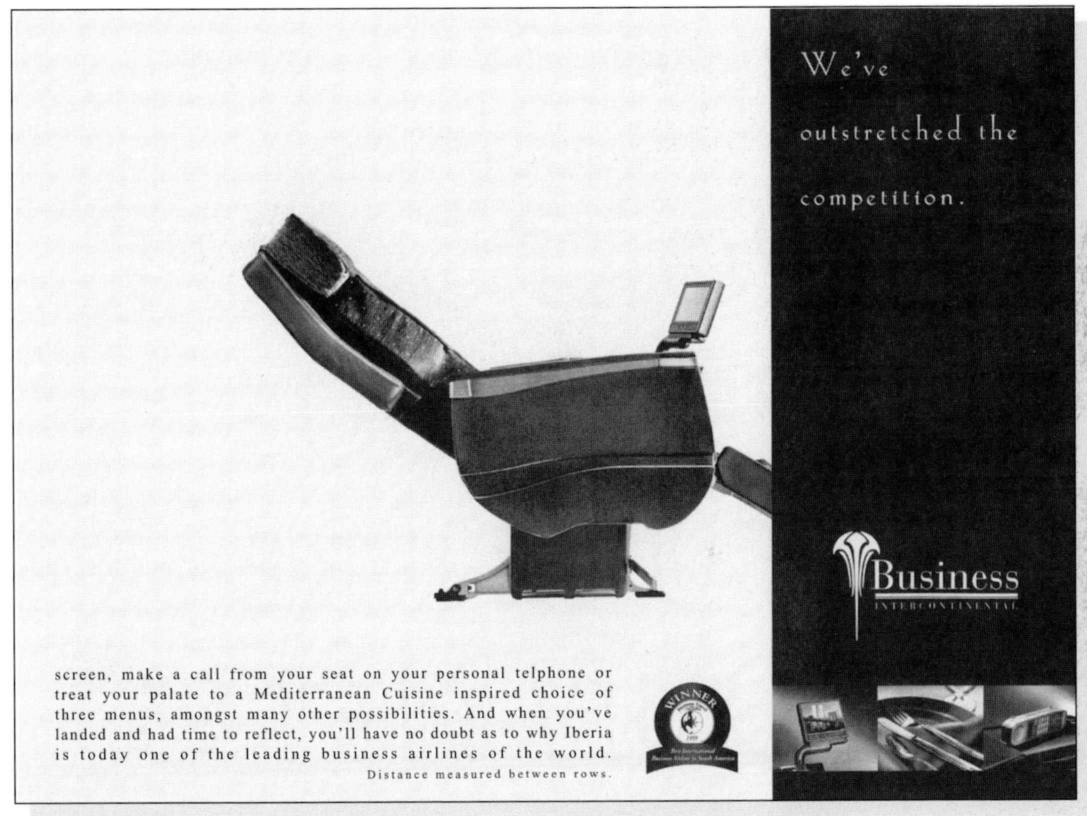
We've
outstretched the
competition.
Business
INTERCONTINENTAL
screen, make a call from your seat on your personal telphone or treat your palate to a Mediterranean Cuisine inspired choice of three menus, amongst many other possibilities. And when you've landed and had time to reflect, you'll have no doubt as to why Iberia is today one of the leading business airlines of the world.
Distance measured between rows.
WINNER

Activity

Now look at Text 5:23. What aspects of culture are noticeable here? Think about the following:

- How does the 'hook' (the writing in large letters above the image of the cheese) link with the phrase 'authentically French'?
- To what extent, if any, do you have to know the French language in order to understand this text?

There is a commentary on this activity at the end of the unit.

Text 5:23

Activity

Text 5:22 presented a playful, rather knowing attitude to its representation of another culture. This shows that texts don't always try to hide their own ideologies. Advertisements in particular can use ideas about representation as part of their persuasive message. This can make the advertised company appear to be very open and truthful.

Look at Text 5:24, where Daewoo presents a message about how car companies have traditionally sold their products. You may recall that in Unit 1, the way one text can refer to or base itself on another was called 'intertextuality'. Explain how Text 5:24 uses intertextuality and refers to the stereotyping of particular groups to construct its persuasive message.

There is a commentary on this activity at the end of the unit.

Text 5:24

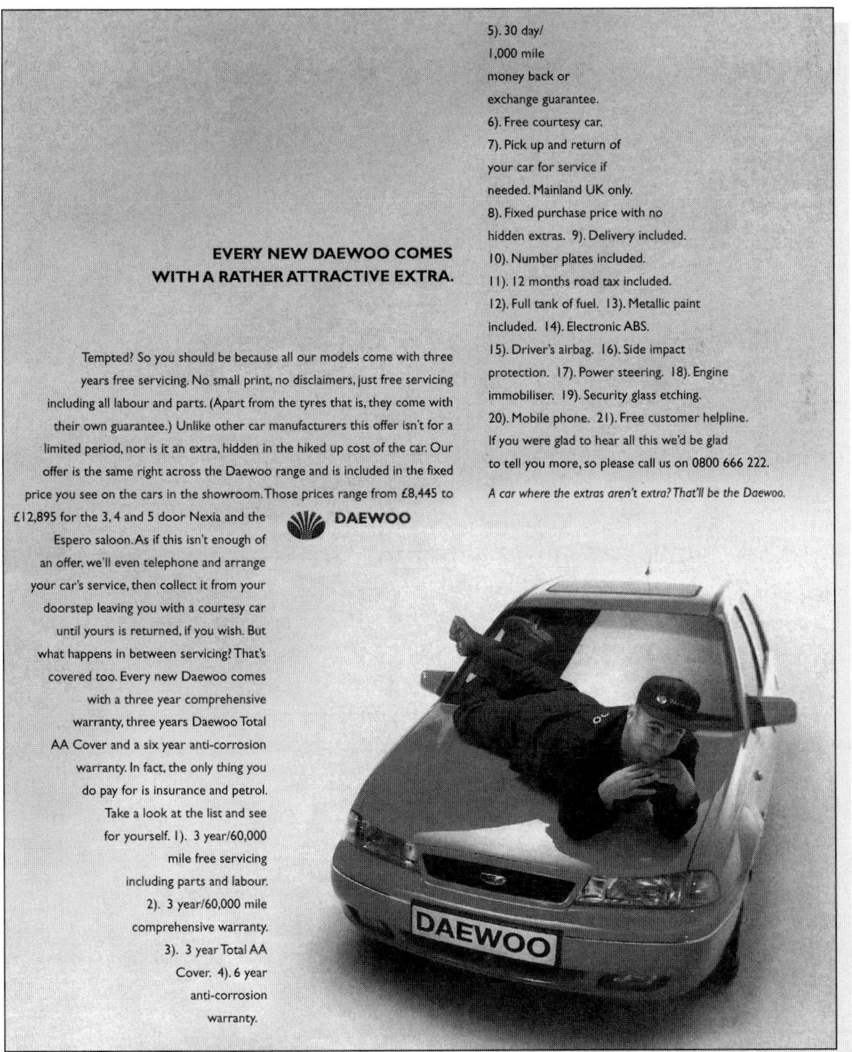

EVERY NEW DAEWOO COMES
WITH A RATHER ATTRACTIVE EXTRA.
Tempted? So you should be because all our models come with three years free servicing. No small print, no disclaimers, just free servicing including all labour and parts. (Apart from the tyres that is, they come with their own guarantee.) Unlike other car manufacturers this offer isn't for a limited period, nor is it an extra, hidden in the hiked up cost of the car. Our offer is the same right across the Daewoo range and is included in the fixed price you see on the cars in the showroom. Those prices range from £8,445 to £12,895 for the 3, 4 and 5 door Nexia and the Espero saloon. As if this isn't enough of an offer, we'll even telephone and arrange your car's service, then collect it from your doorstep leaving you with a courtesy car until yours is returned, if you wish. But what happens in between servicing? That's covered too. Every new Daewoo comes with a three year comprehensive warranty, three years Daewoo Total AA Cover and a six year anti-corrosion warranty. In fact, the only thing you do pay for is insurance and petrol. Take a look at the list and see for yourself. 1). 3 year/60,000 mile free servicing including parts and labour. 2). 3 year/60,000 mile comprehensive warranty. 3). 3 year Total AA Cover. 4). 6 year anti-corrosion warranty.
5). 30 day/1,000 mile money back or exchange guarantee. 6). Free courtesy car. 7). Pick up and return of your car for service if needed. Mainland UK only. 8). Fixed purchase price with no hidden extras. 9). Delivery included. 10). Number plates included. 11). 12 months road tax included. 12). Full tank of fuel. 13). Metallic paint included. 14). Electronic ABS. 15). Driver's airbag. 16). Side impact protection. 17). Power steering. 18). Engine immobiliser. 19). Security glass etching. 20). Mobile phone. 21). Free customer helpline. If you were glad to hear all this we'd be glad to tell you more, so please call us on 0800 666 222.
A car where the extras aren't extra? That'll be the Daewoo.
DAEWOO
DAEWOO

Activity

To enable you to explore the usefulness of contrasting two different texts within the same genre, read through Texts 5:25 (Menu A) and 5:26 (Menu B). They are from very different establishments: A is from a roadside café in the Manchester area; B is from a large chain hotel in Newcastle.

- What ideas about its target audience are suggested by each of the menus?

There is an extensive commentary on these texts at the end of the unit. It is designed as a model answer, to show you the level of detail that a good analysis would provide on texts of this kind.

Text 5:25

Menu A

WAYFARER CAFE

ALL DAY FULL B/FAST WITH B/B
OR TOAST, INC POT TEA

HOMEMADE + 2 VEG, POTS
STEAK + KIDNEY, ALL IN
HOT-POT
HAM SHANK, CHIPS OR JACKET
LIVER + ONIONS
YORKSHIRES/MUSHY PEAS/BLACK PUD EXTRA

APPLE PIE + CUSTARD
BAKEWELL TART
PARKIN

VARIOUS SNACKS
SAUSAGE MUFFIN
BACON BARM
SCOLLOPS + GRAVY
CHIPS + GRAVY/CURRY SAUCE
OR TO ORDER

Text 5:26

Menu B

The Ravenscroft Suite:
GOURMET DINNER DANCE

An interesting warm salad of smoked bacon, wild mushrooms and duck, quickly cooked and bound with a melange of winter leaves sprinkled in a walnut dressing

*

Peeled prawns bound in a tomato enhanced mayonnaise with diced pineapple and walnuts, nestled on a meli-melo of lettuce served in a glass

*

A collection of cured meats and poultry, nestled on a rustic salad and doused in a warm raspberry dressing

*

A terrine of fresh vegetables, sliced onto a coulis of tomato and fresh herbs

***

Supreme of fresh salmon attentively grilled, presented on a cushion of homemade noodles with a champagne sauce

***

Fillets of fresh monkfish spread with a mousse of scampi caressed in cabbage and poached, sliced onto a dry vermouth and avocado sauce

***

Medallions of pork pan-fried and masked in a pink peppercorn sauce accompanied by caramelized kumquats

***

Escalope of turkey folded with cranberry sauce, dusted in breadcrumbs and baked, escorted by a rich Madeira sauce

***

Rounds of venison quickly pan-fried and masked with a sharp blackcurrant sauce with just a suspicion of Juniper berry

***

A tournedos of beef topped with a liver parfait, enrobed in crepinette and oven-baked, served with a Madeira and truffle fondue

Extension activities

1 Collect some written texts in order to explore a particular dimension you have found interesting in this unit.

Here are some starting points, to get you thinking:

- intertextuality – texts that refer explicitly to other texts
- the representation of groups – e.g. gender, age, ethnicity, social class, region
- different types of writing on a common theme. These could include:

  food: recipes, menus, adverts, food labels, poems . . . *drink*: beer mats, wine labels, wine reviews, adverts . . . *relationships*: greetings cards, lonely hearts columns, fiction . . . *travel*: holiday brochures, travel writing, travel guides . . .

2 When you have collected a range of material, focus on an overall question for language analysis which will enable you to contrast a small number of texts for a specific reason. For example, within the area of food, the following contrasts might yield interesting results:

- *Language change*: comparing an older text with a contemporary one from the same genre, what has changed, and why?
- *Spoken compared with written discourse*: spoken (i.e. TV or radio) recipe compared with a written one. You could even compare texts from the same person, as several professional cooks have produced books to accompany their TV series.
- *The functions and features of different genres*: how might the purposes of two types of writing – for example, a persuasive advert compared with an informative food label – be reflected in their language use? Are they more similar or more distinctive than we might think?
- *Texts specifically aimed at different audiences*: how do recipes or menus aimed at children vary from those aimed at adults? Do adverts for food target male and female audiences differently? Do menus aimed at different regional and social-class groups encode ideas about the supposed audience?

Commentaries/Answers to activities

ANSWERS: ACTIVITY p. 142, TEXT 5:1

Texts: A = romantic fiction book 'blurb'; B = advert; C = recipe.

A

Melodie Neil and Jed Martin were old friends.

She knew that he loved her – in a calm settled way rather than any grand passion – and that he would make her a good, kind husband.

In short, when she became engaged to him she knew exactly what she was doing.

So she hated it when that infuriating Keith Scott seemed to go out of his way to suggest that her heart wasn't in the affair.

B

Do you feel that you never get a fair slice of the capital cake?

We do, too.

That's why we created 'Portfolio', a brand new concept in saving.

Portfolio is a high interest investment account that makes your money work for you, while still giving you instant access to your capital.

So that way, you can have your cake and eat it too.

C

Wash and core the apples, taking care to remove all pips.

Slice finely.

Put them into a fireproof dish with the water, and a tablespoon of the sugar.

Ensuring that the lid is tightly sealed, put the dish into a preheated oven, Gas Regulo 6.

Reduce temperature to 3 after 10 minutes.

Allow the fruit to steam in its own juice for a further 15 minutes.

Spoon out the cooked apples and arrange them attractively in rounds on a serving plate.

Mix juice with the brandy, mulled wine, and rest of the sugar.

Pour over the top, and serve with double cream.

ANSWERS: ACTIVITY p. 145, TEXT 5:3

The vehicle was seen proceeding down the main street in a westerly direction = police force

Leading to a spacious and well-appointed residence with considerable potential = estate agency

She went to work, mixing up the six-ten with two parts of 425, and dabbing the mixture through 6 ezimeshes = hairdressing

'This one has a fine shaggy nose and a fruity bouquet with a flowery head', she said = winetasting

He managed to get into a good position, just kissing the cushion = snooker

He said 'Just pop up onto the couch and we'll see what we can do' = medical profession

She pulled down the menu, chose the command by using the cursor, then quit = computers

She said to knead well, roll into a ball and leave overnight to rise = baking

Instead, he mulched well, turned over and left the beds to settle = gardening

Good progress made, but concentration sometimes rather poor; more effort required if success is to be expected in the important months ahead = teaching

COMMENTARY: ACTIVITY p. 146, TEXT 5:4

The kind of metaphor at work here is that of **metonymy,** where two ideas are juxtaposed and linked by association. Here, the underpants pictured stand for maleness – not any one man, but the whole sex. The underpants also represent a specific aspect of male anatomy: the type of cancer the charity is fighting affects a part of the male body covered by underpants. The type of underpants pictured, and the way they are hung out, are also significant in building up the representation. The underpants are not sexy, youthful, designer wear, but a run-of-the-mill, regular, conventional type of Y-front often worn by older men – the very group who are most prone to this cancer. This idea of 'ordinariness' is important to the message of this advert, because it is saying that prostate cancer affects more men than we might think. The idea of general applicability is suggested in a number of ways, including the basic nature of the wooden pegs, and the positioning of the underpants in a series, with their colour-reversed patterns of dark and light cloth and seams.

COMMENTARY: ACTIVITY p. 149, TEXT 5:6

The child's voice is suggested by certain vocabulary items, such as 'knickers', 'shoebag', 'willies', 'smelly', 'Miss', 'Sir', as well as by the direct speech, 'What me Miss? No Miss. Oh Miss, I never did'. In contrast, the adult's language is considerably more complex and abstract: 'untold horrors', 'adept', 'fundamental tortures', 'sweet sainthood', 'total immersion'. The two styles are woven together very cleverly, with subtle shifts occurring within a short space; this can create humorous effects, as in the anti-climax of lines 'The most frightening . . . their willies'.

COMMENTARY: ACTIVITY p. 152, TEXT 5:7

A sense of mystery is created in this text partly by the fact that the reader is unsure who is in the story, and this effect results from the range of pronouns used: you, they, we, it, she, he, one, I. At the beginning, it seems that 'you' means 'one' and that 'they' are 'a ghostly couple'. But then it's uncertain who is talking in direct speech in the second paragraph; also, the second use of 'you' (in the final paragraph) appears to mean, not 'one' as before, but 'they' (i.e. the ghosts). Throughout the whole text, it's unclear exactly what 'it' is that everyone seems to be searching for. The language makes the reader behave like the characters, in that it makes the act of reading an act of searching to locate the meaning.

COMMENTARY: ACTIVITY p. 153, TEXT 5:8

The poem concerns a tragi-comic misunderstanding – a drowning man was ignored because onlookers thought he was cheerily waving at them, when he was really calling for help. This is taken beyond the literal level of a physical drowning to suggest another reading: that we explain away other people's difficulties in rather simplistic ways because we can't face the implications – our own responsibilities, for example.

The misunderstanding is presented by the use of two sets of voices: the 'I' of the dead man, and the 'they' of the onlookers; these voices are presented by a third voice – that of the narrator, who, unlike the onlookers, can hear the dead man speaking.

In using pronouns rather than individual names, the poem suggests that its message has significance for all of us, whoever we are.

COMMENTARY: ACTIVITY p. 156, TEXT 5:10

Text 5:10, the information leaflet, assumes a very wide range of people in its reference to 'you' and 'your' water supply. The fact that 'you' are being addressed in a number of different languages implies a multicultural audience for this text (although English is the primary medium of communication, as evidenced by its placing at the top of the text). There is also a very strong non-verbal representation of the message, via the crossed-out tap symbol. This includes the idea of non-readers in general.

COMMENTARY: ACTIVITY p. 158, TEXT 5:11

The authoritative voice of the text is immediately established by the phrase 'those children of yours': 'those' sets up a distance from the speaker, and 'yours' locates ownership and therefore responsibility for the potential problem raised by the speaker – that of children who may not grow normally.

The main body of the text uses scientific-sounding discourse in the form of many statements to further establish the expertise of the author of the 'open letter' in talking to the recipients – 'mothers of fast-growing children' (therefore all mothers, since few mothers would acknowledge that they had children who were slow-growing).

At the end, the power of authority is reinforced by a command which reminds the reader whose children are being discussed: 'Give *your* children "Ovaltine"'.

COMMENTARY: ACTIVITY p. 160, TEXT 5:12

The British Airways text offers three answers to its initial question, 'Where is everybody?' Opening the first panel offers the first answer – 'here'. This panel is a humorous take on the word 'here', because the 'here' of the reader is obviously different from the various locations listed, such as Cape Town and the Bahamas. The second panel reveals the answer 'there' and offers up a new batch of faraway places; while the final panel – 'everywhere' – completes a now-huge span of locations served by BA. The fact that the sections unfold in time, as the reader opens them, creates a kind of narrative, as each view of where it's possible to fly is expanded by the next textual revelation.

COMMENTARY: ACTIVITY p. 164, TEXT 5:14

The fact that the slogan 'The best. Rest assured.' is in two (minor) sentences means that, by one reading, 'the best' refers to the whole Premier Lodge experience. By this reading, the comparative form 'best' is given no specific reference point, usefully allowing any interpretation of what the hotel chain might be 'best' at. The second sentence then qualifies and endorses this reading, 'rest assured' acting as a discourse marker which tells readers to be confident that this is the truth.

If the slogan is read as one sentence – and the full stops therefore ignored – then the Premier Lodge is making a claim that customers will be guaranteed 'the best rest', in other words, a good night's sleep.

The fact that both these readings can be accessed from the slogan means that they can both exist in a reader's mind, and complement one another. The hotel chain is suggesting it has a good reputation for offering a good night's sleep – a usefully specific claim – while also making a general claim that it is 'the best'.

COMMENTARY: ACTIVITY p. 166, TEXT 5:15

The text uses ellipsis in the form of many minor sentences, including single words ('Justy', 'Precise'), two-word sequences ('Gripping stuff', 'Rotten roads', 'Clean burn', 'Sweet torque', 'Feels right'), and longer sentences where certain elements have been omitted: for example, verbs ('A solitary cat'), and nouns that stand for the subject ('Pulls like a dream'). This, along with other features – notably the fast turnover of items, as if imitating a person's unplanned thoughts, including afterthoughts signalled by 'and' – suggests spoken language rather than writing. On the other hand, the text is set out to resemble a poem visually, with the language arranged in 'stanza' form, fitting in with the idea of the car as 'a poetic little mover'. The text as a whole, including the visual aspects, calls up elements of the detective genre in its suggestions of the loneliness and threat of city meanstreets; the verbal commentary also has the staccato rhythm and dramatic tension of a detective film's narrator. The message of the text, though, is one of reassurance: the car is solid, reliable and secure. The hand in the picture inset is female, with carefully painted nails. This is a vehicle which will protect a genteel woman driver in a man's world: its engine, though little, will growl if necessary; the car is a comfortable outfit; 'Justy' is good with numbers even if its driver isn't.

The text's imitation of spoken language brings the narrator close to the reader, calling up a frisson of fear in order then to be able to dispel it.

COMMENTARY: ACTIVITY p. 175, TEXT 5:18

Possible rewrites:

> The car was driven quickly away from the scene of the crime. The safe had been blown open, the security guard had been shot and left for dead. Emergency services were called and the guard was comforted until their arrival.

> A group of 40 people were surveyed on their attitudes to alcohol. Most of the people surveyed were found to drink more than the recommended level of alcohol per week.
>
> If a mortgage is taken out, the house will be repossessed if monthly payments are not kept up. The building society must be informed if late or reduced payments are going to be made at any time.

COMMENTARY: ACTIVITY p. 177, TEXT 5:21

This text gives an acute sense of a moment suspended in time as the pilot waits to take off; during this moment, he appears to have a heightened perception of his surroundings while looking out through the cockpit canopy. There are several sentence themes that specify spatial orientation: behind me; ahead of me; behind the lights; far away to my right; inside the control tower. At the end, we are brought back to the idea of time passing as the waiting pilot thinks ahead to 'within minutes of my going', at which point we view with him how the surroundings will appear as he takes off. We are brought back down to earth when we are told there would be no 'wandering aviators' that night; finally we are given factual details of time and direction – Christmas Eve 1957, a flight back to Britain. These details bring us back inside the plane, ready for take off.

COMMENTARY: ACTIVITIES pp. 179–83, TEXTS 5:22–5:24

Texts 5:22–5:24 all involve cultural stereotypes of one kind or another. In Text 5:22, the black athlete symbolises the 'outstretching' that is referred to in the advert's hookline. The black figure here is in a fairly stereotyped role, representing physical strength rather than, say, intellectual qualities or business acumen. The figure represents the quality of the airline rather than standing for the type of customer the airline might attract.

Text 5:23 is playfully imitating French language in terms of its written forms, but when the words are read aloud, they 'become' English: 'perfect to share with mates'. However, they become, not standard English, but a kind of English spoken as if with a French accent: 'perfec' instead of 'perfect'; 'wiv' instead of 'with'. The ironic **tag** at the bottom, 'authentically French', tips us the wink that the advert has a playful rather than a serious intent. It could be argued that the language is difficult to understand without some knowledge of French – for example, the words 'chere' and 'ouiv' are not necessarily that transparent. Perhaps the advert, though presenting a kind of cod French, does therefore presume some knowledge of French culture – in which case, getting the joke relies on a notion of being an educated and sophisticated reader.

Text 5:24 refers intertextually to the stereotypical female model draped across car bonnets in the many car adverts of former times. The joke is elaborated by making the model not just male, but a male car mechanic. At the same time, he poses in coy fashion as if traditionally female. The lexical choices in the advertising copy further endorse the joke: readers are offered an 'attractive extra', and are asked whether they are 'tempted'. By showing that they are reversing a known stereotype, the company are perhaps trying to present themselves as enlightened and different from the rest of an industry that has historically been seen as male-dominated and sexist.

COMMENTARY: ACTIVITY pp. 184–5, TEXTS 5:25, 5:26

Graphology/phonology

These two texts represent variations within the menu genre in terms of their layout and organisation. Menu A groups its items in three sections, separated by space: the first section lists main meals, the second lists sweet dishes, while the third offers snacks. Menu B is laid out differently: all the items are equally spaced, but the number of asterisks denotes whether the food described is a starter or main course item. In each case, it is assumed that the reader knows about the organisation of the text as part of his/her reading skills within English-speaking cultural groups: a reader of Menu A would therefore not expect to have to select an item from each of the sections, while a reader of Menu B would not expect the items framed by three asterisks to be snacks.

Menu A uses upper-case letters in a plain typeface, suggesting clarity and straightforwardness, while the italic lower-case script of Menu B carries connotations of artistic purpose.

Menu A uses a range of abbreviations and symbols: b/fast, b/b, inc, veg, homemade, steak + kidney, pots, jacket, yorkshires, pud, 2, +, /. Again, there is an assumption here of shared understanding: there is no need for the text to spell out in any detail what is being referred to. The resulting economy of language suggests little use for the decorative, aesthetic aspect of communication. In contrast, the language of Menu B strives to expand rather than contract: for example, where Menu A uses a plus sign, Menu B renders additive meaning by phrases such as 'accompanied by' and 'escorted by'. Menu B also foregrounds its own language by imitating an artistic construct in its use of sound symbolism – peeled prawns, meli-melo, fillets of fresh monkfish, caressed in cabbage, pork pan-fried . . . pink peppercorn, accompanied . . . caramelized kumquats. The reader could be forgiven for thinking that some of the ingredients are included as much for their alliterative as for their culinary value.

Vocabulary

Menu A contains a large proportion of regional dialect terms, labelling regional food from the Lancashire/Yorkshire area: 'homemade' (a steak pie), 'hot-pot', 'ham shank' (leg of boiled ham), 'Yorkshires' (Yorkshire pudding), 'mushy peas' (baked marrowfat peas), 'black pudding', 'Bakewell tart' (from Bakewell, Derbyshire), 'parkin' (a cake made with black treacle), 'muffin' and 'barm' (both dialect terms for bread rolls), 'scollops' (potato slices dipped in batter and fried). While neither chips nor gravy are regional items, their combination on the same plate is much favoured in the North.

Menu B contains many terms derived from French, including some which are still given French pronunciation – for example: 'melange', 'coulis', 'mousse', 'parfait'. French terms are used to describe particular cuts of meat or fish – 'supreme', 'fillets', 'medallions', 'escalope', 'tournedos'; and the French-derived term 'poultry' is preferred to the Anglo-Saxon alternative, 'chicken'. Dressings and coverings of various kinds – 'mayonnaise', 'coulis', 'mousse', 'parfait', 'sauce' – are of French derivation. French terms also refer to arrangements of food – for example, 'melange', 'meli-melo' (French for 'topsy-turvy'), or particular dishes and items – 'terrine', 'fondue', 'crepinette'.

Beyond the terms related specifically to food, many other terms within the text are French/Latin-based, and have connotations of formality and high status: for example, 'enhanced', 'presented', 'accompanied'. Some terms also suggest sensuality – 'nestled', 'cushion', 'caressed' – while others almost raise the food items to a level of human animacy: the warm salad is 'interesting', the salmon is '*attentively* grilled', the venison carries a 'suspicion' of Juniper, while the turkey is 'escorted', and the beef is 'enrobed'. The picture constructed is one where the food is a sensual experience, but of a high aesthetic level, unfolding within a world of good manners and delicacy, not within an animalistic world of base appetites.

The connotations of the names of the respective establishments provide revealing semantic contrasts: the 'Wayfarer' represents a transport-type café, appearing to suggest a travelling clientele, but offering a very localised fare which needs no explanation, therefore constructing readers who are known and familiar customers; the 'Ravenscroft', on the other hand, suggests ample provision in offering itself as a 'suite', and constructs an audience of sophisticated food experts – 'gourmets' – who have the leisure time to dance as well as eat. The food appears to be explained in some detail, but is couched in language which is not everyday and familiar, and which, in many cases, would need some knowledge in order to pronounce as well as understand.

Grammar

While both texts are lists of a kind, Menu A presents nouns with occasional modification: for example, 'full b/fast', 'ham shank', 'mushy peas', 'Bakewell tart', 'various snacks', 'sausage muffin', 'bacon barm'. In contrast, Menu B presents nouns or noun phrases which are heavily modified, with complex sets of dependencies: for example 'peeled prawns' is qualified by 'bound in a tomato enhanced mayonnaise', which is in turn qualified by 'with diced pineapple and walnuts'; the whole of this structure is then qualified by 'nestled on a meli-melo of lettuce', which is in turn qualified by 'served in a glass'. The effect is of layers of structure where the relationships between the parts of the utterance have to be unravelled; this effect is repeated in each description. The grammar is a linguistic simulation of the food it describes.

One or two aspects of the grammar of Menu B are deviant: for example, 'abound with', 'sprinkled in'. By the time the reader reaches the possibility of being 'caressed in cabbage', there is the distinct feeling that the writer has been overcome by the excesses of his/her own verbiage.

Discourse

The functions of the two texts are clearly different. Menu A offers information, while Menu B is more of a persuasive text resembling an advertisement. Menu A constructs an audience which is a known clientele who expect straight-forward food with few trimmings; Menu B offers food which is dressed up via a text which simulates that elaboration. The audience constructed by Menu B is passing trade rather than regular patrons; such patrons may not actually be sophisticated, but the text suggests that they like to think they are – receptive to and impressed by the high-status connotations of French cuisine, rather than Anglo-Saxon cookery.

Satellite texts

The following satellite texts look at how the ideas in this unit can be applied to particular topics and genres:

The Language of Advertising

The Language of Comics

The Language of Magazines

The Language of Newspapers

The Language of Science

The Language of Sport

The Language of Television

The Language of War

The Language of Work

Unit six

Text and context

Spoken discourse

Aims of this unit

The main aim of this unit is to demonstrate that, just as written discourse has rules which govern its form and help convey meaning, so too does spoken discourse.

These rules have one major difference, however, from the rules which govern written texts, and that is that we are largely unaware of them. In fact in two-way conversations we are unconsciously taking part in a script which hasn't been written yet. As we improvise our way to sharing an experience, explaining ourselves, getting information, telling a joke or even spreading gossip we are negotiating time with our respondent in which to speak, knowing when we have a signal to take a turn in speaking and supporting the other speaker during their turn.

Spoken discourse exists within a social context, and this unit aims to use everyday **speech events** as a starting point from which to recognise that while we may not speak in words, sentences and paragraphs, we do have rules to follow, though they can be broken just as the rules of syntax can be. It's important to realise that spoken discourse should not be judged using the rules of written English: terms such as 'word', 'sentence' and 'paragraph' above, all come from the study of writing. The written form is not an appropriate medium for oral language but, of course, in order to properly analyse speech we need to see it on paper (see Unit 2).

Having signposted some of the features of speech events, this unit will then explore the features of dialogue, go on to consider one-way discourse such as speeches and storytelling, and will conclude with an examination of instant text messaging, a form of speech-as-writing.

Speech events

Imagine how the conversation might go as you take your leave of someone after having had a meal at their house. You might signal your intention of leaving by some line such as 'I must be going', you might express gratitude for the meal, you might say thank you, you might praise the excellence of the food, you might suggest a return visit to your place, the conversation might drift back to an earlier topic or even start a completely new one, you might say thank you again, and then you embark on the 'goodbyes' and 'goodnights' before finally going. In such a situation or **speech event** as this, English speakers will be unconsciously following rules whose purpose is to express thanks, reinforce relationships, leave on good terms and allow a suitable length of time between first suggesting you must go and actually going. Saying you must go and then immediately fleeing the house would be considered inappropriate and rude – certainly in British culture. Conversation exists within a social context and this context determines the shape of the discourse.

However, conversation is not always clear-cut, and sometimes a partial breakdown in communication occurs because intention is misunderstood. What the speaker intends but what the listener hears has informed much of Deborah Tannen's work on gender and conversation (1992). She cites, for example, the case of the woman who had just undergone surgery to have a lump removed from her breast. She tells her female friends that she found it upsetting to have been cut into, and that the operation had left a scar and changed the shape of her breast. Her friends replied: 'I know. It's as if your body has been violated.' But when she told her husband, he replied: 'You can have plastic surgery to cover up the scar and restore the shape of your breast.'

She felt comforted by her friends' comments, but upset by what her husband said. Her friends gave her *understanding* but her husband reacted to her complaint by giving *advice*. His intention was to offer help, but what his wife heard was him telling her to undergo even more surgery.

Intention lies behind a range of specific utterances called **speech acts**. When someone says, for example:

I apologise
I promise
I do (at a wedding)

they are doing something *beyond* what's being said. By saying 'I apologise', for instance, they have performed an apology; there has been a change in the state of things, an act has been carried out.

Speech acts are particularly prevalent and important in the language associated with ritual and ceremony. Here speech acts may contribute to the accepted rules or code of conduct or order that a ceremony has to follow; they often also have legal status. Saying 'I *do*' at the appropriate moment in a wedding ceremony – assuming you meet all the other criteria, being the bride or groom, for example; the choir boy or organist shouting out 'I do!' doesn't count – will get you married in the eyes of the law. The minister also confers legal status when they announce 'I *name* this child . . .'; the judge when they declare 'I *sentence* you to two years' imprisonment'.

Saying, then, is doing and doing is performing. Speech acts are involved in lots of everyday conversation but, of course, not every form of 'I + verb' is a speech act. Take these examples:

I apologise
I promise
I do take
I want.

The first three examples are speech acts but the fourth is not. A way to check this is to put the word ' hereby' between 'I' and the verb and see if it makes sense. If it does then we can consider the form as a speech act. So:

I hereby apologise
I hereby promise
I hereby do take

make sense but

I hereby want

doesn't.

Several attempts have been made to classify the thousands of possible speech acts in everyday occurrence. Perhaps the most useful has been made by Searle (1969) who has suggested five groups:

- *Representatives*: the speaker is committed, in varying degrees, to the truth of a proposition, e.g. 'affirm', 'believe', 'conclude', 'report'.
- *Directives*: the speaker tries to get the hearer to do something, e.g. 'ask', 'challenge', 'command', 'request'.
- *Commissives*: the speaker is committed, in varying degrees, to a certain course of action, e.g. 'bet', 'guarantee', 'pledge', 'promise', 'swear'.
- *Expressives*: the speaker expresses an attitude about a state of affairs, e.g. 'apologise', 'deplore', 'thank', 'welcome'.
- *Declarations*: the speaker alters the status quo by making the utterance, e.g. 'I resign', 'you're offside', 'I name this child', 'you're nicked', 'you're busted punk'.

Look at the following examples: which group does each belong to?

insist
congratulate
I now pronounce you husband and wife
vow
deny

- 'Waiter, I *insist* on seeing the manager' is an example of a directive.
- 'I'd like to *congratulate* everyone involved in making the show such a success' is an expressive.
- 'I now *pronounce* you husband and wife' is a declarative.
- 'I *vow* to obey the rules of this association' is a commissive.
- 'I *deny* all knowledge of the facts' is a representative.

In reality, in everyday discourse, many speech acts do not directly address the listener. For many reasons – because we might be obeying the **politeness principle**, for example, and don't wish to impose – we may ask for something to be done *indirectly*. 'Can you pass the salt?' for instance, is not really a question but a directive; an answer of 'Yes' without any attempt to actually *pass* it would seem totally inappropriate. Forms, then, such as 'Can you pass the salt?' in preference to the more direct 'Pass the salt' are known as **indirect speech acts.** It's possible, of course, to phrase speech acts in various ways – you can, for instance apologise *without* actually using the term 'apologise', as in 'OK I was wrong'; have a bet with someone by saying 'You're on'. Directives can be especially interesting in the gradient they take from direct order to humble question. Imagine that you've got a fly in your soup in a restaurant; a gradient might go something like this:

1 Waiter, get the manager immediately
2 Waiter, I insist on seeing the manager.
3 Waiter, I want to see the manager.
4 Waiter, I'd like to see the manager, please.
5 Waiter, if it's not too much trouble I'd like to see the manager.
6 Waiter, I don't suppose I could see the manager, could I?

Activity

Following the example of the gradient above, try a similar gradient from direct to indirect speech act for the following:

1 *Asking* someone out on a date
2 *Requesting* someone to stop talking in the cinema.

Note that there is no commentary on this activity.

Conversation

When analysing real face-to-face conversations – particularly informal conversations – it becomes clear that the grammatical terminology applied to written English language is inappropriate. For example, the basic unit of clause or sentence with its attendant punctuation is very much a written form and not very helpful in analysing transcriptions of spoken English language. It seems better to refer to spoken turns as utterances. Utterances of course can be of any length but in informal conversation might only consist of one word or even **minimal responses** such as a 'hmm'. Spoken language has its own grammar, its own terminology to describe the way it works.

In most conversations there is very much an unplanned element – and this can apply to both face-to-face conversation, phone conversation and media conversation. Of course participants might have an idea of what they want to say but we react to others' utterances and also our language might well reflect our wish to interact socially. As social beings we negotiate speaking space – taking the floor as it were – and are normally sensitive to the right of others to have their turn in speaking. We are also thinking on our feet and in doing so this accounts for **non-fluency features** such as pauses, fillers and repetition.

In order to analyse a conversation it has to be transcribed and this transcript often looks on the page – and sounds when read out like a play script – quite chaotic.

Look at this conversation between three students on an adventure holiday in Costa Rica (see Text 6:1). They are arriving at a hotel which is unexpectedly luxurious.

The transcription follows punctuation conventions which seem more appropriate than 'written' punctuation conventions. There are no hard and fast rules about how you transcribe talk, and sometimes your transcription will want to focus on certain aspects, but it is obviously important that you provide an accurate key to explain how you have transcribed the talk, and what your symbols mean.

KEY: for all the examples of spoken data presented in this unit.

- The + sign indicates an interrupted turn which continues at the next + sign.
- The = sign indicates an utterance which is cut short.
- A full stop in brackets indicates a 'normal' pause of about half a second; (1), (2), (3) etc. indicate pauses of one second, two seconds and three seconds respectively.
- Upper case letters are used for proper nouns but also to indicate emphasis.
- Square brackets are used to indicate non-verbal sounds such as laughter or inaudible speech.
- Apostrophes are still used.
- Non-standard spellings are used to suggest pronunciation of some common forms, for example 'cos', 'gotta'.

Text 6:1

Three students: Em, Cam, Hat.

Em: I haven't written in my Dan journal yet but I said that I put it in my bag=
Cam: your Dan journal
Em: Dan journal (.) yeah it's+
Cam: aw
Em: +a journal=
Cam: that's lovely
Hat: yeah
Em: cos he's got one too (.) we went shopping together in Wilkos (.) he's got a green one the same and I've got a orange+
Cam: aw that's lovely
Em: +and we even bought pens for writing but I lost the pen
Cam: [laughs]
Hat: ah
Em: oh+
Cam: this is oh=
Em: + brilliant
Cam: I can't believe our luck
Hat: we thought that=
Cam: I know sorry we thought that it would just be what it said in the in the er erm um oh gosh in the erm in the leaflet about what (.) not the leaflet but you know (.) but this has gotta be something at least four star
Hat: oh yeah
Cam: four star hotel
Em: it's really posh
Cam: it costs 150 dollars per night
Hat: Jesus
Em: that's like over 100 quid
Cam: it is per night
Hat: per night yeah
Em: and we're getting it for what
Cam: but I dunno yeah but they're doing this out of the goodness of their heart
Hat: I know
Cam: hearts for purely educational purposes.

Non-fluency features

This text particularly highlights elements of **non-fluency features** which show the participants thinking on their feet and giving them time to decide what to say. There are pauses and these can be *unfilled* or *filled.* Unfilled pauses are silences while filled pauses are vocalisations such as 'er', 'erm', 'um' or sometimes forms such as 'like', 'you know'. Cam uses several filled pauses as she tries to articulate her feelings about the hotel they are arriving at:

> Cam: I know sorry we thought that it would just be what it said in the in the *er erm um oh gosh in the erm* in the leaflet about what (.) not the leaflet but *you know* (.) but this has gotta be something at least four star

Repetition is also present in Cam's utterance as she buys time for thought; if this occurs at the beginning of a new topic of conversation it may also be referred to as a false start. A variation on repetition is when speakers feel the need to go back and qualify what they have just said. This is referred to as **rephrasing**. Cam begins to qualify her mention of the leaflet but leaves it hanging with 'you know'.

Other features present include **response tokens**, which are supportive comments from participants, acting as feedback on what has been said and reflecting the social nature of conversation. They help, too, to make exchanges interactive. They can take the form of **minimal responses** such as 'mm', 'yeah' or perhaps even just supportive laughter. Or responses can be particularly positive, for example, forms such as 'fine', 'great', 'lovely', 'brilliant', 'cool'.

Here there are many examples of both minimal and positive responses. Repetition across the speakers also marks out strong response, for example:

> Cam: it is per night
> Hat: per night yeah.

There is also another interesting use of repetition as a mark of supportive response when Cam softens her interruption of Hat by re-using her words:

> Hat: we thought that=
> Cam: I know sorry we thought that.

This transcription also reflects the non-standard forms of English that can be typical of informal spoken language:

> 'I've got a orange'.

STRUCTURE IN CONVERSATION

The context in which a conversation takes place, the participants involved and the purpose of the conversation will all have effects on the spoken language features. The talk of the students in Text 6:1 demonstrates a shared experience of informal and supportive chat. Sometimes, however, the demands of the context or the demands of the participants will produce a more obviously structured conversation. Text 6:1 had three participants who seemed fairly relaxed about who was holding the floor but turns between participants in some contexts can be quite clearly defined – especially if involving just two people. In this next conversation the turn-taking between the two speakers is more controlled and it features forms such as 'anyway', 'right', 'so' which are called **discourse markers** when they help to organise speech. Often they will come at the start of a new topic.

Activity

Read the text from part of a driving lesson shown in Text 6:2. Pete is the instructor, Sara the pupil.

- How do the spoken language features compare with Text 6:1?
- Comment on the relationship of the two as illustrated by their turn-taking.
- Try to comment, also, on Pete's use of 'okay'.

There is a commentary on this activity at the end of the unit.

Text 6:2

```
Pete: okay look what's coming (.) can we go (.) yes (.) read what's in
      front of you such as what you're heading into (.) there's a car at
      the crossing isn't there (.) yeah
Sara: why isn't the car going
Pete: because the woman hadn't left the crossing (.) yeah (.) DO NOT GO
      until the pedestrian has crossed (3) okay slow down (2) it's all
      about planning ahead Sara (.) observations (5) that Sara would be
      called a hazard (2) okay it's blatantly obvious the lights are on
      red so what
      you going to do about it you're not going to fly through them are
      you (.) yeah (.) look out for pedestrians at all times (5)
```

```
Sara: I'm doing that thing with the handbrake again
Pete: yeah you are I've noticed [laughter] you're pressing the button in
      too soon before lifting it (.) press and release (5) remember when
      we did this last week (10) done any of the hazard perceptions yet
Sara: no
Pete: no (2) why am I not surprised [laughter] what they've done is place
      a camera in the dashboard if you're driving (.) it's lots of video
      clips and you have to point out what's the hazard (.) okay like
      this black car in front which might edge forwards (5) for example
      if a ball comes flying into the road what do you think will follow
      it
Sara: erm a kid
Pete: yes a kid (.) it's things like that okay
```

PATTERNS IN CONVERSATION

Another aspect of structure in conversation concerns sequencing: that is, how one utterance leads to the next and how certain utterances can only occur in a particular order. This is termed **adjacency** and in a two-sequence extract termed **adjacency pairs**. For example, a question expects an answer, a greeting another greeting, a summons may be responded to by an expression of compliance, as follows:

> Sara: why isn't the car going
> Pete: because the woman hadn't left the crossing

and

> Laurence: hi how are you
> Kath: fine thanks

and

> Dad: come on we're going to be late
> Ben: I'll be two minutes.

These patterns of structure often underpin conversational routine although on the surface they may not look neatly cut and dried. For example, consider the following sequence:

Teacher: so what grade did you get
Student: well I thought I really messed up
Teacher: yeah you said it was a hard paper
Student: and I didn't get to finish the last question
Teacher: I know
Student: everyone found it hard
Teacher: yeah
Student: but I got a grade A.

This exchange starts and ends with a question-answer adjacency pair and in between other relevant dialogue takes place. This sequence framed by the question-answer adjacency pair is termed an **insertion sequence**. If, on the other hand, the extra dialogue had little relevance to the framing adjacency pair then it could be termed a **side sequence**. However, even this sequence of utterances is fairly neat; in reality a transcription of a conversation may look quite chaotic but invariably patterns are present and 'rules' are being followed.

Two other common patterns in conversation are **headers** and **tails**. Headers is when what is considered the most significant element is fronted or placed first in an utterance. For example:

Bangkok it's an amazing place
The Beatles they're still my all-time favourite group
The new airport is it open yet

Compare these examples with written versions, for example: Bangkok is an amazing place. In the spoken versions the subject of the utterance is given pre-eminence and has a pronoun referring back to it:

Bangkok (subject) it's (pronoun and verb) an amazing place

Tails reverse the structure of headers but have much the same function, that is to draw particular attention to the subject. Commonly the utterance starts with a pronoun and then this is clarified at the tail or end. For example:

It's an amazing place *Bangkok*
She's my favourite singer *Madonna*
Has she known him long your *friend*

So here we have:

She's (pronoun and verb) my favourite singer Madonna (subject)

These forms of headers and tails are rare in written English, unless authors are trying to represent everyday talk, but entirely acceptable, common and natural in informal spoken English.

PHONE CONVERSATIONS

Adjacency sequencing can sometimes be more clearly identified in the context of phone conversations rather than face-to-face discourse. Schegloff (1986), a researcher working within the tradition of conversation analysis proposed the following routine as that which characterises land line telephone openings in English speaking cultures:

summons–answer

identification–recognition

greeting–greeting

initial enquiries

before first topic introduction.

Explained more fully these are:

- *summons–answer*: phone ring/hello – the ring of the telephone is the summons, and when the called person picks up the receiver and says hello, this counts as the answer.
- *identification–recognition*: in English-speaking cultures, the called person is the first to speak. The fact that they do so allows their voice to be recognised by the caller, who then says, for example, 'Hello Keith?'/'Yeah'.
- *greeting–greeting*: both speakers then exchange greetings, such as 'Hello', 'Hi', 'Good morning', etc. Speakers don't have to exchange exactly the same words, of course.
- *initial enquiries*: these are about participants' health, general state of things, etc. This is the 'how are you?' sequence. For example: 'How are you?/I'm alright how are you?'

Telephone openings are interactionally compact and brief. They also have a perfunctory character, or in other words, participants go through these routines in an automated manner. After these routines a position is established that Schegloff refers to as the 'first topic'. According to Schegloff after identification and recognition are achieved and a set of 'how are yous' are exchanged, the caller uses the 'anchor position' to introduce the 'first topic' or the reason for the call. However, this is not the only possible position for the introduction of the first topic. In fact there are possibilities for the caller and the answerer to pre-empt the introduction of the first topic. Therefore, Schegloff noted, routine openings need to be understood as 'achievements' going through possibilities for pre-emptive first topic, rather than a 'mechanical or automated playing out of pre-scripted routines'.

Interestingly studies in land line telephone openings from other cultures show different routines at work. For example, telephone openings in Iran are very much concerned with enquiries about the families of the participants before first topic introduction. German speakers, unless they have not spoken for some time, often omit the 'how are you?' sequence; or, rather, the first 'how are you?' elicits the introduction of the first topic. For Swedish speakers the identification-recognition sequence is very important and participants self-identify and then give their phone number at the start of their conversation.

Activity

Read through the telephone opening below which is between a student and their tutor. The student has phoned the tutor to get some help with an assignment. The tutor has just returned from America.

- Which parts of Schegloff's model can you identify, and how do they work?

There is a commentary on this activity at the end of the unit.

Text 6:3

The tutor is Steve; the student is Sam (Phone rings; tutor picks up the handset)

Tutor: hello
Student: hi Steve (.) it's Sam
Tutor: hello Sam (.) hi
Student: how are you
Tutor: I'm alright thanks
Student: have you got over jetlag yet

```
Tutor:     um (.) I'm getting there (.) I still feel a bit
           strange (.) but I'll probably be alright in a
           couple of days
Student:   yeah
Tutor:     it's coming back this way (.) it seems not to
           affect me going the other way
Student:   it's (.) that's the thing (.) I can't think of the
           reason why because my brain's so cabbage I can't
           think (.) but you lose time and it does affect you
           coming this way
Tutor:     mm (.) anyway what can I do for you Sam
```

Other aspects of sequencing in conversation that have been researched are **pre-closings** and **closings**, particularly in telephone discourse. Pre-closings are those routines where your interlocutor is warned that you are about to leave. This was referred to briefly right at the beginning of this unit (see p. 198), where protocols for leaving someone's house were discussed. Pre-closings need to preserve the **positive face** needs of your interlocutor (their need to feel valued), yet satisfy your own **negative face** needs (your right not to be imposed on by someone else). All in all, it's a complicated business, made more complex by the fact that different cultural groups have different rules. Closings are the final 'signing-off' routines, where farewells are exchanged.

Activity

Read Text 6:4, the end of a phone conversation between a son and his father. Note the pre-closing routine. Discourse markers can occur as clusters, for example 'so anyway', 'anyway alright' and in phone conversations can particularly initiate pre-closings and closings.

What other features can you find?

Note that there is no commentary on this activity.

Text 6:4

```
Ben:  so anyway the guy I'm staying at er in this b and b it's a lovely
      Irish guy called James Joyce
Dad:  really [ laughs]
Ben:  he keeps calling me 'ah Ben it's James Joyce here+
Dad:  James Joyce [ laughs]
Ben:  +just confirming the dates' (.) he's trying to give me directions
      but I'm not going till September after all this so=
Dad:  alright
Ben:  so anyway I'd better go Dad (.) so I speak to you speak to you
      before the match on Sunday
Dad:  okay (.) what time's the kick off do you know
Ben:  four o'clock (.) you're gonna have to watch it in the pub
Dad:  I know I will do
Ben:  you gonna do that are you
Dad:  yeah
Ben:  you brave enough
Dad:  yeah
Ben:  okay
Dad:  at least we're not playing Charlton
Ben:  yeah and won't have to watch it with those really annoying people
Dad:  so erm
Ben:  anyway alright I'll speak to you later (.) bye
Dad:  take care
Ben:  bye
```

The context in which conversation takes place, the nature or relationship of the participants and the purpose of the conversation will all have an effect on the spoken language features. As seen above, the students' language in Text 6:1 is clearly defined by its non-fluency features and many response tokens; the driving instructor talk in Text 6:2, on the other hand, with its sharper focus and purpose of teaching has a much more structured form. The nature of a teacher-pupil interaction means that discourse markers are clearly evident there.

CONVERSATION IN THE MEDIA

Media programmes which feature discussion or questions have the additional factor of another audience. The nature of the audience and the nature or purpose of the programme will obviously affect the language use and structure. Most programmes will range from a main purpose to entertain to a purpose of informing. Entertain programmes will vary in the amount of factual content; some will almost seem content-less and more like general chat or gossip.

Activity

Read the text from the Scott Mills show aired on Radio 1 which includes a phone-in, shown in Text 6:5. What distinctive features of spoken discourse do you find in this transcript?

Key: A = Scott Mills, main presenter
B = support presenter
C = caller Carrie

Text 6:5

A: right I'm going through a stage of losing everything at the moment
B: right
A: to Norwich er pleasuring some students on Saturday night
B: yeah
A: and yeah well
B: all good
A: yeah brilliant gig+
B: yeah yeah lots of white wine
A: +but no phone now (.) hello Radio One (.) yes hello (.) who's that please
C: hello (.) hi it's Carrie
A: and how can I help you Carrie (.) how are you
C: er I just wondered (.) I was listening to Jo Whiley earlier and she said you upset a taxi driver on Saturday night and I was just wondering was it because you were sick in his cab
A: no (.) I I (.) I've never thrown up in the back of a taxi down the side I have but no+
=B: [laughter] nice nice

```
A:  +basically I lost my phone in the back of the cab on my way back from
    this gig in Norwich right (.) came into Radio One today (.) Jo Whiley
    Moyles and you have all been contacted by the taxi driver
B:  yesterday afternoon I had a call yeah
A:  now I'm waiting for the phone to come back and he says he's sent it
    in and I keep ringing it and it's turned off now but am just thinking
    (1) has he phoned every slightly famous person in my phone book
B:  [laughter] who else is there
C:  [laughter]
A:  Davina McCall might have got a call
B:  Tickle
A:  John Tickle (.) Alistair Griffin might have got a call (.) David
    Sneddon erm (1) well Dermot O'Leary
B:  ooh you do have some famous people
A:  well there's two that I mentioned
B:  Dermot and Davina
A:  yeah (.) but I would um like to say thank you very much to the taxi
    driver cos I thought I had completely lost it (.) but then (.) um er
    at least I know where it is now (.) thanks for phoning everyone in
    the phonebook too cheers (1) how embarrassing
```

Commentary

Although there are three possible participants here this is clearly presenter A's show. He has the most utterances and uses discourse markers to initiate new topics of conversation. Presenter B's role is largely supportive and his language consists mostly of response tokens. The caller's role seems to be to feed Scott Mills a line about upsetting a taxi driver so that he can mention the story of his lost mobile phone. Carrie joins presenter B in supportive minimal response with laughter.

There are elements of phatic conversation, largely social in its purpose and helping to smooth the wheels of communication, for example 'hello', 'how are you'. While still having some kind of agenda – that is to entertain and to maintain references to known people, media celebrities – the programme mimics real informal conversation. As well as pauses, both unfilled and filled, and repetition

A: no (.) I I (.) I've never thrown up in the back of a taxi there is also evidence of ellipsis. Ellipsis is the omission of words considered unnecessary for effective communication. For example 'good day?' meaning 'have you had a good day?' Examples from the radio text include:

> pleasuring some students on Saturday night
> (understood) I was pleasuring some students on Saturday night

and

> but am just thinking
> (understood) but I am just thinking.

Although ellipsis is defined as missing elements, in reality nothing is missing as elliptical utterances contain enough for effective communication.

THE SOCIAL SIDE OF CONVERSATION

Maxims

One area of study that has contributed to our understanding of the assumptions underlying conversation came originally from the discipline of logic and philosophy. This is speech act theory, referred to earlier. An academic figure associated with this school was H.P. Grice, who in 1975 formulated a number of maxims by which he claimed speakers operate in a general sense. Grice posited that conversation was essentially a co-operative enterprise where speakers follow certain unspoken rules that are never spelt out but come to be understood and used as part of the process of language acquisition and early socialisation. He called this the **co-operative principle**, and the associated maxims are as follows:

1 the maxim of *quality*: speakers try to tell the truth

2 the maxim of *quantity*: speakers give the right amount of information

3 the maxim of *relevance*: speakers try to stick to the point

4 the maxim of *manner*: speakers try to present their material in an orderly fashion.

Robin Lakoff (1975) added three further maxims which she termed the politeness principle:

1 Don't impose
2 Give options
3 Make your receiver feel good.

These scholars were not suggesting that we follow the rules above in any simple way; in fact, just as important in their concept of interaction is the idea that we break the rules as well as keep them. Breaking rules, however, proves that rules exist.

Face theory

Research has also been done on another social aspect of conversation which has been termed **face** theory. As well as the maxims detailed above participants are often conscious of how their utterances or messages may be received. Positive face is a term applied to utterances which are specifically designed to give a positive spin to language, to make receivers feel good. Negative face is a term applied to softening an order or an unpleasant comment. This is very similar to Lakoff's maxims.

Activity

Below are some expressions that are often heard in conversations. How does each of the expressions show participants' awareness of some of the rules above? Can you add any further expressions like this to the list?

To cut a long story short

I know you're not going to believe this, but . . .

I'll spare you all the grisly details

Correct me if I'm wrong, but . . .

I know I'm going round the houses here, but . . .

What I forgot to say before was that . . .

I'm not saying we have to discuss this right now, but . . .

Note that there is no commentary on this activity.

Breaking the rules, according to Grice, is a marked activity: it tells us that we need to look for reasons why someone has deviated from what is expected.

Grice calls the process of inference that results from rule-breaking behaviour **conversational implicature**. This means that on the surface we may seem to be breaking or flouting the rules but the sub text in fact is not. For example take this exchange:

A: I'm feeling hungry
B: there's a pub nearby.

On the surface B's response does not seem relevant to A's statement but of course the implication of what B is saying is quite clear: you can get food in the pub which is nearby. This reflects our skill at communication and also our application of social skills.

There can also be conflict between these maxims. For example take this exchange:

Friend A: do you like my new hair style
Friend B: yes it really suits you.

Imagine in fact that friend B doesn't actually like their friend's new hair style and doesn't think it really suits them but doesn't want to hurt their feelings: so they choose to break the maxim of quality while adhering to the principle of making their friend feel good. This white lie confirms the social nature of conversation.

Response tokens have been noted as being features which support conversation and help create interactive exchanges. Like discourse markers they can also appear in clusters – particularly pairs – to reinforce positive response. For example:

A: you can have the car over August
B: great cool
A: just don't crash it.

Tags are another feature which help to create interactive exchanges. In particular in spoken English question tags help to engage the listener and also invite agreement with what is being said. Question tags typically come at the end of an utterance. For example:

She missed her flight *didn't she*
It's a mess *isn't it*

but do not *have* to:

> you're right *aren't you* what you said about the sky train
> that's crazy *isn't it* from an experienced referee.

There are also some fixed tags which do not vary in form, such as 'yeah', 'okay', 'right' and they function as checking devices. For example:

> Pete: if a ball comes flying into the road what do you think will follow it
> Sara: erm a kid
> Pete: yes a kid (.) it's things like that *okay*.

Hedge(s) is a term given to lexis which serves to make utterances less blunt. As such they are also signs of speakers being aware of how they might come across in conversation and how conscious they are in their dealings with others. Expressions which hedge are 'you know', 'I think', 'I guess', 'like', 'kind of'. For example:

> *I think* the train is late

and

> that film was *kind of* weird.

Speakers often do not wish to appear too assertive and this is part of the social function of language. Hedges sometimes encourage listeners to share their feelings; 'you know' and 'I mean' often do this. In this utterance a football commentator is hedging, being less assertive, and also – by doing so – encouraging a sharing of opinion:

> *For me* the one-striker-up-front system isn't working and he's got to change it around second half.

Vague language also softens the assertiveness of speakers' language. Common forms are: 'things', 'stuff', 'and things', 'and stuff', 'or something', 'like', 'whatever', 'kind of'. For example:

> it's more a *kind of* art gallery full of pictures *and things*.

Vague language often assumes common ground and understanding between the participants and can be a sign of sensitively monitored language. For example in the following exchange it would be tiresome to list every possible option:

> Yes but I don't like Thai food
> Okay you can have chips *or something*.

The same form of words can have slightly different functions depending on the context and how they are being used. For example: 'like' is a particularly common word – and can function as hedge, vague language or filled pause. Look at the following utterance:

> Between then and *like* nineteen eighty four I just spent the whole time *I mean* for that whole *sort of* twelve year period *or whatever* I was just working with *lots and lots and lots* of different people.

It is important to try and establish the underlying intention, the subtext to see the intention and purpose of the chosen words. There is often much overlap, however, between function. So in the example above the word 'like' functions as both hedging and vague language. Similarly 'I mean' functions as a hedge but also serves to initiate a rephrasing of the previous few words.

Activity

Text 6:6 is an extract from the TV programme 'Sunday AM'. The interviewer is Andrew Marr; the interviewee Tony Blair. Andrew Marr's opening question here refers to the leader of the Conservative party David Cameron.

- As well as analysing the spoken features present also consider what roles these two participants play and how they try to assert themselves.

Note that there is no commentary on this activity.

Text 6:6

Marr: has he said (.) anything over the last couple of weeks that you could possibly disagree with

Blair: yeah (2) well I do disagree with two (.) distinctive policy positions he's taken (.) one is on (.) saying that schools can bring back academic selection (.) which I think is damaging and dangerous=

Marr: we'll come on to that later

Blair: yes but that's important though because it is an indication of instinct as well as policy (2) and I (.) er I think (.) I'm sure he will change his position but to say he will not join in with other conservative parties in Europe (.) I think is a big (.) big mistake

Marr: slightly (.) I mean that's a relatively minor thing I mean when it comes to+

Blair: er well yeah except if you're in the government then you'd find it a big problem but=

Marr: +immigration (.) getting together with Bob Geldof for poverty (.) erm taking the environment seriously (.) erm when it comes to the NHS saying that he's absolutely pro NHS (2) changing the policy (.) these are all things which make him (.) many people absolutely close to the centre ground people don't need to feel frightened to vote Tory

Blair: well as I was saying if someone comes up to you in politics and says I agree with you (.) er (.) to turn around and say well I'm sorry that's unacceptable [laughs] is a bit stupid

Marr: but you would (.) you would accept (.) you don't buy any of the argument he's some kind of extremist (.) you accept the sincerity of what he's doing

Blair: well I think you've got to test the sincerity (.) that's all I'm saying (.) I put a question mark (.) look (2) what I think in politics is (.) if you end up when someone is obviously trying to re-position their political party (.) and junk a whole load of their old policy (.) if you end up sort of (.) saying this man is the most dangerous thing that has happened to the country (.) you just make yourself look ridiculous

Speeches

Scripted speech, like the oral narrative, is normally 'one way', that is once the speaker has the floor they continues until the end of the speech is reached and the normal rules of co-operation in conversation don't apply or, at least, don't operate in the same way. Of course this is not to say that speakers aren't interrupted, supported or even heckled; indeed in some contexts audience response is expected or even encouraged. The stand-up comic may thrive on feedback or incorporate it into their routine; the Prime Minister needs to deal with it at Question Time in Parliament. That notwithstanding, the scripted speech is composed before delivery and skilful speakers, or their speech writers, use certain rhetorical structures to help them in what is normally the prime aim of a speech and that is to convey a message and convince the audience of a point of view.

Rhetoric, from the Greek meaning orator or teacher, is the art or technique of persuasion, usually through the use of language and this can be in the written or spoken form. In ancient times rhetoric was associated with persuasion in public and political settings – court rooms, assemblies – and this is still the case today, though the medium may have changed to that of television, radio and even podcasting. Its connotations have also changed so that rhetoric can be viewed pejoratively as language designed to persuade at the expense, perhaps, of truth. Sometimes political speeches 'spin' information in order to present a certain stance.

The quotability of a speech can be very important, and speakers may make great efforts to construct what we now term as 'soundbites', short, pithy, sometimes witty chunks of language which catch the ear and the imagination of the media and, through them, the attention and memory of the public. Rhetorical devices take many forms. Alliteration can be an effective device, for example:

> Let us go forth to lead the land we love.
>
> (John F. Kennedy's inaugural speech)

Metaphor, too, can be effective, for example:

> From Stettin in the Baltic to Trieste in the Adriatic, an iron curtain has descended across the continent.
>
> (Winston Churchill, 1946)

The careful and frequent use of pronouns is a common device in helping to make connections between speaker and audience. Here is the opening of Queen Elizabeth's very first Christmas speech to millions of British and Commonwealth listeners in 1952:

> Each Christmas, at this time, my beloved father broadcast a message to his people in all parts of the world. Today I am doing this to you, who are now my people. As he used to do, I am speaking to you from my own home, where I am spending Christmas with my family.'

The Queen stresses her own situation, 'I am doing . . . I am speaking . . . I am spending', but reaches out to her audience, 'to you . . . my people . . . to you'.

Here is a quite different use of pronouns. This is from the eve-of battle speech given by Tim Collins, Commanding Officer, to his British troops in Iraq, 2003:

> We will not fly our flags in their country. We are entering Iraq to free a people and the only flag which will be flown in that ancient land is their own. Show respect for them.

The pronoun use here emphasises the two groups of people involved – the troops and the Iraqi populace – and Collins is keen to stress the purpose of the British and the rights of Iraqis.

In adversarial politics, where speakers might be scoring points off each other, pronouns can be used for other effects. In particular, rousing speeches from political party leaders will use pronouns to make favourable mentions of their own party – 'us' – while at the same time making unfavourable mentions of the other parties – 'them'.

Other rhetorical devices concern patterns in structures and repetition. **Contrasting pairs** are effective, for example:

> We go to liberate not to conquer
>
> (Tim Collins 2003)

Here the second half of the utterance neatly balances the first half – 'to liberate . . . to conquer'.

Lists of three are also popular:

> . . . priorities of the Government in 1987 will be education, education, education
>
> (Tony Blair)

and

> Today, our fellow citizens, our way of life, our very freedom came under attack
>
> George Bush address to the nation after the World Trade Center attack 2001

Activity

Read the following excerpts from speeches, identify the structures being used, and comment on the way the utterances work:

1 Never in the field of human conflict has so much been owed by so many to so few. (Winston Churchill, 1940, praising the Battle of Britain fighter pilots)

2 Ask not what your country can do for you. Ask what you can do for your country. (John F.Kennedy's inaugural address as US President, 1961)

3 Two thousand years ago the proudest boast was 'civis Romanus sum'. Today, in the world of freedom, the proudest boast is 'Ich bin ein Berliner'. (Speech made by John F. Kennedy in West Berlin, 1963)

4 I have a dream that one day my four little children will not be judged by the colour of their skin but by the content of their character. (Martin Luther King's 'I have a dream' speech, Lincoln Memorial, 1963)

5 Government of the people by the people for the people. (Abraham Lincoln's Gettysburg address, 1863)

Note that there is no commentary on this activity.

Activity

Text 6:7 is an extract from the London 2012 Olympic bid presentation to the International Olympic Committee. Here athlete and gold medal winner Denise Lewis – one of several speakers in the London bid team – offers her support.

- How is language being used here in order to convey a persuasive message?
- Pay particular attention to the structures you have just been studying, including the use of pronouns.

There is a commentary on this activity at the end of the unit.

Text 6:7

Mr President, Members of the IOC

I'm Denise Lewis, Olympic Heptathlon champion from the Sydney Games.

I have the pleasure of speaking on behalf of the London Athletes Commission.

I was eight when I was inspired by the Moscow Games.

I dreamt of emulating the athletes I watched. And my dreams came true when I competed in Atlanta, in Sydney and in Athens.

Like every Olympian, I have unforgettable Olympic memories.

And we in London are determined every athlete will leave our city with friendships and memories which last forever.

Our Athletes Commission had to answer one fundamental question: how do you give athletes the best possible Olympic experience?

We said: give us the best Village in the most convenient location. Everything else follows.

Our Village is within walking distance of nine venues. In London, athletes will compete, not commute.

The Village is inside the Park to guarantee the athletes a special experience. Take it from me, it makes all the difference to be as close to the action as possible.

In fact, the whole London plan was conceived with our input. Everything athletes need was designed in from day one. Training venues. Security. And, of course, the needs of Paralympians.

These are the things athletes want.

Storytelling

SPOKEN VERSUS WRITTEN

This section will draw on two real spoken stories in order to highlight some of the common features of the oral narrative. Jonathan's story is about a car crash on the M4; Esther's is about travelling in a plane which is struck by lightning.

Activity

Text 6:8 gives the openings of Jonathan's story, one the spoken version and the other a written version.

- Which is which? (To make them appear the same on the page slashes have been used instead of conventional punctuation.)
- Having spotted which is the spoken version take a few minutes to jot down some of the ways it differs from the written one.

Text 6:8

Extract 1

sometimes I think I'm lucky to be alive / I can't help enjoying really simple things because all the time I'm telling myself that I could be dead instead / once for instance I could have died on the motorway / it was the beginning of my second term of my second year at university / I had spent Christmas with my parents / dad took me to the railway station in Kidderminster / I had to go to Birmingham and then change for Reading / as he shook my hand a yellow Ford drew up / my friend Paul was in it / he smiled roundly and said he had the day off so he'd drive me back to university / I accepted

Extract 2

right well um the whole thing happened er as a result of going back to university one day / this was when I was about nineteen in January 1983 er a friend of mine suddenly turned up er at a railway station my best friend just as I was about to get on the train / back to Reading and said I'll drive you back er I was delighted er partly as it was company and an adventure through half the country / so we started driving back and got desperately lost / we were trying to get back to Reading from just above Worcester we ended up near Bristol

Jonathan Timbers

Commentary

The first extract is written, the second spoken. You might have noted the use of words like 'um' and 'er' in the transcription of the spoken version. These are fillers. Very common in spoken discourse they act as pauses and in effect lengthen the gap between words. In spontaneous speech we are 'thinking on our feet' and the use of fillers allows us to do some forward planning on what to say next. They help to cement ideas together in conversation. Also fillers are often added to the common conjunctions 'and' and 'but'; the pause is then effectively lengthened.

The spoken version seems unnecessarily repetitive, e.g. 'a friend of mine . . . my best friend' and 'I'll drive you back . . . we started driving back', and the chronology is different.

The two extracts are reproduced in Text 6:9 in their punctuated and transcribed versions.

Text 6:9

Extract 1

Sometimes I think I'm lucky to be alive. I can't help enjoying really simple things because all the time I'm telling myself that I could be dead instead. Once, for instance, I could have died on the motorway. It was the beginning of my second term of my second year at university. I had spent Christmas with my parents. Dad took me to the railway station in Kidderminster. I had to go to Birmingham and then change for Reading. As he shook my hand a yellow Ford drew up. My friend Paul was in it. He smiled roundly and said he had the day off, so he'd drive me back to university. I accepted.

Extract 2

right well um the whole thing happened er as a result of going back to university one day (.) this was when I was about nineteen in January 1983 er a friend of mine suddenly turned up er at a railway station my best friend just as I was about to get on the train (.) back to Reading and said I'll drive you back er I was delighted er partly as it was company and an adventure through half the country (.) so we started driving back and got desperately lost (.) we were trying to get back to Reading from just above Worcester we ended up near Bristol

LABOV'S NARRATIVE CATEGORIES

A comparison of spoken and written forms of the same narrative can be very useful in highlighting some of the ways in which oral narratives work. We expect stories to have a beginning, a middle and an end. Oral stories, however, operate in a different context from that of written forms:

attention may have to be attracted from potential listeners and, once attracted, kept. William Labov (1972), in an essay entitled 'The transformation of experience in narrative syntax', posited a six-part structure for a fully-formed oral narrative, based on work he had done on collecting real narratives from New York Black English vernacular culture.

- *Abstract*: signals that a story is about to begin, gets the listener's attention, might ask for permission to tell a story, gives some indication of what the story is about.
- *Orientation*: puts the story into a context, gives the time, place, person(s) involved and situation/activity; the 'when, where, who and what?' of the story.
- *Complicating action*: the main narrative body providing the 'what happened' element of the story.
- *Resolution*: the final events, the 'what finally happened' element.
- *Evaluation*: makes the point of the story clear, suggests why it's worth being told, why it's of interest.
- *Coda*: signals that the story has finished, can also link back to the beginning or return to the present time frame.

With the exception of evaluation, the categories are listed above in the order they would be expected in a typical fully formed narrative. Of course, though, many narratives may lack one or more components or may justifiably have elements which seem to do the work of two components. For example, non-fully-formed narratives may have openings which seem to be both abstract and orientation; or, where stories have been invited by the listener or interviewer, then an abstract would seem to be irrelevant, or even silly. Evaluation can appear at any point in the story.

Activity

Now look back at each extract in Text 6:9. What is the main difference between the way they start?

There is a commentary on this activity at the end of the unit.

Activity

Now have a look at another oral narrative, Esther's story in Text 6:10, and decide whether the elements in it could be labelled according to Labov's categories.

Note that there is no separate commentary on this activity, however both Esther's and Jonathan's stories are discussed on pp. 230–2.

Text 6:10

I remember being on an aircraft (.) when I was about five (.) and I was with my parents coming back from a holiday in Greece (.) and would you believe I mean it sounds ridiculous now but the aeroplane was being hit by lightning and um there was an aircraft above and an aircraft below and we were coming back and it was a massive storm and I can't remember a lot of it (.) I was sat with my mum and my father was sat with my sister behind (.) the lights went off and the air hostesses went absolutely wild everyone was strapped in (.) the pilot explained what was going on but don't panic and there was um a lot of Muslims coming back and they were all saying their prayers and I remember a lady standing up and saying we're all gonna die we're all gonna die and this lady stood up and smacked her across the face and said if we're all gonna die we don't want to listen to you and um afterwards I mean 'cos I was really young I didn't realise (.) I realised there was panic going on in the plane and when we actually landed and the pilot came out and said you were very lucky um (.) it was frightening though very frightening (.) but it doesn't (.) I think it was because I was so young that I've never been frightened of flying (.) never I mean even when I get on an aeroplane now I'm not bothered

Esther Gosnay

The rest of Jonathan's dicing with death is given in Text 6:11 with Labov's labels. A full discussion follows.

Text 6:11

most of this is the main body of the story: the *complicating action*

on the way we managed to park for five minutes er it was a queue of traffic lights (.) and we also tested y'know one or two of the beers of the local area er y'know we found a really good one called Wadsworth Six erm

on the way on the M4 we eventually managed to find the M4 to drive up to Reading again having driven about 100 miles out of our way (.) er Paul managed to switch the heating on the car really high (.) er

and we were travelling about 70 and I suddenly noticed we were beginning to creep onto the hard shoulder (.) *and I couldn't actually believe that I mean I couldn't drive my dad had always driven me nearly everywhere basically apart from a couple of wild nights when I was 17*(.)

and the idea that cars weren't on rails somehow suddenly struck me as unbelievable (.) and er I suddenly realised we were coming off the road (.) and at that point Paul woke up and he then corrected but he over-corrected and so instead of going over the hard shoulder we headed towards the central barrier of the M4 at 70 miles per hour (.) er we hit that (.) er we then proceeded to flip over it (.) into the fast lane of the other carriageway (.) erm

I remember thinking (.) oh shit and having this mental image of y'know steps up to heaven and I think I remember thinking oh shit this is really unoriginal (.) and as we flipped over the central barrier my head went out to the side window and I wasn't wearing a seat belt *as the seat belt rules hadn't quite come in yet* er we then (.) the top of the car hit the fast lane of the other carriageway and I was sort of half way out and half way in the car (.)

it was really interesting when you go outside the window because the air pressure suddenly changes in your ears and I went through so hard it really didn't do too much damage to my face er but I managed to sort of bang the back of my head on the hard shoulder as we flipped over at 70 miles per hour (.)

I also recognised that the car was about to roll on top of me (.) and sort of sever my head (.) so I managed to push myself out and sort of my arms suddenly developed this incredible strength and just pushed myself out the side window (.)

erm I couldn't really see at all *and had there been any traffic coming immediately on the hard shoulder course I'd be knocked over and crushed but* erm er I was in a complete daze and started looking for my glasses which had

complicating action = series of narrative clauses, ordered chronologically, with verbs in the simple past

except: *embedded speech* = the classic form might be: 'this is it!'

except: *evaluative commentary* = a comment by the speaker on the events

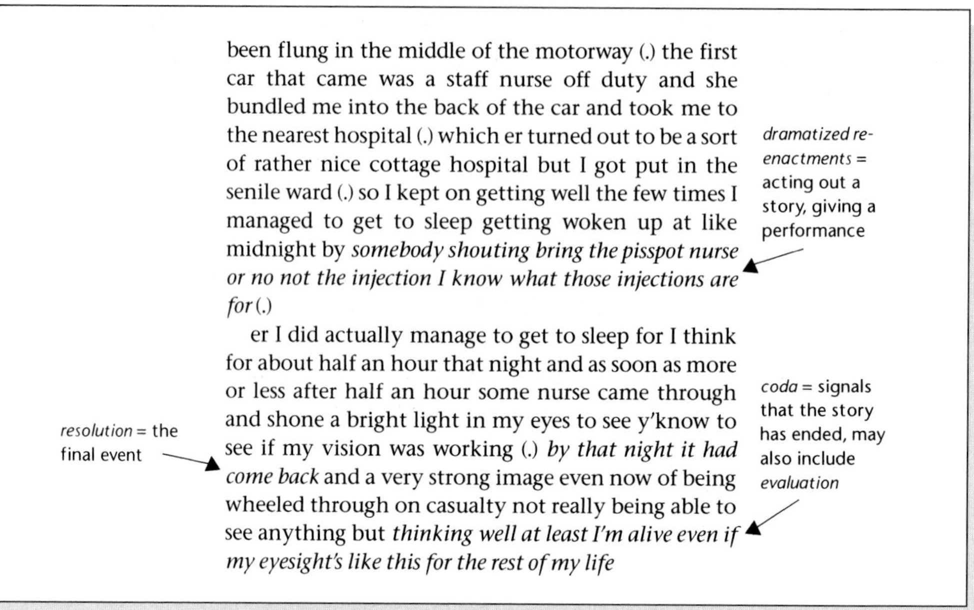

been flung in the middle of the motorway (.) the first car that came was a staff nurse off duty and she bundled me into the back of the car and took me to the nearest hospital (.) which er turned out to be a sort of rather nice cottage hospital but I got put in the senile ward (.) so I kept on getting well the few times I managed to get to sleep getting woken up at like midnight by *somebody shouting bring the pisspot nurse or no not the injection I know what those injections are for* (.)
er I did actually manage to get to sleep for I think for about half an hour that night and as soon as more or less after half an hour some nurse came through and shone a bright light in my eyes to see y'know to see if my vision was working (.) *by that night it had come back* and a very strong image even now of being wheeled through on casualty not really being able to see anything but *thinking well at least I'm alive even if my eyesight's like this for the rest of my life*
dramatized re-enactments = acting out a story, giving a performance
resolution = the final event
coda = signals that the story has ended, may also include *evaluation*

DISCUSSION OF TEXTS 6.9–6.11

Evaluation covers anything which is not strictly narrative, anything above and beyond the 'blow-by-blow' account of what happened; it's anything which is not strictly necessary in relating the events, the 'we did this and then we did that and this happened and then that happened'. It is of course pervasive in most narratives (and sometimes the most interesting element) and it takes many forms. The two broad areas most useful for us to consider can be labelled evaluative commentary and embedded speech.

Perhaps the most common form, evaluative commentary, as the term suggests, is a comment by the speaker on the events. An example of this occurs early in Esther's narrative even before the story proper starts:

> and would you believe I mean it sounds ridiculous now

where she takes momentary time off from the story proper to underline her assertion that the aeroplane she was travelling in was being hit by lightning and she also uses this comment to deflect any doubting listeners. It's as if she's saying 'Yes I know all this sounds a bit far-fetched or exaggerated, but it really happened!'.

Jonathan does something similar in his car-crash story. With the car in which he was travelling drifting out of control, he offers the frank admission that

> the idea that cars weren't on rails suddenly struck me as unbelievable.

Evaluative commentary can also add extra interesting information. As Jonathan crashes and is forced through the car window, he comments:

> it was really interesting when you go outside the window because the air pressure suddenly changes in your ears.

Also under this heading you might find comments such as:

> I really thought my number was up

or any other idiomatic expression meaning impending death. Any comment, too, which aims to underline the seriousness of the situation, such as:

> we were very lucky; or

> two seconds later and it would have hit us

can be considered as evaluative commentary.

Another form of these 'time outs' from the bare bones of the story is embedded speech; this may well add interest too, and heighten the dramatic presentation of the story. The classic form would be:

> I said to myself, 'This is it!'

Of course in reality such clichéd responses are rare. But any words articulated as direct speech, indirect speech or even left as thoughts would count as evaluation. We find an example at the end of Esther's story:

> when we actually landed and the pilot came out and said you were very lucky,

and, on collision course at 70 miles per hour for the central barrier, Jonathan tells us:

> I remember thinking (.) oh shit and having this mental image of y'know steps up to heaven and I think I remember thinking oh shit this is really unoriginal.

A further point on embedded speech is worth making. Labov does not regard speech as part of the narrative core; he only counts what is done rather than what is said. This may be problematic, however. It may well be difficult, if not impossible, to divorce some speech from the narrative flow as if it just doesn't contribute to 'what happens'. Obviously the pilot's comment above *is* outside of what is essentially happening: the plane being hit by lightning; the events would have happened anyway. But there will be cases when the speech *is* part of what happens and does precipitate events, bring things to a head, or whatever; we may be driven to action by what someone says. To take a well-known example from the world of film, surely Dirty Harry's taunt to the gunman he's facing of 'Make my day, punk!' *does* influence the action and cannot, therefore, be considered extraneous or unnecessary to the plot. It seems, then, sensible to differentiate between speech which is central to the core of the story and speech which is not. Dirty Harry's speech, therefore, would be complicating action, and the pilot's comment would be classed as evaluation. Relevant to this, it seems sensible, too, to consider at this point the work done by Wolfson (1982) on storytelling as dramatised re-enactments. She writes:

> When a speaker acts out a story, as if to give his audience the opportunity to experience the event and his evaluation of it, he may be said to be giving a performance.

Wolfson also draws attention to dramatised categories which seek to provide a more vivid and involving experience of that story, while exploiting special performance features as resources for highlighting the story's main point. Further examples from Esther's story seem more accurately described as dramatised re-enactments rather than the more general term embedded speech:

> the pilot explained what was going on but don't panic;

and

> a lady standing up and saying we're all gonna die we're all gonna die.

Activity

Write a linguistic analysis of the narrative in Text 6:12. In the process consider how helpful Labov's categories are; and focus on the role of the embedded speech/dramatised re-enactments in the story.

Note that there is no commentary on this activity.

Text 6:12

well Gabriel (.) who's a little on the impulsive side (.) met this bloke when she was sixteen (.) moved in with him the next day but that's beside the point (.) she met this bloke on Saturday night (.) he said ooooh come out to the pub like on Saturday lunchtime (.) so she went out (.) started drinking with this sort of rugger-bugger type (.)

so eight pints later she was in the curry house like this (.) and she funnily enough she slumped over her chicken tikka or whatever (.) and erm what they did all these ten blokes hid round the corner like in the kitchen of the curry house and they got the manager to come and wake her up and say all your mates have gone (.) you've got a hundred quid bill (.) you've got to pay (1) she'd only met this bloke the night before (1)

and she was going like (.) oh my God I haven't got anything here (.) take my jewellery (.) take my watch (.) I'll (.) I'll come back with the money as soon as I've been to the bank later (.) he was going no no I'm not going to let you leave the premises (.) I'm going to call the police (.) all this sort of stuff (1)

anyway they waited till she was on the point of hysterics and they all came out going ha ha what a good joke (.) like this (.) it's not a very nice story is it (.) she's still with him (.) that's four years later (.) and that's his bloody nicest feature (.) that's the nicest story she can tell about him

Jessica Gardner

Computer mediated communication (CMC)

One of the main links between speech and internet instant messaging is the fact that they take place in 'real time'. In spoken conversations we are aware that our language will immediately shape the discussion and have a direct effect. Speech, face-to-face or on the telephone, is part of a communication where all of the participants are present, whereas the internet allows us to address a wider audience. Instant messengers bridge that gap by allowing users to choose whom they address and the conversations are also immediate, thus instant. This has directly affected the language of MSN as users are required to convey detailed information in the quickest way possible.

MSN language has many of the features of spoken language: the turn taking mechanisms, discourse markers, response tokens – as well as some of its non fluency features: pauses, ellipsis. It has also created its own spelling conventions – basically a shorthand phonetic spelling system as well as a system to indicate prosodic features.

Openings in MSN language closely replicate face-to-face conversation and land line telephone openings.

A typical structure is:

A – greeting
B – replies with a greeting
A – asks how B is at that moment in time
B – responds to the question and gives thanks, then asks how A is
A – responds to the question and gives thanks
A – initiates the first topic of conversation, usually as a question.

For example:

A: hiya!
B: hiya!
A: u ok?
B: yeah thanks, you?
A: fine tar chick
A: so wot u bin up 2?

As in oral conversation the closing lines of a MSN exchange follows a sequence which prevents the conversation closing abruptly or unexpectedly. Pre-closing signals appear so that MSN endings particularly mirror phone closings.

A typical structure is:

A – states they have to leave
A – gives a reason for leaving
B – agrees or acknowledges that A is leaving
A – closes the conversation
B – mirrors the closure

this can be repeated several times.

For example:

A: anyway ive g2g ive got 10 hours of pushign trolleys and then a pirate party to go to 2moz so I need sleep
A: wats ruths mob??
B: bye bye xxx
B: umm, ill email it you
A: cheers me dears
A: bye
A: xxx
B: bye x.

Note the misspelling of 'pushing' which reflects the speed of typing and the overlaps of dialogue which reflect the slight time delay in text messaging. Some punctuation features from written language also appear.

Prosodic features

Intonation is represented in various ways to replicate the non-verbal aspects of speech. Participants can alter the way they compose their voice and this can change the meaning of the word. Capitalization and the repetition of punctuation marks can help suggest prosodic features. For example:

'NOOOOO' and 'WHAT!!!!'

Here the capital letters symbolize shouting and the use of exclamation marks help stress the word. The exclamation marks can suggest several things: either the person cannot believe what has just been said, or is confused and finds the conversation humorous, or can indicate sarcasm. Without intonation conversations through MSN can sound very matter of fact and blunt, and misinterpretation is also possible. Repetition can also suggest pace, for example: 'Julie? JULIE?'

Clippings

Word clippings are often used in MSN utterances as they save time and are less effort than typing the full word. Saving time is the biggest practical constraint influencing the style of writing via MSN. Clippings can also create a personal and informal tone. Examples would be: 'lil' for 'little', 'hun' for 'honey', 'k' for okay'.

Blendings

These, again, help to save time and can also form part of an individual's MSN idiolect, or personal writing style. Examples are: 'whasup' for 'what is up', 'cudda' for 'could have', 'wudda' for 'would have', shudda' for 'should have', 'dya' for 'do you'.

Phonetic spellings

Various influences on spelling affect MSN lexis and are similar to spelling choices used in text messaging. As well as spelling words phonetically and reducing the number of letters needed to communicate, numbers themselves are used to shorten words. Some examples: 'u' for 'you', 'c' for 'see', 'l8a' for 'later', '2geva' for 'together', '2moz' for 'tomorrow'. There is also scope for suggesting accent or dialect. For example: 'im' for 'him', 'satdi' for 'Saturday'.

Internet messaging is different to text messaging, emails and internet forums. An email is not intended to be read immediately and therefore an instant reply is not required; users of instant messengers behave as if they are with or talking to the participants. MSN language shares features from both spoken language and text messaging.

Other common features are:

- **Vague language.** For example:

  A: yea bt *like* wen we had dinna *n stuff* – kept catcHin her just starin in to space n lookin down.

- **Interrupted constructions.** For example:

  A: wen u nxt seein Paulo?
  B: erm possibly Friday bt
  A: cool
  A: wat u gna do coz u sed u dint av enuf money, onli for sat

Instant messaging, then, has its own particular features but also its own 'rules' which users abide by. The idea of maxims, seen earlier in this unit, can be adapted to reflect the understood principles behind MSN messaging

These are:

- *The maxim of honesty and deception*: a participant has the flexibility to offer contributions with as much or as little similarities to their 'offline' lives as they wish. Similarly participants are warned to question the quality of others' contributions.
- *The maxim of anonymity*: users are reminded that personal information divulged over the internet is available to anyone in the world. Therefore, contributions should be made with caution.
- *The maxim of subject matter*: contributions may be made at any time on any issue. The author does not need the consent of other users to communicate.
- *The maxim of ambiguity*: the contributions are open to interpretation and are ambiguous due to the global semantic differences in the English language. Users may choose to use this fact to their own advantage.

Activity

This unit concludes with some MSN text. What spoken features can you find? How does this text differ from written forms?

Text 6:13

```
H:   hehe :D!!!! how cool!!!
E:   sooo that was my yesterday
H:   :D
H:   cool
E:   how was your yesterday/tpday?
E:   nuffin special
H:   only got three lectures left :)
E:   oooh still home?
H:   yep
E:   do you have to clear everything out?
H:   nope
H:   got my room right through till july
E:   oooh that's really good!
E:   did you have to pay extra for that?
H:   didn't get a choice
H:   they just allocate you a room and you pay for however
     long the let is
H:   depends on where you are as to length
E:   how much do you pay? If you don't mind me asking
H:   2342
H:   60
H:   £2342.60
E:   for a year?
E:   whats that a week? as when we went york seemed really
     cheap
H:   yup
H:   about 50 60ish
E:   is it 40 week let?
H:   yeah think os
E:   on 40 weeks its £58.55
H:   that sounds about right
```

Commentary

There is much ellipsis here, as you might expect, for example:

> 'only got three lectures left'

and

> 'depends on where you are as to length'

where initial unnecessary words are ellipted:

> '*I have* only got three lectures left'

and

> '*it* depends on where you are as to length'.

Prosodic features are common: 'hehe' to indicate laughter, exclamatives are used for emphasis: 'how cool!!!' and words are lengthened: 'sooo', 'oooh'. Emoticons are used to express emotions: ':)' for a smile, ':D' for laughter.

There are also response tokens to smooth and encourage communication: 'cool', 'yep', 'yup'.

Interestingly spelling is generally standard; even 'three' is spelled fully. The exceptions: 'nuffin' is a clipping to suggest accent and 'tpday' and 'os' reflect the speed of typing.

Rules are very fluid in this medium and as long as communication is maintained then the actual forms do not give concern. Finally, in terms of written conventions there is no use of upper case and punctuation, also, is fluid. Full stops and apostrophes are ignored yet question marks are prevalent, at least in this example.

Guidelines for your own research

Before embarking on research of your own, the following guidelines should be read.

SOME GUIDELINES ON COLLECTING SPEECH

(a) You need to get permission before taping potential informants.
(b) Having got this, and having established the best site for the tape recorder, don't be disheartened if your subjects seem unduly conscious of being recorded, making the early exchanges seem unnatural as spontaneous conversation.
(c) Treat the first few minutes as a 'warm up'; most people will soon forget that a tape recorder or dictaphone is present and relax into 'normal' conversation.
(d) We can never be entirely sure, however, what is 'normal' conversation because once we start to observe or record it we encounter what's known as the 'observer's paradox', that is, how far does the act of observing conversation influence its outcome? Does conversation perform for the observer? Only by recording surreptitiously can we get close to what may be natural conversation.
(e) Having said that, should you inadvertently record someone without him/her knowing beforehand – if, for example, s/he happens to join a group after recording has started – then ask that person's permission to use the material gathered when the recording is over.
(f) Finally, always preserve the anonymity of your informants and change the names.

SOME GUIDELINES ON COLLECTING CMC AND MEDIA DIALOGUE

Participants' contributions to chatrooms and discussion forum spaces belong to them and should be treated in the same way as speech, above. You need to ask permission to use material, and if this is given, you should preserve the anonymity of the contributors. This is particularly important for material from this context because users' locations can be traced if you are sloppy about erasing their details.

Media dialogue can be accessed easily through audio clips streamed over the internet or as downloadable podcasts. If you intend to use any of this data for publication you should seek permission to do so.

SOME GUIDELINES ON TRANSCRIPTION ...

... and a key to transcription features used in spoken data in this unit. Normal punctuation doesn't apply as this is seen as very much a written feature. Speakers are better described as using utterances rather than sentences so different symbols are employed to indicate how conversation is structured.

- The + sign indicates an interrupted turn which continues at the next + sign.
- The = sign indicates an utterance which is cut short.
- A full stop in brackets indicates a normal pause of about half a second; (1), (2), (3) etc. indicate pauses of one second, two seconds and three seconds respectively.
- Upper case letters are used for proper nouns but also to indicate emphasis.
- Square brackets are used to indicate non verbal sounds such as laughter or inaudible speech.
- Apostrophes are still used.
- Non-standard spellings are used to indicate the words are actually said.

Extension activities

1 Exploring the style and pattern of everyday speech events can prove valuable, fruitful and interesting. Consider also whether different sociolinguistic categories may affect rules such as: ethnicity; age; gender.

2 Examine the ritualistic language of ceremonies such as weddings, baptisms, funerals. Oscar, Britpop, Booker Prize or similar award-winning ceremonies are televised. The language of the courts, medicine and other professions are also possible areas for investigation.

3 The narratives given by Jonathan and Esther were in response to the question: 'Can you tell me of a time when you were in a life-threatening situation?' Jessica's story, on the other hand, centres around a friend's discomfiture. Collect a range of narratives – e.g. when someone's life was in danger, a story about someone you know, a funny story. Do they follow the same structure? Does the nature of the narrative influence the relative importance of each category?

4 Compare spoken and written versions of the same narratives. It's better to ask for a spoken version first; then having got that on tape ask your informant if they would give you a written version. It's also more interesting to choose informants from different backgrounds and of different ages.

5 Political speeches are readily available from political party headquarters and the internet. Analyse them from the page or, if they are being broadcast on radio or TV, consider the speaker's sense of timing and response to applause.

6 Consider how the audience affects the nature of the formal speech: for example, examine transcripts of speeches made just for broadcast. These include the Queen's Christmas message and party political broadcasts. Speeches given by authority figures forced into resignation can also be very interesting, mixing the personal with the public voice. Also consider speeches given at sensitive times, for example after a national crisis/disaster.

7 Research participants engaged in general conversation. It is often better when people are actually doing something so that the conversation has focus, for example a small group of children engaged in a group activity.

8 Research the concept of sequencing and adjacency in some speech from a particular context. For example, it has been suggested (Coulthard, 1992) that the teaching situation often produces three-part exchanges of teacher question, pupil response and teacher feedback. Tape some material from the teaching situation to see whether this pattern is prevalent. Team talks given by sport coaches can also be very interesting.

9 Research phone conversations. Compare phone calls for different purposes, for example social calls compared with instrumental calls, that is calls for a specific purpose: ordering something, asking for information. Look for differences in answerphone calls, mobile calls, landline calls, etc.

10 Research media discourse, for example interviews or chat shows or reality shows. Other interesting areas are film or TV dramas which try to replicate spontaneous conversation.

11 In CMC compare different uses of language depending on context and the role of the participants.

Commentaries/Answers to activities

COMMENTARY: ACTIVITY p. 205, TEXT 6:2

There are fewer non fluency features present here and this reflects the instructional nature of the context. The long pauses, which might be problematic in a purely social context, are quite natural. The driving instructor in organising the lesson and the learning is structuring the conversation quite clearly. Mostly he uses 'okay' as a discourse marker to initiate a new piece of advice, for example

> Pete: okay look what's coming
> okay slow down.

Discourse markers also help to maintain a listener's involvement and this is obviously important in a teacher-pupil context. Pete's final 'okay' functions as a checking question. Elsewhere he is asking questions as part of his strategy to teach and he either gives the answer himself or makes it plain he wants Sara to supply the answer. His use of laughter is interesting; here it functions to soften any implied criticism of Sara's driving or preparation. This conversation illustrates the power held by the driving instructor and he dominates most of the exchanges.

Work on teacher–pupil exchanges has been done by Sinclair and Coulthard on what is known as exchange-structure theory. (See Extension ideas, p. 242.)

COMMENTARY: ACTIVITY p. 209, TEXT 6:3

Summons and answer, identification and recognition are all present, as are mutual greetings. Note that the tutor offers three greetings, an opening 'hello' for 'voice display' purposes when picking the phone up, another 'hello' when Sam's voice is recognised, then a 'hi', which acts possibly as a move towards increased informality and friendliness.

The speakers move quickly to the initial enquiries stage, but then this stage is extensive, with the student apparently anxious to show concern for the tutor's health; note that this is not reciprocated. Perhaps the student feels obliged to show this concern because the purpose of the phone call is to ask for help: the student therefore needs the tutor to be positively oriented to the upcoming request. The student's self-disparagement ('my brain's so cabbage . . .') could be seen as further evidence that preparations are being made to ask for help.

Despite the suggestions above that the initial enquiries stage is oriented towards the request for help, the student doesn't seem able to initiate this first topic. (It is normally the caller's responsibility to make the shift from initial enquiries to first topic, remember.) Or perhaps if the tutor had allowed more time, this would actually have happened. In the event, the tutor takes over with a rather more business-like 'what can I do for you', and uses the student's name, which could mark a shift towards increased formality. The rest of the conversation goes on to deal with the real purpose of the phone call – the fact that the student has been struggling with an essay.

COMMENTARY: ACTIVITY p. 223, TEXT 6:7

This text has been taken from the London Olympic Bid website where written punctuation conventions have been followed. It is clear, though, that this speech is a collection of short 'bite-size chunks'. One of the main features employed is the use of pronouns. Denise Lewis introduces herself:

> 'I'm Denise Lewis, Olympic Heptathlon champion'

and then continues to use the first person singular 'I' form – in total seven times – to reinforce her position as someone with a view worth being heard in this context. Halfway through there is the switch to first person plural – 'we', 'our' – so as to suggest the views of all athletes. The final section is also framed by a question:

> 'how do you give athletes the best possible Olympic experience?'

and concludes with:

> 'these are the things athletes want.'

Patterns in lexical choices abound. For example:

> I was eight
> I was inspired
> I dreamt
> I watched.
> In London, athletes will compete, not commute.

The words 'Olympics', 'London' and 'athletes' are continually repeated. The overall impression is of the needs of athletes being at the forefront of the planning for the games in London, and of athletes having a special experience to leave lasting friendships and memories.

COMMENTARY: ACTIVITY p. 227, TEXT 6:9

The opening of Extract 1 seems to be justifying its existence; it's saying why it's being written, why it's worth reading. Finally, it's giving some idea of what the story is going to be about: almost dying in a motorway crash. The oral narrative of Extract 2 jumps straight into the story and refers to the incident with no specific detail as 'the whole thing happened'. This is the abstract of the narrative.

The next part of each Extract seeks to establish the *time* that the incident took place; e.g. Extract 1: 'the beginning of my second term of my second year at university . . . [at] Christmas'; and Extract 2: 'going back to university one day . . . when I was about nineteen in January 1983'. Also the *place*; Extract 1: 'the railway station in Kidderminster . . . had to go to Birmingham . . . then change for Reading'; Extract 2: 'a railway station . . . the train back to Reading'. We learn about the *persons* involved; Extract 1: 'parents . . . dad . . . my friend Paul'; Extract 2: 'a friend of mine . . . my best friend'. Finally we are told of the circumstances, the *situation,* i.e. being driven back to university. All these details help to place the story in context and can be labelled orientation.

The story proper, the 'what happened' element, known as the complicating action, only gets going in Extract 2: 'so we started driving back . . .', etc.

Satellite texts

The following satellite texts look in detail at ideas covered in this unit:

Language Change looks at changing telephone routines.

The Language of Children looks at how children acquire the rules of conversation.

The Language of Comics looks at a genre which makes extensive use of represented talk.

The Language of Conversation is central to this unit, as is *The Language of Speech and Writing.*

Language and Gender looks at how aspects of gender can affect conversation.

The Language of Humour looks at rule-breaking for comic effect.

The Language of ICT and *The Language of Websites* look at aspects of computer-mediated communication.

The Language of Politics looks at political speeches.

Language and Region looks at regional features of talk.

The Language of Work looks at workplace talk.

Unit seven

Applications

Aims of this unit

This brief final unit aims to give you some guidance on where to go next in your development of analytical skills.

The core book you have been reading is intended as a foundation course in language analysis. Meanwhile in the book's 'Extension' sections we have been signposting possible directions for further research in a wide range of areas.

Now that you have come to the end of this book, you are in a position to think about specialising in particular areas or aspects of language use. Indeed, if you are on a language course involving coursework/research, it will probably be a course requirement to undertake a piece of research of your own. So where do you start? Here are some questions to think about.

WHICH ASPECTS OF THIS BOOK HAVE I FOUND MOST INTERESTING?

If you are going to do a substantial piece of independent work, it has to be interesting enough for you to stay with it for some time. This means that you need to start by asking yourself which aspects of language you find most interesting, intriguing, creative, perplexing – in short, those aspects that engage you most strongly. These might be quite structural, to do with things like signs and sounds, grammar in a certain context, new words in technological settings, they might be more to do with language use as it relates to a certain topic such as sport, war or politics, or they might be a bit of both such as seeing how language works in the media, in geographical regions or in new technologies.

You can start by looking back through this book and noting down those texts and discussions that affected you the most: what questions were raised in your mind by them? The Intertext satellite books then offer many additional ideas for starting research of your own. Finding a library with a full set of these books, and then browsing through them, will offer you a very wide range of possibilities.

Here is a full list of current titles:

- *The Language of Advertising: Written texts*
  (second edition, 2002)
  Angela Goddard
- *Language Change*
  Adrian Beard
- *The Language of Children*
  Julia Gillen
- *The Language of Comics*
  Mario Saraceni
- *The Language of Conversation*
  Francesca Pridham
- *The Language of Drama*
  Keith Sanger
- *The Language of Fiction*
  Keith Sanger
- *Language and Gender*
  Angela Goddard and Lindsey Meân Patterson
- *The Language of Humour*
  Alison Ross
- *The Language of ICT: Information and communication technology*
  Tim Shortis

- *The Language of Magazines*
  Linda McLoughlin
- *The Language of Newspapers*
  (second edition, 2002)
  Danuta Reah
- *The Language of Poetry*
  John McRae
- *The Language of Politics*
  Adrian Beard
- *Language and Region*
  Joan C. Beal
- *The Language of Science*
  Carol Reeves
- *The Language of Speech and Writing*
  Sandra Cornbleet and Ronald Carter
- *The Language of Sport*
  Adrian Beard
- *The Language of Television*
  Jill Marshall and Angela Werndly
- *The Language of War*
  Steve Thorne
- *The Language of Websites*
  Mark Boardman
- *The Language of Work*
  Almut Koester

WHAT TYPES OF MATERIAL WOULD IT BE POSSIBLE FOR ME TO COLLECT?

It's good to be ambitious in research, but you also need to be realistic, particularly if you have a busy schedule and you are trying to juggle a language research assignment with many other demands. So think about the language that you have the means to access, and where there are no ethical problems in the process of collection. Sometimes people assume that they need to go far afield for material, because they interpret the idea of 'objectivity' as a notion that researchers need to be removed from their object of study. This is a false premise.

You will require data to analyse as part of your research. The best studies often tackle data from areas well known to the researcher, but where the analyst is open-minded rather than simply distanced. The important issue is to explain your relationship with the data clearly.

So think about what data you have close to hand. You may well have material that you have overlooked, or that you are discounting because you are assuming you are too involved with it.

WHAT KINDS OF QUESTIONS CAN BE ASKED ABOUT DIFFERENT SORTS OF DATA?

The 'wh' question words we use in ordinary language are also at the basis of research, for example: *What* tends to happen in spoken, written, multimodal interactions such as these? *How* does this text work? *Where* do texts like these come from and how do we know? *Who* uses this kind of language? *When* do we use language like this? In a small-scale piece of research you will not be able to ask all these questions but they give a broad indication of what you can be looking for in your research.

WHAT OTHER RESOURCES CAN HELP ME?

You need to focus on texts not as objects that have dropped out of the sky, but as pieces of communication that exist within a system of discourses. The smaller topic-based books that are part of the Intertext series each focus on a type of discourse, present some of its important aspects, and suggest ways to research it.

There are also many other books which can be of help. The list below is inevitably just a starting point, but all the books have been recommended by the authors of these units, so come well recommended. While they have been linked to a specific unit here, they may well have wider applications too.

Unit 1

Chandler, D. (2004) *Semiotics: The basics*, Routledge, London.

Unit 2

Gillen, J. (2003) *The Language of Children*, Routledge, London.
Hughes, A., Trudgill, P. and Watt, D. (2005) *English Accents and Dialects*, 4th edn, Hodder Education, London.

Wells, J.C. (1982) *Accents of English*, vols 1–3, Cambridge University Press, Cambridge.

Unit 3

Ross, Alison (2006) *Language Knowledge for Secondary Teachers*, David Fulton Publishers, London.
Sinclair, John (2003) *Reading Concordances*, Pearson Longman, London.

Unit 4

Carter, R. and McCarthy, M. (2006) *Cambridge Grammar of English: A comprehensive guide to spoken and written grammar and usage*, Cambridge University Press, Cambridge.
Hewings, A. and Hewings, M. (2005) *Grammar and Context*, Routledge, London.
Jackson, H. (2002) *Grammar and Vocabulary*, Routledge, London.
Swan, M. (2005) *Grammar*, Oxford University Press, Oxford.

Unit 5

Cutting, J. (2003) *Pragmatics and Discourse*, Routledge, London.
Mongomery, M., *et al.* (2007) *Ways of Reading*, 3rd edn. Routledge, London.

Unit 6

Carter, R. and McCarthy, M. (2006) *Cambridge Grammar of English: A comprehensive guide to spoken and written grammar and usage*, Cambridge University Press, Cambridge.
Maybin, J., Mercer, N. and Hewings, A. (eds) (2007) *Using English*, Routledge, London.

In addition to books, students are increasingly turning to the internet for help, sometimes in the provision of data, and sometimes for support with ideas and critical readings. While the internet can be an amazing resource to use in the search for data and ideas, there are issues to consider with its use. Books tend to have been through a process of quality control: this does not necessarily mean that they are accessible, interesting or even 'right' in all that they say, but they offer a certain reliability. The more open and democratic nature of the internet, however, where any individual can become an author, does mean that readers have to be very selective and critical before they accept what they read: thinking about the source of the material, for example, is always sensible.

URLs are always susceptible to change, so those mentioned below are liable to alter: because they are largely institutional, though, they should be easy to track down in their new guise. The following sites, if used judiciously, should offer plenty of potential for help with researching your own ideas. As an activity you could take each in turn and see what it has to offer in the field of English Language and Linguistics, and the topics covered in this book. It is also worth keeping your own list of useful 'favourites'.

Dictionaries

www.oed.com – a standard work

www.urbandictionary.com – an online dictionary of contemporary slang

www.yourdictionary.com – an American site with all sorts of linguistic activities

www.netlingo.com

Translation

http://babelfish.altavista.com – this site offers to translate text from one language to another

Newspapers

Most newspapers, whether national or local have a website. The following are just a few:

www.reuters.com – an international news agency

www.pressassociation.co.uk – a news agency for the UK

www.timesonline.co.uk – *The Times* (UK)

www.independent.co.uk – *Independent* (UK)

www.thesun.co.uk (UK)

www.dailystar.co.uk (UK)

www.mirror.co.uk (UK)

www.nytimes.com (USA)

www.latimes.com (USA)

timesofindia.indiatimes.com (India)

Other media sites

Television companies all over the world have their own sites. You could start with:

www.bbc.co.uk

www.sky.com

www.cnn.com/

Corpus searches

www.natcorp.ox.ac.uk

http://uk.cambridge.org/elt/corpus/cancode.htm

Emoticons

http://randomhouse.com/features/davebarry/emoticon.html

Historical archive

http://news.bbc.co.uk/onthisday

Speeches

www.americanrhetoric.com

www.wfu.edu/~louden/Political%20Communication/Class%20 Information/SPEECHES.html

Others

www.london2012.org – about the Olympics in London

www.june29.com/HLP – a collection of language links

http://eserver.org – a wide ranging site on English topics based at Iowa State University

www.bartleby.com – literature texts

references

Chandler, D. (2006) 'Identities under Construction' in J. Maybin and J. Swann (eds) *The Art of English: Everyday creativity*, Palgrave Macmillan and The Open University, Milton Keynes.

Coulthard, M. (ed.) (1992) *Advances in Spoken Discourse Analysis*, Routledge, London.

Crystal, D. (1995) *The Cambridge Encyclopedia of the English Language*, Cambridge University Press, Cambridge.

Giddens, A. (1993) *Sociology*, Polity Press, Oxford.

Grice, P. (1975) 'Logic and conversation', in P. Cole and J. Morgan (eds) *Syntax and Semantics, vol. 3: Speech acts*, Academic Press, New York, pp. 41–58.

Halliday, M.A.K. and Hasan, R. (1976) *Cohesion in English*, Longman, Harlow.

Labov, W. (1972) 'The transformation of experience in narrative syntax', in W. Labov (ed.) *Language in the Inner City*, University of Philadelphia Press, Philadelphia, PA, pp. 354–96.

Lakoff, R. (1975) *Language and Woman's Place*, Harper & Row, New York.

Schegloff, E. (1986) 'The routine as achievement', *Human Studies*, 9 (2–3): 111–51.

Schmitt, N. (2000) *Vocabulary and Language Teaching*, Cambridge University Press, Cambridge.

Searle, J. (1969) *Speech Acts: An essay in the philosophy of language*, Cambridge University Press, Cambridge.

Sinclair, J. (2003) *Reading Concordances*, Pearson, Harlow.

Tannen, D. (1992) *You Just Don't Understand: Men and women in conversation*, Virago, London.

Thurlow, C., Tomic, A., Lengel, L. (2004) *Computer Mediated Communication*, Sage, London.

Wells, J.C. (1982) *Accents of English*, vols 1–3, Cambridge University Press, Cambridge.

Wolfson, N. (1982) *CHP: The conversational historic present in American English narrative*, Foris Publications, Cinnaminson, NJ.

index of terms

This is a form of combined glossary and index. Listed below are some of the key terms used in the book, together with brief definitions. These terms are shown in **bold**. Not all terms used in the book are glossed here as some of them receive extensive explanation in the units themselves. As this is not a complete index of linguistic terms, it should be used in conjunction with other reference books.

acronym
A word composed of the initial letters of the name of something, usually an organisation and normally pronounced as a whole word. For example, NATO (North Atlantic Treaty Organization).

active voice
see **voice**

adjacency
The positioning of elements in a conversational exchange so that one follows on from another. For example, greetings are nearly always followed by greetings in an **adjacency pair**.

adjacency pair
see **adjacency**

anaphoric reference
see **reference**

anthropomorphism
A view that an animal or an object has feelings like those of a human being. Anthropomorphic descriptions occur regularly in literary texts where a similar term used is personification.

bound morpheme
see **morpheme**

bricolage
Literally means 'handiwork'.

cataphoric reference
see **reference**

clause
A structural unit which is part of a **sentence** either as a main clause which can stand alone and be equivalent to a sentence or as a subordinate or dependent clause. For example, 'The owner, who lives abroad, has written to all the neighbours' consists of a main clause 'The owner . . . has written to all the neighbours' and a subordinate clause 'who lives abroad'.

closing
Words and phrases used to indicate that a conversational sequence is ending. For example, routine expressions like farewells ('bye then') are closings. (*See also* **pre-closing**.)

cohesion
Cohesion is a term which describes the patterns of language created

within a text, mainly within and across sentence boundaries and which collectively make up the organisation of larger units of the text such as paragraphs. Cohesion can be both lexical and grammatical. **Lexical cohesion** is established by means of chains of words with related meanings linking across sentences; **grammatical cohesion** is established mainly by grammatical words such as 'the', 'this', 'it' and so on.

conjunction
A general term which describes words which link sentences and clauses together, indicating temporal, spatial, logical and causal relationships. Words such as 'and', 'but', 'therefore', 'because' are conjunctions. Conjunctions are also termed 'connectives'.

connotation
The connotations of a word are the associations it creates. For example, the connotations of December, mainly within British and North American culture, would be of 'cold', 'dark nights' and 'Christmas parties'. Connotations are often either individual or cultural.

contrasting pair
Words or phrases which are put together rhetorically but contain opposite meanings.

conversational implicature
What is really meant rather than what is actually said. So, for example, someone who asks 'Is there a café near here' actually means 'I'm hungry'.

co-operative principle
Refers to the way in which most conversations are conducted in a coherent manner with participants acting towards one another as efficiently and collaboratively as possible.

deictics
Deictics are words which point backwards, forwards and extra-textually and which serve to situate a speaker or writer in relation to what is said. For example, in the sentence 'I'm going to get some wine from that shop over there', the main deictic words are 'that' and 'there'.

derivational morpheme
see **morpheme**

discourse
A term used in linguistics to describe the rules and conventions underlying the use of language in extended stretches of text, spoken and written. (Such an academic study is referred to as 'discourse analysis'.) The term is also used as a convenient general term to refer to language in action and the patterns which characterise particular types of language in action, for example, the 'discourse' of advertising.

discourse marker
Spoken words and phrases which help to organise speech, especially turn taking.

ellipsis
Ellipsis refers to the omission of part of a structure. It is normally used for reasons of economy and, in spoken **discourse**, can create a sense of informality. For example, in the sentence 'She went to the party and danced all night', the pronoun 'she' is ellipted from the second **clause**; in the dialogue 'You going to the party?' / 'Might be', the verb 'are' and the pronoun 'I', respectively, are omitted with the ellipsis here creating a casual and informal tone.

emoticons
An emoticon is a sign to express a certain emotion that is created by using a keyboard.

endophoric reference
see **reference**

epenthesis
The process of inserting vowel sounds to separate consonant sounds.

exophoric reference
see **reference**

face
see **positive face** and **negative face**

finite verb
A finite verb or verb phrase can occur on its own in a **clause** or sentence and is normally marked for tense and mood. A non-finite verb only occurs in a subordinate **clause** and normally lacks explicit **reference** to time or person. For example, 'Walking through the town, we came across an old pub' contains a non-finite verb 'walking' and a finite verb 'came'.

formality
A level of language use which refers to a particular social context or situation. Formal language is used in social situations which are distant and more impersonal; informal language is used in social situations which are intimate and casual.

free morpheme
see **morpheme**

glottal stop
Technically this describes the audible release of a closure at the glottis. The effect of this can be heard in certain pronunciation of words like bottle and butter.

grammatical cohesion
see **cohesion**

graphology
The arrangement and visual appearance of written text.

header
This is when an element in speech is placed at the front of a statement for added significance/emphasis, e.g. '*England*, what a team'.

hedge(s)
Hedges are words and phrases which soften or weaken the force with which something is said. Examples of hedges are: 'kind of', 'sort of', 'by any chance', 'as it were' and 'admittedly'.

homophone
Words which have the same pronunciation but which differ in meaning. For example, 'threw' and 'through'.

hypernym
see **hyponymy**

hyponymy
Hyponymy is the relationship which exists between specific and general words. For example, 'rose' is a hyponym of the more general word 'flower'. General words such as 'flower', 'animal' and 'vehicle' are also sometimes called **hypernyms**.

iconic
A direct representation of something (contrast **symbolic**).

indirect speech act
see **speech act**

inflectional morpheme
see **morpheme**

initialism
A feature of words in which whole words are abbreviated to initial letters. For example, 'incl.' (for 'including').

insertion sequences
Conversational acts which interrupt or forestall **adjacency pairs**. For example, a question–answer routine can be interrupted by further questions, requests for clarification, objections, etc.

intertextuality
The way in which one text echoes or refers to another text. For example, an advertisement that stated 'To be in Florida in winter or not to be in Florida in winter' would contain an intertextual reference to a key speech in Shakespeare's *Hamlet*. (*See also* Unit 1.)

lexeme
Lexeme or 'lexical item' is sometimes used in order to avoid difficulties of referring to 'words'. For example, the abstract lexeme 'walk' underlies all the separate instances 'walks', 'walked', 'walking'; the idiom 'smell a rat' is also a lexeme in so far as it functions in the manner of a single word.

lexical cohesion
see **cohesion**

metaphor
A word or phrase which establishes a comparison or analogy between one object or idea and another. For example, 'I *demolished* his argument' contains a comparison between argument and war, and also underlines the idea that arguments can be constructed like buildings.

metonymy
This involves the association of two things (such as objects, ideas, etc.) with one thing referred to as though it were the other. So, for example Number 10 Downing Street is the official home of the British Prime Minister. By metonymic association, a reference to Number 10, can stand for a reference to the Prime Minister and even his government, e.g. 'Number 10 today announced a tax on luxury cars'. A similar effect can be achieved visually when news reporters stand outside Number 10 to introduce a news item.

minimal pair
Two words which are separated by a single sound.

minimal response
A brief **response token**.

morpheme
A morpheme is a basic unit of grammar in that it can function to mark a grammatical feature or structure. For example, 'walks' contains two morphemes: 'walk' and 's', the latter morpheme marking the tense and person of the basic or root morpheme 'walk'. Morphemes are normally divided into **free morphemes** and **bound morphemes**, the former occurring also as single words and the latter only occurring meaningfully when joined to the free morpheme. Thus, 'unselfish' is a word made up from three morphemes, a free morpheme 'self' and two bound morphemes 'un' and 'ish'.

Morphemes are often studied as inflectional or derivational forms: **inflectional morphemes** are morphemes such as 's' and 'ed' (bound morphemes) which indicate grammatical meanings; derivational morphemes are morphemes such as 'ship' and 'dom' which can form specific grammatical categories – in these cases nouns such as 'friend*ship*' and 'king*dom*'.

morphology
see **morpheme**

multimodal
Describes communication systems which use more than one mode, i.e. visual signs alongside the written word.

negative face
Utterances which are designed to make hearers disapprove/feel negatively. Speakers try to avoid negative face by not allowing themselves to be imposed upon. 'I'd rather not but just for you', or 'Well, I'm a bit busy this weekend but . . .' are typical phrases which avoid too much negative face.

non-finite verb
see **finite verb**

non-fluency features
Aspects of speech which break the flow but serve the purpose of allowing thinking time. Pauses and fillers are typical non-fluency features.

noun
Nouns are a major class of words which are regularly inflected or otherwise marked to show plurals ('ship'/'ships'; 'mouse'/'mice'; 'child'/'children') and to indicate possession (the dog's lead).

noun phrase
A group of words which describe a **noun**. 'Old pop-singers with long hair are still making records', for example, contains a noun phrase with the core noun 'pop-singers' pre-modified with the word 'old' and post-modified with the words 'with long hair'.

passive voice
see **voice**

phatic
Talk which has a specific social purpose but less specific meaning.

politeness principle
A principle of conversation in which speakers indicate respect for each other by adopting appropriate strategies to maintain polite and smooth-running interaction.

polysemy
A semantic process by which certain words have several meanings. For example, the word 'lap' is polysemous, meaning, for example, to lick up a liquid, a circuit of a track, part of the body, etc.

positive face
Utterances which are designed to make hearers approve/feel positively. Speakers try to preserve the positive face of the people they are talking with by not, for example, seeming to impose on them. Phrases, 'Do you mind if . . .' or 'I know this is inconvenient but . . .' help to preserve positive face. (*See also* **negative face**.)

post-modifiers
Words or phrases which come after a noun or verb and add a sense of detail.

pre-closing
Words and phrases which are used to indicate that a conversation is about to be brought to a **closing**. For example, 'I must be going, I'm late already' is a pre-closing move. (*See also* **closing**.)

pre-modifiers
Words or phrases which come before a noun or verb and add a sense of detail.

present participles
Verb forms ending with '-ing'. (*See also* **verb**.)

pronoun
Words which normally substitute for nouns and noun phrases. For example, 'I', 'you', 'it', 'they', 'their', 'some', 'any', 'this', 'myself' and 'which'. Personal pronouns such as 'I', 'you', 'we', 'they' and 'us' are especially significant in texts.

reference
Reference is the act of referring to something (often called a **referent**). Many words also allow reference to each other and establish links and patterns across a text. Different types of reference include: 'anaphoric' and 'cataphoric' reference. **Anaphoric reference** points backwards; for example, the grammatical word 'he' in the following sentence: 'I saw the man. *He* was wearing . . .'. **Cataphoric reference** points forwards; for example, the word 'here' in the following sentence: '*Here* is the nine o' clock news'.

Reference within a text is generally referred to as **endophoric reference**; reference to the world outside the text is generally referred to as **exophoric reference**.

'Demonstrative reference' involves **deictics** such as 'these', 'those', 'here' and 'there' which refer back and forth within a text or **speech event**.

'Comparative reference' involves reference within a text when one thing is compared to another; for example, 'Ann is *fitter than* Jill'.

referent
The thing being referred to.

rephrasing
Going back over something that has already been said and saying it differently for further elaboration, emphasis etc.

response token
Comments from participants in a conversation which respond to what is being said.

semantic field
A group of words which are related in meaning, normally as a result of being connected with a particular context of use. For example, 'chop', 'sprinkle', 'salt', 'dice', 'wash', 'simmer', 'boil', 'herbs' are all connected with the semantic field of cookery.

semiotics
Human communication by means of signs and symbols.

sentence
A difficult term to define because the structure of sentences differs according to whether spoken or written language is used. Traditionally, a sentence has a subject and a main **verb**, though in literary texts a sentence can be a single word; in spoken English, however, structures such as 'over here', 'if you like' and 'perhaps' can constitute a sentence. (*See also* **clause**.)

side sequence
This is where an **adjacency pair** is interrupted by a sequence which has little strict relevance to the pair itself.

speech act
A speech act refers to what is done when something is said (for

example, warning, threatening, promising, requesting). 'I declare the meeting open' in this sense does what it says. An 'indirect speech act' has a meaning which is different from its apparent meaning. For example, the question: 'Is that your coat on the floor?' could *indirectly* suggest that the coat should be picked up.

speech event
A use of language in a social context in which the speakers normally follow a set of agreed rules and conventions. For example, telling a joke, recounting a story or purchasing stamps in a post office are all speech events.

substitution
Substitution allows a speaker or writer to substitute one word or phrase for another in a text. 'Do' is normally used to substitute for verbs or verb phrases, whereas words like 'so' can be used to substitute for whole clauses. For example: 'Are you going to the party?' / 'I would do but I'm a bit tired.'

symbolic
Something is symbolic when it suggests associations rather than refers to something directly.

synonymy
Synonyms are words which have equivalent meanings. For example, 'cheap' and 'inexpensive'.

tag
An element attached to the end of an utterance, often in the form of a question.

tail
'Tail' is the opposite of **header**, so placing an item at the end of a statement, but still for added effect, e.g. 'You've got to admit it, they're a great team *England*'.

tense
Tense is a very important grammatical category and is mainly associated with the **verb** in a sentence. English has two primary tenses, the present tense and the past tense. (The future is normally referred to by means of modal **verbs** such as 'will' and by adverbs or adverbial phrases such as 'tomorrow' or 'on Monday'.)

vague language
As the term suggests, this is language that is essentially unspecific in meaning but which can be an important part of social communication.

verb
A verb is a major category of grammar. Verbs can be either main verbs or auxiliary verbs. For example in the sentence: 'I do intend to go to the match', 'intend' is a main verb and 'do' is an auxiliary verb. Auxiliary verbs cannot normally stand on their own, whereas main verbs can (e.g. I intend to go to the match). Verbs also have other forms. Here, for example, 'to go' is an infinitive form of the verb 'go'.

Verbs can be inflected to show tense. For example 'She works hard' (present tense); 'She worked hard' (past tense) – and can also form present and past participles: working (present participle); worked (past participle). Participles can be used as modifiers: 'The working day'; 'A worked example'.

A progressive form of the verb indicates an action which is continuous. For example, 'I was walking home' is a past progressive form of the verb 'walk'.

verb voice
see **voice**

voice
Voice is a grammatical feature which indicates whether a subject in a sentence is the agent of an action or is affected by the action. Voice can normally be either active or passive. For example: 'The dog bit the man' (active); 'The man was bitten by the dog' (passive).

In the passive **sentence** it is of course still the dog which bites and in this sense the dog remains the underlying subject of the sentence; but the man is given greater emphasis in the passive sentence. The passive voice also allows the 'by-phrase' to be omitted, thus deleting any **reference** to an agent, for example: 'The man was bitten'.

Such structures allow the responsibility for an action or event to be concealed. In a text the choice of active or passive forms is often connected to questions of **theme** and **cohesion**.